PERSPECTIVES ON COLLEGE STUDENT SUICIDE

Ralph L. V. Rickgarn
University of Minnesota

Death, Value and Meaning Series
Series Editor: John D. Morgan

Baywood Publishing Company, Inc.
AMITYVILLE, NEW YORK

Copyright © 1994 by the Baywood Publishing Company, Inc., Amityville, New York. All rights reserved. Printed in the United States of America.

Library of Congress Catalog Number: 94-41
ISBN: 0-89503-153-1 (cloth)
ISBN: 0-89503-154-X (paper)

Library of Congress Cataloging-in-Publication Data

Rickgarn, Ralph L. V.
  Perspectives on college suicide / Ralph L. V. Rickgarn.
    p.   cm. - - (Death, value, and meaning series)
  Includes index.
  ISBN 0-89503-153-1. - - ISBN 0-89503-154-X (pbk.)
  1. College students- -Suicidal behavior- -United States.   I. Title.
II. Series.
HV6545.8.R53 1994
362.2'8'0835- -dc20

                                    94-41
                                    CIP

*Dedicated to the many students,
particularly those in the Suicide Support Group,
who have helped me understand their
perspectives on suicide and how to effectively
respond to them in their time of need,
and,
with thanks to my wife, Glenys,
and our daughter and son-in-law,
MerLynne and Patrick,
for their support and understanding.*

Foreword

Clinicians who frequently work with young adults are often impressed with the potential for multiple tragedies to unfold before their eyes. Not only does the young adult considering suicide cast a shadow over everything that the clinician will say and do, but also the potential tragic loss of future social, academic and interpersonal achievements looms larger than life, itself. Very carefully clinicians must pick their words with a great deal of trepidation and selectivity, considering the correct language and strategies to apply in preventing the young person's suicide. The added burden is often not spoken but is the additional impact that the young person's death has on survivors. The profound and almost indescribable impact for those who survive, must also be taken into the clinical considerations that a clinician, friend, or relative selects when they intervene to help.

Perspectives on College Student Suicide is a very thorough review of this situation. This is an insightful perspective of the tragic loss of young human lives just as they are embarking on complex academic, social and vocational choices. This book expertly examines all issues, without omitting any one important aspect. What makes this challenging and confrontational approach so compelling is the dramatic and personalized viewpoint from many students. Nothing is more riveting than reading the words of the students at various steps along the pathway to self-destructive behavior. The author has skillfully used the student writings and words to underscore the many useful clinical points that he has established from his own personal and professional experiences.

The beginning three chapters effectively provide an accurate backdrop and the necessary demographic, clinical, and systems theories that are required for any clinician who wants to provide help to troubled college students. The comprehensive nature of this information is clearly and succinctly presented. I was struck with how well integrated the author makes this system so understandable, and at the same time, also so very practical. The background information culminates in a very clearly presented set of chapters on the mythology and the etiology of suicide [Chapters 4 and 5]. These chapters complement the background data and give the author a chance to present his own theoretical emphasis on what he sees as creating suicide in a particular individual. The description of hopelessness, and in particular, locus of control in Chapter 5 has been presented in such clear and practical terms that anyone intervening on behalf of a student would be able to recognize these features.

This book provides complete information on prevention [Chapter 6], intervention [Chapter 7], and postvention [Chapter 8]. These three chapters complete the necessary information in working within the college system and on behalf of individual students. The author has successfully combined a systems approach with the essential steps one should take in working with the vulnerable individual. Till now, this chapter on prevention is perhaps one of the most comprehensive and systematic reviews of this topic for college settings, to appear in print. The intervention chapter provides a broad and thorough approach for everyone to apply to a suicidal individual within the college system. Chapter 7 must be mandatory reading for all resident assistants, student counselors and others who will encounter suicidal students.

Chapter 8, the postvention chapter, examines both the system and the specific individual factors that are activated when a suicide tragedy occurs on campus. The author does not ignore any one component of the system nor the interactive aspects of each of the individual elements. This allows for a very thorough analysis and an understanding of how important it is for individuals in a system to react once a suicide occurs. All aspects of the bereavement and mourning process are appropriately and sensitively discussed.

Too often when clinicians and friends encounter a suicidal young person, we do not have a book to guide us on how to handle the various aspects of what we are confronting. That was the case up until now. This book will guide you through the demanding, frightening, and challenging circumstances that a student's suicide or threatened suicide will impose on those of us who are willing to fully respond to what we are compelled to hear.

Barry D. Garfinkel, M.D., F.R.P.C.(C)
Division of Child and Adolescent Psychiatry
University of Minnesota Medical School

Contents

Introduction

I've decided on Thursday. Actually I picked Thursday a couple of days ago and I'm just trying to see how it sits. It really is hard to make myself wait, to walk around, talk to people, make plans for next week or next month. In a way it feels good to have made the decision but it's also very scary too. Do I really want to die? That's what these 4 days are for, to try to discern that better.

— a student's diary

We talked a lot and she said she had these feelings that were always there. And I told her that I'd always listen. What I don't understand is why she didn't believe me.

— a friend

I've never felt so alone, so rejected, so . . . angry. Wasn't there something, even a little note that said "Why" so I can somehow try to understand. I need to know why, I need to know . . .

— a parent

I understand suicide from a clinical point of view. But, it's so damn difficult when your . . . my client commits suicide. It's the ultimate slap-in-the-face. It says I can't help and that's all I've been trained to do and all I ever wanted to do.

— a psychologist

No man is an island, entire of it self;
every man is a piece of the continent, a
part of the main; if a clod be washed away
by the sea, Europe is the less; . . . any man's
death diminishes me, because I am involved in
mankind. And, therefore never send to know
for whom the bell tolls, it tolls for thee.

— John Donne
(Coffin, 1952) [1]

Perspective is the relationship of aspects of a subject to each other and to the whole. This well-known selection from one of John Donne's meditations provides an example of this definition of perspective as it relates to our involvement with each other. Our loss through any person's death, particularly by suicide, diminishes us, creates different relationships, more closely bonds some people, and rends others apart. The subject of this book is college student suicide. However, to gain one perspective on this subject we need to understand the relationships that exist between an array of unique persons, different educational institutions' staff and faculty and the process of suicide itself. That brings us to a second definition of perspective, a point of view. Each person who is involved with a college student has a different point of view regarding the issue of suicide. Sometimes the differences are inconsequential, but at other times there may be major differences that have significant consequences for each other individually and collectively. A third definition of perspective is a technique for representing three dimensional objects and depth relationships on a two dimensional surface. In this book I have attempted to construct a format that would present the subject of college student suicide in a somewhat different manner. It seems to me that we often choose to view a student's suicide as an isolated, unfortunate incident. That, however, is not the way it happens. Rather, the effect of a suicide on the campus is much more like the effect that takes place when a stone is thrown into the water. There are ever widening rings as the ripple effect spreads out across the water. When these ripples reach a solid object like a shoreline they tend to disappear. However, they create marks upon the beach and create erosion in the land. That action is the metaphorical equivalent of the affect that is present on the campus following a suicidal action. There is an erosion, a wearing away of our feelings of invulnerability and immortality. It is a process that is more than just the incident. With the words of students as they speak, write, and think about their suicidal experience, I hope to create a group of three dimensional personages who will "pop-up" from this two dimensional page and become real individuals who can heighten our awareness of the effect suicide has upon individuals and the campus as an entity.

However, even as suicidal behavior is a process, a series of changes and actions which result in ideations, attempts and completions, so is the collegiate experience a process, a movement toward knowledge and understanding, concluding with the awarding of a degree testifying to this newly acquired experience and body of knowledge. In a utopian world, these two processes would be independent of each other, and suicide would possibly not exist. Unfortunately, we do not live in a utopia and there are a significant number of instances where they interrelate. How this interrelationship occurs, what effect it has upon various aspects in the life of a student and the educational institution and what might be done to alleviate the negative and affirm the positive aspects of this interrelationship is also a part of this book.

This book is not written for any single segment of the academic institution. It is written so that administrators might have a better understanding of who is coming to the campus and, once they arrive, what is needed to provide more than academic support to the men and women who are endeavoring to achieve so much—intellectually, physically, socially, spiritually—in such a short period of time. It is written so that staff in student support services, particularly residence halls, fraternities and sororities and other community living situations, can learn more about how to cope with students who exhibit various suicidal behaviors and how to act effectively at these critical moments. It is written to provide staff in counseling centers with information on the development of support groups for suicidal students and survivors. It is written so that faculty will become aware of signs of distress and understand that their interventions can have an important impact upon the student who is academically competent but becoming less effective because of stresses within his or her life. It is written for clergy who work on or adjacent to the campus so that they can develop a further understanding of this phenomenon and reach out to their parishioners both in moments of crisis and in moments of grief. It is written for campus security/law enforcement officers to facilitate their understanding and enable them to empathically intervene with attempters and sympathetically with survivors. And, it is written for students so they will come to understand they are most likely the first people who will become aware of the fact one of their peers is contemplating suicide and know how to approach and meaningfully engage him or her in a positive outcome. This is not intended to be a clinical book. Rather my intention is to present materials that will develop a sense of awareness, and a sense of competence for activities related to prevention, intervention, and postvention together with some suggested tools for the task.

I suspect that some persons reading this will regard this as too much of a "broad brush" approach to a complex issue. That may be a weakness of this approach. But, I would again remind the reader that it is critical that all parts of the academic community work together if we are to affect the lives of college students in any meaningful manner. For those who are contemplating or engaging in suicidal behaviors this is a critical point.

As a book about college student suicide, this book begins with suicidal students' views about college and suicidal behavior with their own words. This may seem a peculiar way to begin a book, but if we are to understand these students we need to hear what they have to say. Assuredly this chapter does not represent all students. It represents those students with whom I have had contact and who are at some point on a continuum of suicidal behavior and who I believe have some important views to express. They give us their perspective. Chapter two takes a different perspective toward college student suicide in that the material presented is a portrait of what the prospective student body may be like. Basically, this chapter says, "Look who's coming to college." And, this time, it's not test scores and class rankings that are the major issues. The issues are the stressors and precipitating factors toward suicide that already exist before the student sets foot on the campus for the first day of school and may continue to be distressing factors in his or her life. Chapter three is devoted to the incidence of suicide using available information in an attempt to construct perspectives on the potential and actual incidence of attempted and completed suicide among some of the major constituencies that comprise the student body. Chapter four reviews the mythology of suicide, its origins and its effects upon our individual and collective efforts to engage in interventions with suicidal students. Chapter five offers a perspective on the etiology of suicide and the development of a continuum of suicidal behavior. Chapter six, seven, and eight present information on prevention, intervention, and postvention including programs, suggestions and strategies that can be used by all members of the campus community. While prevention, intervention, and postvention are presented as separate entities, in fact they are all interrelated and necessary to a complete programmatic effort on the campus. Chapter nine is a review of the psychological, ethical, and legal consequences of the actions that may be taken toward suicidal students. It is one way in which students make some determinations about the capacity of the campus to assist them in their plight. It is also intended to help the reader focus the material in the previous eight chapters and make a decision on whether their particular campus will become a caring, supportive environment academically and psychologically. Chapter ten provides a selected bibliography of books, journals, and organizations relating to suicide and death.

We are all aware that suicide is a mental health issue on the campuses of colleges and universities throughout the United States. However, suicide is more than just a mental health issue. Suicide has a powerful emotional impact that can be seen in its various incarnations. As a concept, suicide tends to be dominated by mythology, a magical, mystical approach that permits distancing and non-involvement. As a word, suicide evokes apprehension and anxiety. When suicide is spoken of with another person, it often creates a desire within the listener to avoid or detach themselves from the discussion. As a behavior—considered, attempted, or completed—suicide evokes very powerful reactions. An atmosphere is created where discussion or involvement with the suicidal person is inhibited. Anxiety, uncertainty, hesitation, and resentment are but a few of the different emotions that may be experienced by the person who receives this information be it another student, a resident assistant, an instructor, or a member of the clergy. For each person who becomes involved there will be a different, highly individualized perspective.

- For the student who is contemplating suicide there will be the perspective that varying degrees of hopelessness and helplessness make it appear that there is little reason to continue living.
- For the roommate and/or friend there will be the perspective of being placed in the very difficult situation of not wanting to be involved, but recognizing that if nothing is done they may lose a friend. This is particularly true if he or she has been placed in the compromising position of having promised "not to tell anyone" and now realizes the matter is beyond his or her control.
- For the residence hall staff there is the perspective of needing to obtain assistance for the student while at the same time coping with their own emotional issues and stress as well as the needs of other residents who may now know or will become aware of the situation.
- For campus security staff, answering a call for an attempted or completed suicide creates a concern about properly handling a situation that will often be riddled with emotional trauma for those persons who discovered the situation as well as the difficult task of the notification of the family.
- For clergy there may be the need to react to a suicidal student who has come to seek assistance in the resolution of his or her problems. There also may be the need to comfort those who are grieving the loss of a friend while at the same time coping with their own religious values relating to life and death.
- For counseling center staff, a suicidal student presents a potentially volatile situation that requires significant emotional energy and time investment both in the initial intervention and in the ensuing counseling sessions.
- For administrators, an attempted or completed suicide brings the perspective of having to cope with family, staff, reporters, attorneys, and others who have different and sometimes competing agendas.

- For parents, there are intense personal perspectives as they attempt to understand the "why?" of an attempted or completed suicide while they are attempting to deal with their own grief and that of the rest of their family and friends.

These are simplifications of the perspectives of these individuals and they are not the only individuals who will be involved when suicide is contemplated, attempted, or committed. However, even from this very cursory overview, clearly there are many different perspectives that must be explored to fully understand not only the behavior that has resulted in the suicidal action but the reactions of those who are involved at one degree of intimacy or another with the suicidal person. All of these are important in our consideration of the various perspectives of college student suicide.

However, there is yet another perspective. What may there be about the collegiate experience, the college or university setting, that contributes to a student's suicidal behavior? We need to be aware of those policies and procedures that create stresses as well as any diminution of services for those who are most vulnerable. We need to be aware of those students who cannot keep pace psychologically. Instead of an "explosion" from them we are more likely to witness an "implosion" as they find it impossible to "explode." Most likely we may have a combination of factors creating a psychological and physical overload, where without the benefit of some type of "fuse" self-destructive behavior occurs. An institutional introspection is necessary to discover and alleviate as many of these factors as possible.

Throughout this book, the perspective of the student will be the dominant focus. Using this perspective and other pertinent materials, both para-professional and professional persons may gain insight and information on how to appropriately act and react to suicidal situations on the campus. The perspective of some other persons also will be presented to facilitate an understanding of the physical and emotional reactions that take place during this stressful time. Throughout this book there will be direct quotations from students. Some of them are paraphrased to preclude any identification of the person(s) and the true name of the person quoted has not been used. Their classification will be used as this may be pertinent to understanding the context. This is a somewhat different approach, but it is a way to understand more fully the perspective of the persons involved. It is a way to make it easier to understand the emotions of the suicidal students as they present in their words their perspectives, their distortions—which are their realities unless someone intervenes—and their realities. Some quotations are of fleeting thoughts, some are complex views from students moving toward possible suicidal actions, some are from those who have attempted or taken a fatal action that was interrupted and some are from suicide notes. They come in the form of statements, of poems, or of diary entries. All of them allow us the opportunity to view the world from their perspective as we work to intervene and prevent suicide on the campus or as we work to cope with the aftermath of a completed suicide.

Lastly, I would like to draw attention to what I consider to be a very significant and disturbing perspective. That perspective is how we view the current suicide rate for our young men and women. Between 1960 and 1980, the suicide rate for persons in the fifteen to twenty-four years of age group significantly increased moving from 5.2/100,000 to 12.3/100,000. In 1990 this rate increased to 13.2/100,000. In the 1980s there were many calls for massive suicide prevention programs as we were losing the tremendous potential human resources of our nation through youth suicide. In addition, there was also the impact of the attempted suicides that reflected a tremendous sense of turmoil in the young men and women of this age group. Suicide became the second leading cause of death, exceeded only by accidents, in the college age population. I have been particularly struck by the fact that while the calls for extensive suicide programs has subsided, the rate has not decreased. The general response is that the suicide rate has flattened out or stabilized in recent years. Unfortunately the suicide rate has flattened out at the high end.

What I have become aware of is that we have accepted this elevated rate as normal. To me that is a very disturbing thought. Then, I read Senator Daniel Patrick Moynihan's article, "Defining Deviancy Down" [2]. Moynihan looked at the American social crisis and talked about it in terms of denial and normalizing. He pointed out that we are redefining deviancy and creating new categories of normal behavior to cope with current elevated levels of various behaviors. Moynihan noted, for instance, that our current homicide rates have peaks that attract some attention but the current average levels would have been considered epidemic in the 1960s. As various problems and the rates associated with them continue to increase, we define the normal in a different way, down.

What does it mean to deviate? A dictionary definition is "to oscillate about or more increasingly away from a designated norm, as from a specified course or prescribed mode of behavior" [3, p. 361]. Something that is deviant differs "from a norm or from the accepted standards of society" [3, p. 361]. I do not want it misconstrued that I am applying the concept of "deviant" to the suicidal person. Rather I want to use the term to take a hard look at the deviations we have made to consider the actual numbers of young men and women who are engaging in various suicidal behaviors as "normal."

"Normal" has become the 1990s rates of suicide regardless of race, sex, age, or any other factor. It is a clear case of deviating, of defining "normal" down (or up as you choose to perceive it). In any case, the result is that we are engaging in denial. Denial that suicide is really a problem. Indeed, it has been easy to replace it with a concern for a new epidemic, HIV and AIDS, rather than be concerned about both. There are beginning to be some inextricable links between diagnosis of HIV+, AIDS and suicide and it will be interesting to see what becomes the new "normal" for these medical and mental health issues.

We need to be aware that the suicide rate for persons in the fifteen to twenty-four years of age bracket is now at the highest rate ever. This is not normal. Yet, two recent, major books on college students make no reference to suicide. In Pascarella and Terenzini's book, *How College Affects Students: Findings and Insights from Twenty Years of Research,* we will find one reference to suicide [4]. There is research to indicate that educational institutions do create stressors which have a negative impact on some students. And, some institutional policies may exacerbate the depressed and suicidal states of students. Winston, Anchors and Associates' *Student Housing and Residential Life: A Handbook for Professionals Committed to Student Development Goals* also makes no reference to depression and suicide [5]. There are references to rape, alcohol use and abuse, AIDS and date violence. While there is some discussion of developmental crises and developmental dissonance, critical issues related to depression and suicide are strikingly absent. I trust that this is an unintentional oversight by the authors and editors working with large volumes of material. However, I believe that it can serve to illustrate our sense of denial toward those issues with which we have great discomfort, issues of suicide, dying and death. If this is combined with our acceptance of the increasingly high rate of suicide as the normal human condition, it is an unfortunate circumstance. I would hope that the material in this book will challenge the concept that we are going to view these elevated rates as our new normalcy. And, most of all that the material will encourage less denial of this significant problem and create an activist attitude among all members of the academic community—students, staff, and faculty.

Throughout, it is important to remember that suicide must be viewed in the context of a behavior, that attempted or completed suicide is the culmination of a process that results in a traumatic event for both the individual and all of those people with whom there are connections. Whether we are students, administrators, housing services staff, counselors, police officers, clergy, student personnel staff, or any other person involved in the academic community, we need to attempt to understand why college students attempt and commit suicide as an integral part of being a caring community. At a conference I heard a speaker remark that dying and adolescence were both transitional phases that were characterized by changes, losses and separation and combined with a search for meaning and identity. While that certainly appears true of our college age population, it is equally true for all of us who search for new meanings for in truth, our education ends only with our last breath.

REFERENCES

1. C. M. Coffin (ed.), *The Complete Poetry and Selected Prose of John Donne*, Modern Library, New York, 1952.
2. D. P. Moynihan, Defining Deviancy Down, *American Scholar*, pp. 17-30, Winter 1993.
3. W. Morris, *The American Heritage Dictionary of the English Language*, American Heritage, Boston, 1969.
4. E. T. Pascarella and P. T. Terenzini, *How College Affects Students: Findings and Insights from Twenty Years of Research*, Jossey-Bass, San Francisco, 1991.
5. R. B. Winston, Jr., *Student Housing and Residential Life: A Handbook for Professionals Committed to Student Development Goals*, Jossey-Bass, San Francisco, 1993.

CHAPTER 1

Suicidal Students' Views of College and Suicidal Behavior

> I think of college as a form of witness protection program. It means I can come here and be who I want to be. I don't have to be someone who other people want me to be. I don't have to behave the way they think I should, or am expected to. I don't have to be the person I was in high school. I can start over. I can be who I really want to be. But, it's not exactly turning out that way.
>
> —Mark (freshman)

Why do young men and women enter college? What are their views on college life both before they arrive and while they are attending the institution? Why do young college men and women attempt and commit suicide? What are their views on suicide both before they arrive on the campus and after they have entered into the life of the institution? Most often, what is written about college and university life is from the point of view of the general student population, the great, supposedly homogeneous mass that moves at one pace or another toward the goal of graduation. However, within the student body, there are those individuals for whom life before entering the institution or during their campus experience does not appear to resemble that of their peers. These are the students who have experienced one level or another of depression and/or suicidal behaviors before their arrival on campus or are experiencing these phenomena during their collegiate years. For them, the campus perspective is quite different. What is going to occur throughout this book is that you will be exposed to the collegiate experience from the point of view of these students. It is their context and perspective that we need to examine to develop a complete picture of the dynamics of college student suicide and to engage in productive prevention, intervention, and postvention efforts.

Why do students attend colleges and universities and what are their perceptions of these institutions and the life that goes on within them both before and after matriculation?

1

Students enter colleges and universities for a variety of reasons. Most of the time it is assumed that their enrollments are based solely on the desire to enhance their educational status, to learn new skills so that they can obtain better jobs, pursue advanced degrees or to fulfill some life-long ambition. There is great anticipation and anxiety surrounding this momentous life change. The fantasies of collegiate life that are developed contain both the elation of anticipated success and new discoveries and the fear of many unknowns and potential failure. Their new independence also means that old support systems may not be as intact and immediately available as considerable distances often separate students from their families and friends. This may invoke varying degrees of feelings of isolation and vulnerability. Positive feelings of self-esteem may be shaken by the realization that there are now a significant number of strangers whose abilities appear equal to or better than their own and who have the same expectations of good grades and future employment possibilities.

Regardless of their own internal or external strengths and support systems, any student who enters a college or university encounters significant stressors. His or her ability to cope with the stresses that will occur throughout the collegiate career will be a measure of success in more than academic work. Often the phrase, "the best years of your life," is assigned to these significant developmental years of a student's life. However, these are years that are fraught with incredible personal, physical, social, spiritual, and sexual changes and complications. Any adult who realistically recalls these years in their own life, may well empathize with the student who responded to such a suggestion with "if these are the best years of my life, I don't want to see the rest of it."

In 1969, Chickering wrote *Education and Identity* in which he defined seven vectors of development or tasks that needed to be accomplished during adolescence and early adulthood [1]. These were: developing competence; managing emotions; developing autonomy; establishing identity; freeing interpersonal relationships; developing purpose; and developing integrity. He also pointed out that students come into the institution hesitantly, but they become independent rather soon. An analogy which Chickering used is as apt today as when it was written. He stated that this independence is that of hogs on ice.

He is on slippery new territory and without familiar footholds; he responds with thrashing or bewildered and anxious immobility. Free of accustomed restraints or outside pressures, he exhibits random activity or rigid adherence to behaviors appropriate to former situations. The dominant impression is instability [1, p. 12].

Indeed, anyone subjected to similar massive changes in their life would very likely react in similar manner.

What are students' perceptions of colleges and universities? Indeed, for the great majority of students their view is that these are institutions of higher learning where they will be involved in the process of developing a fuller understanding of their chosen field of study. It is anticipated that this work will enable them to secure employment that will satisfy both intellectual and material status. However, there are other perceptions of these institutions that may effectively interface or actually conflict with the concept of a college or university as intended by the faculty or administration. Other than a place for education, students may perceive the institution as a different vehicle, one that will serve their other perceived needs. I would submit that for a number of students, college may be viewed as a "refuge," as a "family requirement," as a "proving ground," as a *"coup de grace,"* as a "sanctuary," as "freedom to experiment," and as a "milieu."

To gain an understanding of these needs, their related experiences and to place them in a context, some vignettes of students are presented here. Their own words provide an explanation of their views of their collegiate experience and their suicidal behaviors.

COLLEGE AS A REFUGE

There are students like Mark who was quoted at the beginning of this chapter who view college as a refuge from another condition or place. Mark entered a major university with motives that were not immediately obvious. He came to the attention of residence hall staff because, while previously quite gregarious, he seemed to be withdrawing from activities. He also had expressed to his friends and to the residents assistant considerable unhappiness about his academic work. In a discussion with the resident assistant, it became clear that he was very unhappy. Mark had developed some low level suicidal ideation because the "witness protection program" didn't offer him exactly what he had believed it would. He had assumed that without anyone knowing who he was, he would be able to get rid of the expectations that had developed in his home community. However, he now found that even with a supposedly new *persona,* there still were expectations from other people. Certainly, they appeared to be different from those which existed in his family and home community. At this point they did not have the same intensity. Nevertheless, he found it impossible to escape expectations and his lack of coping skills resulted in the return of many of the suicidal thoughts he had experienced during high school. It was necessary for him to learn how to cope with expectations and develop and maintain his own identity so he could function effectively as a young adult who wouldn't need a "witness protection program."

COLLEGE AS A FAMILY REQUIREMENT

Not all students arrive on campus as the result of an independent decision by themselves or an interdependent decision between themselves and their parents. Students arrive on the campus bearing family expectations as to what they will study and what they will become. Sometimes these expectations are very positive. At other times they can be very negative and potentially destructive forces in the student's life. Quite often these students come from families dominated by physicians, dentists, lawyers, and corporate leaders. For these students their academic career and life plan have been predetermined by their parents. The student may express his or her feelings as follows:

> No one ever asked me what I wanted to do with my life. I cannot remember a time when it wasn't a "given" that I would be just like my father, my grandfather, my great grandfather and whoever came before that. I was always going to be young Dr. Mallory. Oh yes, young Dr. Mallory III. And my family is already talking about IV. Well, no son of mine will ever have to go through this because there isn't going to be a IV. I don't even think there's going to be a III much longer. I just don't want to be a doctor and I don't know how to get out of it without doing something like just ending it all.
> —George (junior)

Within this family there was an assumption that this young man would be a medical doctor given the pattern for males in the family. It was never discussed, it was just assumed. So, George was enrolled at a university with a prominent medical school so that he could proceed to his M.D. degree without interruption. Certainly he was intelligent and capable enough to achieve this goal if he had wanted to do so. However, he had other career aspirations. He loved to work with children and wanted to earn a Ph.D. in child psychology. The problem was how to discuss these ideas with a family that had foreclosed all options and was paying for his college education under the assumption that he would obtain the M.D. degree. George believed that if he decided to go against his parents' wishes they would no longer pay for his college education. Without this funding, he believed that he would have to drop out of school and work to get enough money to continue his education. That, in turn, would interrupt the flow of his academic work and he was afraid that this would make it difficult to get the grades he needed for entry into a graduate school. These unresolved predicaments led him to consider suicide as an option. For George, the major tasks of his collegiate career were to develop his own identity, autonomy and integrity and the skills that would enable him to successfully negotiate his separation and individuation from his family.

COLLEGE AS A PROVING GROUND

Other students arrive with quite different expectations from their families. Sometimes the expectation is that they will not, or should not succeed and the student is forced to prove that they are capable. In some ways this conflict is the reverse side of the "college as family requirement" coin.

> I've lasted an entire year and I'm back for another and nobody wants to give me any credit for this. All they expect is that I will fail, that I'm not smart enough. I think mom really wants me to make a go of this. But dad thinks it is really a waste of time—and his money . . . a damned high priced MRS. degree as he puts it. Well, if I don't make it, I won't be a problem and I won't fail at that.
> —Celia (sophomore)

Celia's last statement was a less than veiled threat. If she did not succeed, she would not return home to be ridiculed and accused of wasting hard earned moneys. Rather she would make certain that she would succeed in what she presumed would be the last act of her life. For her, college was a constant battle to prove herself, particularly to her father. In addition to normal college stresses, there was the stress of having committed herself to a guaranteed course of action should she not succeed in her college studies. This foreboding commitment created an undercurrent of insidious stress for her. Celia had a very clear concept and academic plan for her field of study. Her task was to achieve a sense of identity enabling her to manage her relationships with her family, particularly her father.

Now, if these last two examples seem incredibly stereotypical situations, they are. They are stereotypical because these expectations exist and in unfortunate numbers. It is very important for anyone working with students to recognize that whatever advances have been made in the development of new options and alternatives for young men and women, stereotypes and stereotypical expectations exist and students are caught up within them. This creates a significant discontinuity in their lives and we need to know not only where they want to go, but from whence they came. Otherwise we will be less effective in our work with them.

COLLEGE AS *COUP DE GRACE*

Some students have very high expectations of themselves based on their high school experience. Their past successes, both academic and extra-curricular, may have been almost routine. Their expectations were that their college experience would be the crowning achievement of their student careers. Now they find their new experiences are not matching their expectations. Consequently, new and difficult predicaments are being created and require responses.

> It was all so easy. Well, to be truthful it wasn't always that easy. But, I got the A's I wanted and needed to get here. Now, I work harder than I have ever worked before and nothing is working out for me. I couldn't even tell my roommate that I got a C in the last two midquarters that we have together. He got a A and a B. I just told him that they must have lost my test since I couldn't find it. Then today! I got back my biology midterm with an F! I never got less than a B in high school. Let's face it, I just can't make it here and I won't go home and work at some dumb job. I don't understand it. I just feel hopeless.
>
> —Maria (freshman)

In college recruitment materials the "new competition" that students will face is not mentioned. The broad spectrum group from high school has now been replaced with the select percentage who are accustomed to receiving the A's and B's in a routine manner. The shock of a lesser grade, and particularly a failing grade is not only disconcerting, but a major tragedy. While colleges and universities are busy recruiting the "best and the brightest" there also should be an awareness of these students' impending needs that have been brought about by significantly increased levels of competition. Maria is in the process of attempting to achieve intellectual competence but this competence is threatened by other individuals creating a crisis of self-esteem. Maria's tasks of clarifying purpose and developing her own integrity are linked with learning to manage her emotions and gaining self-control.

COLLEGE AS SANCTUARY

Other students arrive on the campus with the assumption that campuses are islands of tranquillity and safety where the threats and actions taking place in the "outside world" can be avoided. For them, the campus takes on a completely different atmosphere once this concept is violated.

You must really think I'm naive . . . no just plain dumb, dumb, dumb, dumb. I thought he was a real friend. Everybody thinks he is just the most wonderful guy, he's so nice and does little things for all the girls in the dorm. And then he did this to me. I don't know why I'm telling you, but I have to talk to someone. No one is ever going to believe me. I tried to call my mom, but when she answered the phone I couldn't speak. I just hung up. I felt so . . . I just wanted to die and didn't know how to do it. But, if I have to go on living here and listening to everyone tell me how lucky I am to have him for a friend or have him walk around and stop and talk to me in the cafeteria like nothing ever happened, I will find a way to do it!

—Ann (sophomore)

What the hell made him think he could do that? What the hell gave him the idea that I might be gay? I trusted him. He *was* my best friend and we'd often go out drinking so when he flew into town and asked me to meet him as his motel I didn't even think twice. I drank way too much and he said I was too drunk to drive home. He was probably right! So, I just took off my shirt and jeans and fell into bed . . . and asleep. I woke up with no shorts on and he was doing . . . I pulled on my clothes and ran to the car asking myself all kinds of questions while I was driving. I was so angry, so ashamed that it was all I could do to keep from hitting something with the car. Why did he do it? How could I put myself in such a position. Guys are supposed to be able to take care of themselves.

—Sam (senior)

For both individuals there was a violation of trust by a friend resulting in a sexual assault. For both of them, there were feelings of shame, guilt, and powerlessness. The perceived helplessness associated with each of their circumstances created situations where they felt that life was intolerable and each began to look for solutions that included the possibility of suicide. The supposedly carefree days of college had suddenly been destroyed and replaced with the reality of lost innocence and concerns, even fears, of being labeled in a derogatory manner should their peers ever discover that these incidents had taken place. For Sam and Ann their personal identities had been attacked. Sam was concerned that he would be labeled as a homosexual should any of his friends discover what had taken place. Ann was concerned that she would be regarded as "easy" if the incident became known. The concept of trusted interpersonal relationships had been severely violated. For both of them the tasks of managing emotions, redeveloping their integrity and learning to trust new interpersonal relationships would be paramount.

COLLEGE AS FREEDOM TO EXPERIMENT

College life is also a period where experimentation and exploration continues as the individual strives to learn of their place in the "adult world." This process is intensified because the apparent freedom from parental and other constraints is exemplified by the "who'll know?" fantasy. For many, movement through these periods of experimentation and exploration proceeds without significant distress. For others, the new freedom may result in situations that are beyond their current coping skills.

> God, I don't know how it happened. Oh, shit, I do know how it happened, I'm not that dumb! I just didn't think it would! Jill didn't either! But, she went to the doctor Monday and found out she was pregnant. Up in smoke, both of our careers! Catholics don't have abortions! Our parents will just kill us! We just talked and cried last night—all night. We just couldn't see any way out. We even talked about "going for a drive," you know, a high speed drive. An accident, that's all. But, everything else is going wrong so we'd probably just end up getting crippled and making things even worse. We wanted to make sure it would work, no more failures. Isn't there another way out, we really don't want to cause any more pain. And we can't go on this way, something has to happen!
>
> —Mark (freshman)

Sexual experimentation without any contraceptive protection (they supposedly understood the rhythm method) created a situation where parental and religious expectations were not met and their careers seemed in total jeopardy because of an unwanted pregnancy. The immediate crisis, compounded by seemingly inflexible parameters, produced a panic situation that fortunately was not acted upon during the night. During that time, the introduction of the element of the fear of another potential failure contributing to an already impossible situation was a major factor in deterring a contemplated double suicide. With the possibility of suicide still in the background, Mark's exploration for another way to cope with this situation had begun. For Mark and Jill the management of emotions relating to both sexuality and aggression was to become significant tasks. As their choice became to marry and raise the child, there was also a significant need to develop further their interpersonal relationships as well as that with their parents.

It is important to remember that sexual experimentation is not confined to heterosexual activity. As students seek to define their sexual identity, homosexual and bisexual activity also take place. Students have often remarked that they are not certain "where" they want to be. The greater openness and acceptance of gays, lesbians, and bisexuals on the campus have enabled more students to present themselves as they are. However, recently there also has been a significant lack of tolerance shown on campuses. This presents a conflicting milieu for these students. There are times when the desire for acceptance as a total person clearly outweighs the potential risks of being known as a homosexual. Students seeking their full identities are at risk without significant support systems.

> My roommate wanted to know why I didn't have sex with this woman last night. He said she didn't believe it was because I didn't have a condom. And he told me she thought I was gay. I asked Jim what difference it would make if I was gay. He said it wouldn't matter because he knew other gay guys in the hall. So, I told him I was gay. Jim just looked at me and said, "You're kidding!" I told him I wasn't joking and asked him not to tell anyone else. He just said he had to go study at the library and left. He never came back that night. When I met him at team practice I asked where he had been, he said he had studied and stayed at a friend's apartment. Well, now he's asked to change dorm rooms and asked coach not to assign us together on team trips. I asked him if he had told them and he said he hadn't said a word. But, somebody is going to wonder what has happened between us. I mean we were like brothers. We've known each other since grade school and I know if he tells anyone it will be his dad. And my dad and his dad are best buds and I know it will get back to my dad. I just know it is going to get out. Then, it will be all over. If that happens I might as well kill myself and spare everyone the pain.
>
> —Frank (junior)

A quiet relevation to a trusted friend, who appeared to be accepting of a gay lifestyle, became a fearful experience. Jim was apparently accepting of gay men who were at a distance. Jim now distanced himself from Frank in a manner that was perplexing to anyone who knew the two men. The unspoken reasons for room reassignment had led to rumor and speculation. The concern that Jim would eventually tell his father of the reason for these actions would lead to Frank's father's knowledge of his sexual preference was becoming an intolerable uncertainty for Frank. He knew his father's attitudes toward homosexuality was one of complete disgust. He saw no reasonable resolution to his situation. Frank had decided that if his fears were realized he would take the action that he saw as bringing the least amount of pain to those involved, his suicide. For Frank the task of deciding whether to openly acknowledge his homosexuality was a major task in the development of his own identity and integrity.

Yet, there are also purported experiments that may conceal a more deadly purpose. An example of this took place in a residence hall where Bill's behaviors had become of concern to some residents and the residence hall staff. While he did not drink often as a freshman, Bill's behavior changed significantly during his sophomore year. Again, he did not drink on a regular basis. However, about every three weeks, Bill would consume prodigious amounts, particularly of "white lightning." Usually Bill drank until he passed out and he told friends that he often "blacked out." This behavior had become "legendary" among the students in the hall. His friends "took care of him" so he wouldn't get in trouble with staff or be taken to detox. When they learned of these incidents, staff would discuss the binge drinking habits with Bill. These conversations had little effect as Bill insisted he didn't have a drinking problem, wasn't doing anything that was different from any other male resident and he had not violated any hall rule since staff had not found him drinking. Bill was referred to the hall director. In his conversation with the hall director, Bill gave some indications that there was more than an abusive alcohol situation present. Bill remarked that he appreciated the efforts of students who would "take care of me." He said that he knew he had some real friends and that, at last, he had met someone who cared about him and really "wanted him around." Other statements indicated Bill believed no one really wanted him around. When the director said, "It seems to me that you are trying to kill yourself through this behavior." Bill had this response:

> I don't know how you figured that out, but you're right. There are some things going on right now that I don't think I want to talk about. I've never been the son my parents wanted. Seems like I was always the one who would get in trouble. I've heard some people say that my folks would be better off if I just had an accident or something while I was drinking. Now, they've never said anything like that, I think my folks do care. But I know I'm a real s.o.b. at times and I think it would be best if I wasn't around to cause any more problems and that's when I got the idea. Just put it this way, my folks can deal with a dead drunk, they can't deal with a dead suicide.
>
> —Bill (sophomore)

Indeed, had he died during one of his binges, the coroner would most likely have certified Bill's death as due to acute alcoholic poisoning. The real reason would have been a carefully disguised suicide. Bill believed that an accidental death caused by alcohol would end his pain and also preclude as much pain as possible for his parents. For Bill the development of self control and establishment of healthy interpersonal relationships and clarifying his purposes in life were to be his major developmental tasks.

These "socially acceptable suicides" can happen in a variety of ways—alcohol, accident, high risk activity. These are self-destructive behaviors that may not appear to be suicides but in fact are. Students use their intellect to devise these self-destructive behaviors so that they and their families will not be stigmatized with the suicidal death. At times this deception can incorporate the symptoms of another disease.

> I've read all about bulimia and anorexia. I know what the symptoms are and how people are supposed to act. And, I can act. I've always been able to take any part and make it mine. So, people will never know what I'm doing. They'll just think 'poor little Jean. I don't know what ever made her so ill.' I'll just do what it takes. And it won't be much fun but pain killers will help. They'll all be so sorry for me. They'll never know why and they don't need to know. All they'll know is I died of an eating disorder and that's all I want them to know.
>
> —Jean (senior)

Jean was another student attempting a disguised suicide. As she put it, "I know that I won't be condemned for dying from an eating disorder. It will just be an unfortunate situation. They'd never say that if I committed suicide." For Jean, acting was her only interest and she had been unable to secure a part after several tryouts at university and local theaters. Jean was having a difficult time achieving competence in her chosen field which could mean a change in career choices. As her identity was tied to being an actress, issues of developing a new identity and purpose in life would become major tasks for her. For her, the greatest acting of her life was to take place while she was dying. If college could not be her "ticket" to the theater stage, it would become the stage for her final act.

COLLEGE AS MILIEU

For some students the choice of a college or university is based on its size. Does it fit them? Is the institution too large or too small? Did they make the right choice? Or, did they have all the requisite information to make an intelligent choice. Much has been written on the relationship between an individual and his or her environment. Huebner discussed the interaction of students and campus and noted there has been a movement toward "determining whether students are able to use the college environment for personal, intellectual and social development" [2, p. 139]. There is a generalized consensus that a large institution may be too impersonal and provide little or no support for a student. Students often migrate from a large institution to a smaller one for this reason. However, at times the situation is reversed and a student will leave a smaller institution to gain a broader field of study or some anonymity at a larger institution. At any educational institution there are students who feel suicidal and attribute much of their discomfort to the institution's size.

> This place is just so damned big! Nobody here really cares what happens. I'm gone, another number comes in and takes my place. We're just a lot of numbers. So, nobody here will notice when I'm gone. I could die right in the middle of campus and they'd just haul me off—maybe there'd be little notice somewhere on the back page of the campus paper would say that somebody had committed suicide on campus. You see, nobody cares!
>
> —Kara (sophomore)

> This place is like living in a glass bowl! I wish everybody would just mind their own business. I came here because I thought I would like a small college where I could make some life-long friends. I'm not real proud of what my dad does for a living but I didn't think anyone would find out here, hundreds of miles from anywhere. Now nobody wants to associate with me. I've never felt so alone. I eat alone and no one comes to see me in my room. I can't tell my dad why I want to change schools. And I can't deal with all the behind the back comments. I can't trade in for another family and I can't live with this one in a place like this. Reminds me of a play—*Stop the World, I Want to Get Off!*
>
> —Lester (freshman)

Institutional size affects students differently. The amount of discomfort in any institution creates a situation where a student begins to look for a way to relieve the anxiety. There is a complex interaction at work between the student and his or her environment. The behavior of the student is a result of this interaction. In this instance there are tasks for both the student and the institution. The development of competencies that will enable him or her to function within the institution is important. However, it is equally important as a task for the institution to understand how it contributes, negatively or positively, to the environment. The collegiate environment must include possibilities for the development of not only intellectual skills, but also skills of personal and social development. If the institution fails in those tasks, the developmental tasks of students will be made all the more difficult.

Students enter colleges and universities for a wide range of reasons. Not all of these reasons are consonant with the institution's mission of intellectual enrichment, but they may be more closely allied if the institution also genuinely seeks to provide for the general welfare of students. Students perceive a college or university as more than an intellectual endeavor, it is where they hope that they can work through developmental tasks (even though they are not perceived in those psychological terms) and become a whole person. Students also perceive failure in their multiplicity of efforts and at times do not have sufficient coping mechanisms to support them. If, at this point, they withdraw to the extent that their options and alternatives become limited to just two—living or dying—the risk of suicidal behavior becomes very high. If they are unsure about the sensitivity of the human environment to their pain, they engage in behaviors to determine if there is someone who cares—the "cry for help" whether it be verbal or non-verbal. If students sense there are resources available to them and these resources appear empathic, genuine and capable, they may seek assistance in the resolution of their pain rather than attempt or commit suicide.

What are these students' views on suicide? In the chapter on prevention (chapter 6), the research data on students' views on suicide is presented. From the quotations presented above, it would appear that while there is an ambivalence toward a suicidal action, there is a fairly pervasive acceptance that suicide is a viable alternative. I have always been struck by one particular student's comments on suicide. While maintaining his ambivalence toward suicide, he was always very aware when he was approaching a critical state.

> When I reach a certain point the world changes for me. It is no longer a three dimensional world. It becomes a two dimensional world. Everything is flat! There is no depth! It's like I am going to walk right into a 'wall' because I can't go beyond what I see. When this happens I know that I need to do something because I know what the alternative is. I know it sounds very strange, but that's what happens. Does this happen to other people?
>
> —Ray (graduate student)

There are significant variations in attitudes toward suicide among suicidal students as will be seen from the student observations throughout the book. Each variation reflects the uniqueness of that individual. That is why suicide is regarded as a most individualized and personalized action.

> I know it's wrong. I know it's not the solution that I need. I know I can't do it to myself. I've tried and I just throw up the minute I start taking something. I just can't do it! Yet, I feel so damned awful that I want all my feelings to just stop. How can I want to die so badly and still keep fighting dying?
>
> —Mary (sophomore)

Mary's strong ethical views about suicide were a major element in her physical reaction to the ingestion of drugs. At this point in her suicidal process her belief that it was wrong to commit suicide effectively counterbalanced the psychological pain that she was experiencing. For her (and eventually her therapist) this powerful belief system was an effective ally in the resolution of her personal crisis. However, this type of belief system is not always present to assist in the prevention of a suicidal action.

> I've decided that it's just another way to die. It isn't right and it isn't wrong. People shouldn't judge what you do until they have experienced your life, you know . . . . that old bit about walking in the Indian's moccasins. That's how I feel about it. At least you were right, you can't know exactly how I feel. Hell, I don't even know exactly how I feel! Two of my friends did it. One of them was a really good friend and I really don't know how they felt either. I wish I knew. But, they weren't bad guys, they just hurt a lot like a lot of us do. Well, right now I wouldn't do it. But that doesn't mean that I won't in the future because like I said, it's just another way to die.
>
> —Elliott (junior)

Elliott's views on suicide were non-judgmental. That also coincided with his general view of life—people should not judge each other but take them at "face-value." His view of suicide would place him in a higher risk category because there were apparently no inhibitions. Perhaps the suicide of his friends created a need to insulate himself through this attitude. Further discussions on his point of view became impossible when he was hospitalized for severe depression while living with his parents during the summer.

Students' views of college and suicidal behavior are as diverse as the student body. We can know what they are by being alert, by asking questions, by genuinely caring and by providing the resources that are needed to facilitate the developmental growth of students. To do this is to provide the potential for positive perceptions and behaviors among the vast majority of students. To do less is to invite potential disaster for both students and the institution.

I will conclude this chapter with four days from Sharon's diary. Sharon engaged in a potentially lethal suicidal action, was found by her friends and taken to a hospital where she recovered. She gave me a copy of the pages from her diary which described what she anticipated would be her last four days of life. I believe that these thoughts provide us with an intimate view of a seriously suicidal person. The diary was intended to be read following her death to explain why she committed suicide.

Monday

I know I have to do this. I never thought of it before in my impulsiveness but this time I'm not being impulsive and some how I've got to let you know that. I keep telling myself that there is nothing I can say at this point that will be enough, yet I have to try. In a way it reminds me of a story that we read in Spanish last week. The woman didn't want to give an explanation because she knew no one would believe her anyhow. In a way that's how I feel because my reasons are both so simple and yet so complex, but what I really want to do is somehow to redeem myself—or at least explain myself. That's what you're looking for anyway isn't it?

I write this on a Monday afternoon (the 12th). I want to put thought into this ahead of time. Why did I do it? Simply put, because it hurts too much. But it's more than that. I go through these phases in my life when I'm suicidal and it's going to keep coming back and keeping hurting. What makes me feel this way? That's what I haven't quite figured out. It has to do with not being good enough, special enough maybe. This isn't coming out right. See, what you must know too is that I feel loved. I know it's there from my friends and my family. I don't know how though to use that. And there wasn't anything any of you could have done!! I didn't tell you, I didn't send out any signs. It's the fact that there are people caring about me that makes it so hard. If I hadn't all these people in my life I would have done it much sooner. I *have* thought about how it would affect you, I've thought about you collectively and individually as well and all I can say is—I'M SORRY. This is without a doubt the MOST SELFISH thing I've ever done. But I can't keep living just for other people. I've done that my whole life and most especially in the last two years.

Why do I hurt? I guess I'm not exactly sure why. It seems to me though that I always hurt. The littlest things can make me happy sometimes. But I'm also sensitive—"it's my biggest asset and my biggest fault." I over-react. Actually it's not action it's feeling. I just feel too much and too hard. And I don't want to go through my life this way—I can't and I won't. I feel like there is so much I want to say now and I just can't think of how I want you to be able to know the Sharon, Sherri or Shar that I never let you know before—the part of me that had to end up like this. It's weird to be writing this now, even though I plan to wait a few days—and it probably makes you think I'm just that much weirder. Please don't remember me that way. Every time I walk outside, talk to someone or get a hug I wonder—what the hell am I planning on doing. And it hurts. It hurts to think I'm going to leave you, the sunshine, etc. But I can't bear the living anymore, I really can't.

When I feel depressed like this it's so hard to interact and then I'm even more angry with myself because it's just a cycle getting more and more down on myself. I know I'm a good person and I try really hard to be better. Maybe it's just sometimes I see so many neat people around me and it discourages me. I'm not good *enough*. I don't care *enough*. I don't give *enough*. And GOD KNOWS I try.

Speaking of God, that's a whole other story. I really *have* lost my faith—I know it sounds crazy to say that. I'm not saying that God doesn't exist, but *I* can't pray to him or worship or whatever. It hurts because I know what I'm missing yet it's just not there for me. Too bad, because I probably could use it now.

I love you all a lot and I tried hard to show you and I'm so sorry for this. But I just can't live anymore. I don't know why it is but I'm just not strong enough. Please don't think of me as crazy. I'm not crazy and this was not an irrational or an insane act. I've thought about it for a long time. Just think about it. How have I been towards you this week? Not irrational, maybe only just trying to say good-bye. If there is anything I would like to do now it would be to *make* you understand and have compassion, not pity or anger. Just understand. But I can't make you do anything, I can only hope. All I can imagine is that you must be so angry at the hurt I have caused. Again, all I hope that is that it will heal and that it may make you a stronger person—could that be my last gift to you? It's kind of like when John Brantner committed suicide. (Note: Brantner was a university professor who committed suicide.) I can't remember exactly what the paper said but it was a good legacy that he left.

Only you can make yourself happy—and I just can't do that for myself.   I LOVE YOU & I'M SORRY

Tuesday

I've decided on Thursday. Actually I picked Thursday a couple of days ago and I'm just trying to see how it sits. It really is hard to make myself wait, to walk around, talk to people, make plans for next week or next month. In a way it feels good to have made the decision but it's also very scary too. Do I really want to die? that's what these 4 days are for, to try to discern that better.

I do know that I don't want to live. I don't want to experience any more of the pain of life. And the funny thing about that is that I've probably had it pretty easy up until now, comparatively speaking. I look at other people and what there is to deal with out in the "real world" and I just know I don't want to do it. It really makes me depressed to walk across the campus and see the people who work there. I think about the daily "rat race" to move up, to compete, constantly having to negotiate one thing or another. I don't want to do it. I'm already so tired of having to perform at school, turn things out, jump through hoops. And life is only going to get more complicated, more demanding. I don't want to keep feeling the hurt, struggling with feelings of suicide which I believe will somehow always be there.

I wrote yesterday that I'm a good person which may be true to some extent but not really. Everyone loves me from what I *do* not who I *am*. I feel like I am constantly having to prove myself through some sort of action or from giving of myself. That's what I get my self-worth from but I realize now that that isn't really any good. I need to feel that people will love me for just who I am and that's where I realize that I am really not good. I'm not a good enough person for someone to love me for just who I am and I finally realized that I couldn't "compete" with those who are. I'm sorry I couldn't give more, no wait. I was giving. I'm sorry I couldn't *be* more.

Wednesday

Today I wanted so much to be able to say good-bye to you but I didn't know how. I really struggled with my decision but I do not want to live. I think that if it's hard now I could drop out of school for the quarter—but I don't ever want to deal with school, with all the "rat race" things I talked about before. Is there any part of me that wants to live? I guess there must have been something because I came so close to telling my therapist—"here, this is what's really going on—SAVE ME!" But I thought a lot about it and I don't want to be saved. So I got passed this hurdle, I'll just have so much—and worse things yet—to deal with. No, I can't do it, I must go.

I've thought about goals that I have had, to get married and have a family. That was so important to me, how is it that I can let go of it so easily now? I just can't imagine anything in life that can make up for all the hurt that gets thrown at you, all the struggle etc.

I really wish I could do something about the guilt I'm supposedly going to cause. I'm so sorry about the hurt that I caused. You must believe that there wasn't anything you could do. I didn't let *anyone* know what was going on, that my depression was really going to lead to suicide. I didn't want any help!! If I would have wanted help I knew there were many people I could turn to. I know you were there for me just like I tried to be there for you. But I *didn't* want the help and I didn't let you in. My rationale for this is that if you knew and then something happened you would feel guilty for not having done enough. See this all happens because of what was going on inside my head and I didn't let it out. Please don't feel guilty. Be angry with me or be hurt if you must but don't feel guilty.

Thursday

It's a rainy morning, how appropriate. As I took the bus up there I had a chance to look at the world, downtown, the community where I grew up. It's such a cold lonely world.

I really don't have much else to say, it's covered pretty well as I read over what I've written so far. These 4 days have gone by pretty fast, after dragging so at the beginning. Sometimes I think I must be crazy, the methodical way I'm going through this. But I don't feel crazy, this was a rational act done by a rational person, remember that. I made a choice. *GOOD-BYE*

Now if you are really mad at me don't read any further because I want to say something about my funeral, which may seem even more morbid than anything I've written thus far. The most important thing to me is that I be cremated—and this is something I've said before. Don't waste money on a funeral, don't even spend money on a casket for reviewal if you don't have to. I don't want to be buried in the ground. Spread my ashes over some body of water, a lake or river. I loved to swim. Out there in the middle of a lake, it was there I felt most free.

I suppose you'll have to have some sort of church service, even though I haven't gone for months. They tell me that the Catholic Church will do funerals for suicide victims now because the funeral is really for the survivors. Do Michael's bird song, and also that song that goes—Surely it is God who saves me, I will trust in him and not be afraid . . . . that song really did save me once, too bad there isn't a God for me now.

Make sure my money, that little of it that there is goes to people who are really needy, give it to the poor and homeless in the Twin Cities. I am painful aware of that need. If anyone wants any of my stuff, let them have it. I guess I won't be needing it anymore.

WHERE AM I GOING NOW!

Many of the thoughts expressed by Sharon will be found throughout this book. It is my hope that these perspectives will make it possible to intervene with other students like Sharon before they write the last four days in their diary.

REFERENCES

1. A. W. Chickering, *Education and Identity,* Jossey-Bass, San Francisco, 1969.
2. L. A. Huebner, Interaction of Student and Campus, in *Student Services: A Handbook for the Profession,* U. Delworth, G. R. Hanson, and associates (eds.), Jossey-Bass, San Francisco, 1980.

CHAPTER 2

Portrait of a Student Body:
Potential Antecedents for Suicide

Whether the incidence of suicide among college or university students is precipitated by events that have taken place before their matriculation, by events during their collegiate years or a combination of the two may be difficult to ascertain. The existing psychological state or the risk factors that are present within those students who are entering the institution should be of considerable importance and concern. They will affect the role of student services, particularly those persons who are in direct contact with students (e.g., advisors, counselors, resident assistants, hall directors, nurses, physicians, campus security, etc.) while they are enrolled.

There is evidence of a number of high risk factors as antecedents for potential suicidal behaviors present among students entering a college or university. These students probably have never discussed their adverse personal circumstances with anyone unless it has been with their peers. Consequently, they may arrive at the institution with a considerable amount of "psychological baggage" needing resolution. A review of some of the latest available data (generally from 1985 forward) presents a portrait of a student body at risk.

In 1989, the Minnesota Department of Education began a student survey project among students in grades six, nine and twelve. The Minnesota Student Survey (Prevention and Risk Reduction Unit), is to be conducted every three years with the following goals:

- "To get a more accurate picture of students' perspectives.
- To ascertain the level of a variety of problems that confront students.
- To assist educators, parents, and communities with responding to young peoples' needs.
- To monitor the effectiveness of prevention efforts.

• To establish a standardized mechanism for evaluating students' concerns and problem behaviors across communities and over time" [1, p. 6].

The comparison sample consisted of 85,322 students in 1989 and 96,116 students in 1992. The race/ethnicity of these students in 1992 was 85 percent Caucasian, 4 percent biracial/other, 3 percent Asian American, 3 percent African American, 3 percent unknown, 2 percent Native American and 1 percent Hispanic. The information reported here is for high school seniors, the potential college freshmen.

RISK FACTOR

Personal Chemical Use and Abuse

The study found alcohol use among seniors had declined from 54 percent to 41 percent between 1989 and 1992 for those individuals who used alcohol at least once a month. Those who had used marijuana or other non-prescription drugs during the past year changed from 22 percent in 1989 to 18 percent in 1992. Likewise, the percentage of those who used alcohol or other drugs on a weekly basis dropped from 35 percent to 24 percent. Fewer students reported that they were drinking to the point of intoxication. In 1989, 43 percent of the seniors reported intoxication at least once a month and 40 percent reported having five or more drinks on a typical occasion. In 1992, those who reported intoxication decreased to 30 percent and those who had five or more drinks decreased to 35 percent. Even with these positive changes, the study found that there was cause for concern because the proportions of users who are involved in serious problems show much smaller declines in usage.

> By far, the highest rates of alcohol and other drug use are among students who frequently engage in antisocial behaviors. Those who report feeling alienated from their families have the next highest elevations of use. Adolescents with a history of suicide attempt, sexual or physical abuse, depression, anxiety, low self-esteem, or family alcohol/drug problems all show significant elevations in use compared with adolescents without these problems. . . . The smallest declines are seen among those adolescents who feel alienated from their families, who have been sexually abused or who frequently engage in antisocial behaviors [1, p. 16].

The combination of these risk factors and the use of alcohol or other drugs creates a potentially dangerous situation.

The relationship between alcohol abuse and suicidal behaviors has been clearly demonstrated. Wright investigated the incidence of serious suicidal thought and its relationship to family stress, drinking and drug abuse problems among both high school seniors and college students [2]. He found "both high school and college students who reported ST's (serious suicidal thoughts) were significantly more likely than their classmates to think of themselves as having a drinking problem, a drug-abuse problem, and to remember their childhood as being unhappy" [2, p. 577]. Seriously suicidal students reported drinking and drug abuse problems three to six times more often than their classmates.

In a psychological autopsy of twenty children and adolescents aged twelve to nineteen who had committed suicide, Shafii, Carrigan, Whittinghill and Derrick found 70 percent of the suicide victims were reported to have frequently used non-prescribed drugs or alcohol [3]. Robbins and Alessi found alcohol abuse was significantly associated with suicidal tendencies, the number of suicidal gestures, the seriousness of suicidal intent and the medical lethality of the behaviors [4]. "Substance abuse in a depressed adolescent appears both to increase the risk of multiple attempts and to add to the risk of a medically serious attempt" [4, pp. 591-592]. Kinkel, Bailey and Josef found chemical substance use was a solid indicator for a potential suicide attempt [5]. They investigated use by males and females and found there were differing reactions to the heavy use of these chemicals.

> These studies lend credence to the view that the impact of some drugs (alcohol, marijuana) can move women rather than men further along the continuum of self-destructive behavior and loss of control, which may make a suicide attempt more likely" [5, p. 57].

Murphy also examined the role of substance abuse in suicide [6]. He reported "67% of the suicides under the age of 30 years were identified as substance abusers" [6, p. 594]. Berman and Schwartz found two thirds of the adolescent drug users ($n = 298$, age range 13–19) reported suicidal ideation, 30 percent reported having made one or more attempts which is about three times the number of attempts in normal adolescents [7]. Forty percent of the attempters had used drugs within eight hours of the attempt. They noted that although depression was reported as prevalent prior to the beginning of drug use, "suicide ideation and behavior increased significantly during the years of drug use. If substance use is intended as a self-medication of an underlying depression, it evidently fails miserably in accomplishing this purpose; instead, it appears to potentiate suicidality" [7, p. 313]. Felts, Chenier and Barnes used data from 3,064 respondents in the 1990 North Carolina Youth Risk Behavior Survey to examine the relationship between adolescent drug use and suicidal behavior [8]. They found drug use (particularly crack/cocaine) was related to increased ideation and other suicidal behaviors.

Downey chose to explore the hypothesis that increased use, misuse and abuse of drugs were part of a constellation of factors that has resulted in an increase in youth suicide [9]. Reviewing the literature and the research done in this area, she noted reports indicated there were significant correlations between alcohol use, drug use or a combination of the two and suicidal behavior. She came to the conclusion that, in fact, drug abuse may be a form of slow suicide. However, there comes a point when even drugs fail to deaden the intense psychological pain. They also fail to fulfill the unmet needs of the individual. At the point, "when chemicals fail to provide the sought after relief and solution to one's problems, suicide can then become the one and only way out-THE LAST EXIT" [9, p. 266].

Valois, Vincent, McKeown, Garrison and Kirby analyzed types and predictors of violent behaviors among 2,299 eleventh and twelfth grade students (48% males; 52% females) in South Carolina [10]. They found binge drinking (5 or more drinks on 1 occasion) in the last thirty days was self-reported by 52 percent of the Caucasian males and 34 percent of the Caucasian females. Twenty-five percent of the African American males and 15 percent of the African American females reported the same behavior. They noted the use of alcohol and other drugs dramatically increased the risk of violent behaviors including suicide. The authors suggested campuses request incoming freshman complete the CDC's (Center for Disease Control) Youth Risk Behavior Study or the Problem Behavior Index (Donovan and Jessor, [11]) as a way to assess target outreach and prevention efforts on the campus.

It is patently clear that there is a significant correlation between alcohol/drug abuse and suicidal behaviors. It is also clear that there are a considerable number of potential college students who will bring these characteristics with them as they matriculate. Students may be abusing alcohol and/or other drugs to provide an escape from problems that are creating an intolerable situation or as a disinhibitor for a suicidal action or as a "signal flare" of their level of distress. It is important to determine the underlying cause and its connection with potential suicidal action as a necessary element in intervention efforts.

Parental Chemical Use and Abuse

The Minnesota study also looked at another potential risk factor [1]. Students were asked about family alcohol and drug problems and there was only a slight decline in the three years between surveys. Seniors reported that alcohol and/or drug problems among family members changed slightly. Problems in 25 percent of the seniors' families in 1989 decreased to 22 percent in 1992. Viewed separately, seniors reported that family drug problems changed from 9 percent in 1989 to 8 percent in 1992, or virtually no change. The family alcohol problems showed only a 2 percent decrease to 20 percent in 1992. The report noted

> family alcohol and drug problem questions were included primarily to determine the risks faced by students rather than to serve as a comparison of rates of family problems over time. Students who report family substance abuse are more likely than other students to be regular users themselves [1, p. 32].

Pfeffer reported that both fathers and mothers of attempters exhibited more alcoholism than the parents of non-attempters [12]. Leenars and Wenckstern noted that a central factor associated with adolescent suicide is a malfunctioning family system which includes alcoholism [13].

Consequently, colleges and universities may find students who are at risk because of this external risk factor that may defy all efforts at change.

Sexual Abuse and Assault

Sexual abuse is another risk factor for potential suicide. The Minnesota study asked about lifetime experiences with sexual abuse [1]. Intrafamilial sexual abuse was determined from a "yes" response to the question "Has any older or stronger member of your family ever touched you sexually or had you touch them sexually?" As might be expected, female seniors reported a higher percentage (6.9%) than male seniors (1.9%). Extrafamilial sexual abuse was determined from a "yes" response to the same question as above with "adult or older person outside your family" substituted for the family member in the question. Again, female seniors had a higher percentage of experiences (15.8%) than males (3.3%). For female seniors there was an increase of 2.2 percent between 1989 and 1992. Some students reported they had experienced both intra- and extrafamilial sexual abuse. The overall rates showed 19 percent of the females and 4 percent of the males were victims of sexual abuse during their lifetime.

Hall and Flannery surveyed adolescents between the ages of fourteen and seventeen and found 12 percent of the females and 2 percent of the males said they had been raped or sexually assaulted [14]. They noted many adolescents may be unsure of what rape is or fear reporting it which may lead to under reporting. A poll of 1700 sixth to ninth grade students conducted by the Cranston, Rhode Island, Rape Crisis Center's sexual assault awareness program found 24 percent of the boys and 16 percent of the girls surveyed said it was acceptable for a man to force a woman to have sex if he had spent "a lot of money" on her [15]. If the couple had been dating for more than six months, 65 percent of the boys and 47 percent of the girls said it was acceptable for a man to force sex with a woman. Attitudes are formed at an early age and this example of attitudes toward sexual assault would indicate a definite possibility of under reporting as the action would be considered "normal" or at the very least "acceptable."

Riggs, Alario, McHorney, DeChristopher and Crombie engaged in a study of high school students to determine if students who reported having made a suicide attempt would be more likely than their peers to report physical and/or sexual abuse and other risk taking behaviors [16]. They surveyed 650 students of whom 600 (92%) completed the questionnaire. Twelve percent of the students reported they had made a suicide attempt. In the entire sample, abuse was judged to be high with 6.2 percent reporting physical abuse and 7.1 percent reporting sexual abuse. Students who had made suicide attempts were more likely to report physical abuse (22% vs. 4%) or sexual abuse (25% vs. 5%) than their non-suicidal peers. They were more likely to have either been pregnant or have impregnated someone (30% vs. 7%). And, they were more likely to be substance abusers (52% vs. 24%). From these data, Riggs et al. suggested students who engaged in risk taking behaviors and who were abused were more likely to be at risk for suicide attempts.

The prevalence of survivors of sexual abuse among college students was reported by Witchel [17]. The number of student survivors (females and males) ranged from 19 percent to 34 percent in the reported studies. An important point made in this work is that this is not a new phenomenon on the campus. Gagnon reported a survey of 1,200 college females revealed that over 28 percent reported they had a sexual experience with an adult before they were thirteen [18]. Incest and sexual abuse remain very secretive events that create significant distress for the survivors who are present on the campus.

These studies indicate there are a substantial number of victims of sexual assault/incest and it is important to look at the potential consequences. Smith and Crawford found among female students only 2.6 percent stated that they had been raped/sexually abused [19]. However, among ideators the percentage who had been raped/sexually abused was 6.0 percent, among suicide planners 10.9 percent and among actual attempters 24.2 percent. Curran stated a "high incidence of suicidal behavior has been reported in association with teenagers who have been sexually or physically abused or are victims of incest" [20, p. 114]. Hoberman and Garfinkel reported girls are more likely to commit suicide after an assault and there is an increasing association between assault and suicidal behaviors [21].

Shaunesey, Cohen, Plummer and Berman surveyed 117 hospitalized adolescents (51 males; 66 females) to determine the relationship between sexual and physical abuse and suicidality [22]. These adolescents were between the ages of thirteen and eighteen and were 82.4 percent Caucasian, 12 percent Hispanic, 3.4 percent African American, and 2.2 percent otherwise identified. They found "adolescents who had experienced any form of abuse made significantly more suicide attempts than did adolescents who had not experienced abuse" [22, p. 118]. They also found that more severe and a greater frequency of abuse led to more severe suicidal thinking and a greater number of attempts.

Part of a risk assessment of a sexually assaulted person should be a determination of the level of suicidality. Feelings of powerlessness and helplessness are typical factors in the emotional state of the sexually assaulted person. They are also an integral part of the emotional state of the suicidal person. A suicide support group was facilitated by staff of the University Counseling Service and Housing Services at the University of Minnesota. All the female participants in the group had been victims of sexual assault or incest during their lifetime (most before their matriculation at the University). They had all attempted suicide and some continued to exhibit varying levels of suicidal ideation at the beginning of the group. It appeared that the impact of incest and sexual assault had generally not been managed through the use of any professional service. Thus it remains a potentially explosive issue for the victim until resolved.

Physical Abuse

Part of the risk assessment in the Minnesota study, was to determine the number of students who had been physically abused within their family or who have witnessed abuse within the family during their lifetime [1]. Eighteen percent of the seniors reported having been a victim of or witnessing family violence with some having experienced both. This figure was 1 percent higher than reported in the 1989 survey.

Shafii, Carrigan, Whittinghill and Derrick found 55 percent ($n = 11$) of the suicide victims they studied had experienced parental absence or physical or emotional abusiveness [3]. Deykin, Alpert and Mc-Namarra likewise found that exposure to child abuse or neglect was associated with suicidal behavior in adolescents [23]. Wright noted "college students who reported ST's (serious suicidal thoughts) were, in addition (to having family drinking problems), significantly more likely than their classmates to state they had been physically abused by a parent, and had many conflicts with their parents" [2, p. 577]. Curran also indicated this is a high risk group for suicide [20].

Physical abuse is often coupled with the use/abuse of alcohol by the perpetrator of the violence. Alcohol use/abuse is also a tactic used by the victim to attempt to alleviate the physical and psychological pain that has been inflicted upon them. This results in the creation of a significant suicide risk. In a summary note to the Minnesota study, risk factors were quite in evidence [1].

> One in five students surveyed report a family alcohol or drug problem. One in eight have been physically abused by an adult in their household. One in seven have seen another family member physically abused. And by age 15, one in 6 females and one in 25 males have been sexually abused. Combining these experiences means that over a third of adolescents have had to deal with the traumatic effects of sexual or physical violence, or alcohol/drug problems in their family [1, p. 4].

Ideation and Other Suicidal Behaviors

Levels of emotional distress and self-esteem were also surveyed by the Minnesota study [1]. There was a slight increase in the most serious levels of emotional distress as "measured by responses to a series of six questions about general mood, stress, sadness, discourage-ment or hopelessness, nervousness, and satisfaction with personal life" [1, p. 26]. There was also an increase for serious low self-esteem as students reflected a negative opinion of themselves. The study noted there is usually a correlation between emotional distress and low self-esteem and alcohol/drug use/abuse. However, in this study alcohol use had declined while emotional distress had increased slightly making "it clear that prevention of alcohol and drug use will not by itself address the emotional health problems that confront today's young people" [1, p. 26]. The report also challenged the assumptions that decreased use of alcohol/drugs will result in fewer problems with self esteem.

> Since the rates for self-esteem problems have been more stable over time than those for substance use, it can be argued that low self-esteem is more likely to lead to substance use than substance use is to produce low self-esteem [1, p. 26].

The Minnesota study also showed an increase in the lifetime incidence of attempts among some high school seniors [1]. Between 1989 and 1992, females increased from 16 percent to 18 percent while males remained at a consistent 8 percent. The study reported "adolescents who report a suicide attempt are among those at highest risk for alcohol and other drug use. Suicidal behavior is highly correlated with sexual and physical abuse and serious family problems" [1, p. 27].

A previous Minnesota study presented more specific data on students in grades seven to twelve [24]. During the last month, 18 to 21 percent of the students stated they had felt depressed and 22 to 25 percent stated they were dissatisfied with life. Likewise, during the last month, 17 percent of the males and 29 percent of the females in the metro areas had thought about committing suicide. In the non-metro areas, 13 percent of the males and 24 percent of the females reported suicidal ideation. In their lifetime, it was reported that 6.7 percent of the males and 14.2 percent of the females had attempted suicide and, within the previous year, 2.8 percent of the males and 5.8 percent of the females had attempted suicide. More specifically, by the senior year, 10 percent of the males and 23 percent of the females in the metro area had attempted suicide. In the non-metro areas of Minnesota, 6 percent of the males and 15 percent of the females had attempted suicide.

Smith and Crawford's pilot study of "normal" high school students (n = 313) in the Midwest found 62.6 percent of these students reported some degree of suicidal ideation or action [19]. Suicide attempts had been made by 8.4 percent of the group. Approximately 90 percent of those who attempted suicide did not seek any medical assistance demonstrating the difficulty in ascertaining accurate data on attempts.

Harkavy-Friedman, Asnis, Boeck and DiFiore studied students in an academically select public high school in New York [25]. Of the 380 students completing the survey, 201 (52.9%) stated they had considered suicide and thirty-three (8.7%) stated they had attempted suicide at least once. Males constituted 51 percent of the ideators and females constituted 76 percent of the attempters. Of the suicide ideators (n = 201), 51.2 percent were Caucasian,[1] 23.4 percent Asian American, 11.4 percent African American, 9.4 percent Hispanic and 4.5 percent other. The percentage of students within the total sample of each racial group who expressed suicidal ideation was similar. Significantly, more Asian students reported having persistent suicidal thoughts (i.e., thoughts that lasted for at least 7 consecutive days) (58.0%) followed by Caucasian (54.2%), Hispanics (51.3%) and African Americans (46.0%).

Of the thirty-three students who stated they had attempted suicide, 48.5 percent were Caucasian, 21.2 percent were African American, 15.2 percent were Hispanic, 12.1 percent were Asian American and 3.0 percent other. They made from one to six attempts with twenty-one (63.6%) attempters having made at least two attempts. Overdosing and wrist slashings were the most commonly reported methods for attempters. A greater percentage of African American (14.0%) and Hispanic (13.5%) students had attempted suicide than Caucasian (8.4%) and Asian Americans (4.9%). The percentages of the total group are:

	Total	Ideators	Attempters
Caucasians	50.0	51.0	49.0
African Americans	13.0	11.0	21.0
Hispanics	10.0	10.0	15.0
Asian Americans	21.0	23.0	12.0
Others	6.0	5.0	3.0

It would be expected that Caucasians would constitute the largest percentage of ideators and attempters and they do. However, other racial groups showed some surprising rates such as the percentage of African Americans who attempted suicide. Statistical data are helpful, but it is important to remember that the suicidal individual does not always fit the statistical pattern.

This survey also produced some surprising results in the relationship between religious preference and suicidal behavior.

---

[1] Unless otherwise specified, the following definitions shall be used in this text for racial and/or ethnic groups: African American = black, non-Hispanic peoples; Asian Americans = Asian and Pacific Islands peoples; Caucasian = white, non-Hispanic peoples; Hispanic = Caribbean, Central and South American peoples; and Native Americans = American Indian and Alaskan Native peoples.

	Suicidal Ideators (n = 201)	Suicide Attempters (n = 33)
Catholic	27.9%	45.2%
Protestant	17.9%	15.2%
Jewish	17.9%	21.2%
Other	16.4%	15.2%
None	19.4%	3.0%

While there is no indicator of the degree of religiosity in this study, the data relating to religion is surprising. The Catholic Church has long been one of the strongest opponents of suicide, teaching that suicide is a sin. Yet, the highest percentage of ideators and attempters state that they are Catholic. Likewise, the Jewish faith has also taught that suicide is unacceptable. However, the second highest percentage of attempters is Jewish. Persons who are working with suicidal individuals need to clearly understand that religion is not necessarily an inhibitor of suicidal behavior as is clearly demonstrated in this study.

It is obvious that not all the high school students in these studies will be attending a college or university. Consequently, there is a need for a "tighter" focus, a more explicit focus on those students who will most likely attend a college or university. This can be done through the use of data obtained from surveys conducted by *Who's Who Among American High School Students* [26, 27]. The students who were surveyed in their twenty third annual survey of high achievers (1992) (n = 2,092) had a "B" or better GPA and present a profile that should be of concern to administrators, faculty, counselors, and residence hall staff as 97 percent of these students stated that they intended to enroll in colleges and universities following their graduation.

The profile was derived from a survey of 1,527 women and 565 men aged sixteen (23%), seventeen (74%) and eighteen (2%) who were 81 percent Caucasian (n = 1,695), 7 percent African-American (n = 146), 5 percent Asian-American (n = 105), 3 percent Hispanic (n = 63) and 8 percent listed as other (n = 83).

To the statement "I have considered committing suicide," 30.8 percent of the students responded affirmatively. This is a 4 percent increase over the response of the previous year. A significant finding in this area was that 44 percent of the Asian-American students (n = 46) had considered suicide compared with 40 percent of the Hispanic students (n = 25), 31 percent of the African-American students (n = 45) and 30 percent of the Caucasian students (n = 509).

The reasons students gave for their suicidal ideation were general depression (47%), school pressures (16%), fights with parents (11%), the break-up of a relationship (9%), divorce or family problems (8%), having a friend commit suicide (1%) and unsure or don't know (5%). Among those students who gave school pressure as a reason for considering suicide the highest percentage was Asian-American students (34%). As noted previously, Asian-American students had the highest percentage of ideation. This is an important correlation particularly if academic pressure continues to be a major stress for these students as they enter colleges and universities. Among the other student groups, 15 percent of the Caucasian students, 11 percent of the Hispanic students and 10 percent of the African-American students gave school pressure as a reason for suicidal ideation. Ten percent of all students who considered suicide gave school pressure as a reason for suicidal ideation.

Those students who had suicidal ideation gave the following as reasons that they had reconsidered: 67 percent worked it through themselves or just started to feel better, 18 percent talked with a friend, 3 percent talked to a hotline or a professional counselor, 2 percent talked with a parent and 7 percent were unsure or didn't know how they had resolved the situation. It is important to note that only 3 percent sought professional assistance.

The survey asked "I have tried committing suicide." Five percent of the students ($n = 105$) stated that they had made an attempt. This is a 1 percent increase over the response in the 1991 survey. While there is a general impression that attempted suicide is predominately a Caucasian phenomenon this was not what was reported by these students. Hispanic and African American students each had the highest percentage of attempts—9 percent (Hispanic $n = 6$, African American $n = 13$), followed by Asian-American students with 8 percent ($n = 8$) and Caucasian students with 4 percent ($n = 68$).

The reasons that were given by these students for attending college may be part of the academic pressure felt at the time of the survey as well as a continuing issue during their college years. The top three reasons were 1) that they would need a college degree to get a good job (97%), 2) that they believed that their education was not complete (95%) and 3) that their parents wanted them to go to college (80%). The last reason was considered a significant finding by the study.

One risk factor for suicidal behavior was included in the survey. As noted earlier, rape or sexual assault has been shown to be a factor for suicidal behavior. The following data were not reported in the previous risk factor section because it pertains specifically to this high achiever group and may be more indicative of risk factors present in entering freshmen. In this survey, 14 percent of all female students stated that they had been raped or sexually assaulted. There was variation between racial groups with 25 percent ($n = 15$) of the Hispanic, 21 percent (n = 31) of the African-American, 13 percent (n = 25) of the Caucasian and 9 percent (n = 9) of the Asian-American female students reporting rape or sexual assault. Date rape was a significant factor with 4.6 percent of the women stating that they had been a victim of date rape. These victims stated that they knew the assailant because they had dated previously (40%), were friends (29%), or were casual acquaintances (18%). Eleven percent stated that they had just met the assailant. Alcohol consumption was involved in 31 percent of the date rapes. Both parties had been drinking in 14 percent of the cases, only the assailant drinking in 13 percent and only the victim drinking in 4 percent of the cases. Only 4.2 percent of the victims reported the assault to police. There was no indication if the students had received any counseling or other assistance.

Another risk factor is alcohol and drug consumption/use which is being reported here for the same reasons as the sexual assault data. The reported use of alcoholic beverages by this high achiever group was that 8 percent drank on weekends, 9 percent drank monthly, 29 percent almost never drank and 52 percent reported that they did not drink. Ninety-two percent of the students surveyed stated that they had never tried marijuana. This is a positive factor. The newest data from the Public Health Service showed that "heavy use by high school seniors decreased from 33 percent in 1987 to 29.8 percent in 1991, while college students' heavy drinking behavior appeared to increase, from 41.7% in 1987 to 42.8% in 1991" [28, p. 80]. Thus, it appears that the good news of a decline in a risk factor during the senior year in high school is offset by an increase during college. Whether this is a part of the usual experimentation or a result of stress factors is an unknown.

The *Who's Who* survey was taken during the spring of 1992 and is a sample of high achievers who were juniors or seniors and who represent slightly over 6 percent of the twelve million high school students in 1992 [27]. The racial/ethnic backgrounds of these students closely resemble those of the freshman classes in American colleges and universities for the 1992-93 academic year as reported in *The Chronical of Higher Education* (Fact File, [29]). The *Chronicle* survey indicated 92.2 percent of the students graduated from high school in 1992. The reported percentages were:

	Who's Who [27]	Chronicle [29]
Caucasian	81.0	82.3
African American	7.0	9.1
Asian American	5.0	3.1
Hispanic	3.0	3.3
Other	4.0	4.0

(Note: The *Who's Who* data for "other" were not further delineated. The *Chronicle* data were further defined as 1.7 percent Native American, .7 percent Puerto Rican American and 2.6 percent other.)

One significant allied item was that 9.1 percent of the freshman students in the *Chronicle* survey reported they frequently felt depressed (males 6.2%; females 11.6%) [29]. The remainder of the data from the two studies is incompatible for purposes of comparison.

Offer and Spiro conducted an epidemiological study of mental health and mental illness among a random selection of students in three Chicago area high schools [30]. From their study they concluded "the day a college opens its doors to the incoming freshmen and freshwomen, 20% of those students will be emotionally disturbed or have significant psychic distress" [30, p. 213]. They pointed out that colleges need to focus not only on academic development but must also develop effective mental health programs to intervene with this group of students.

Suicidal behaviors are not caused by any single factor. There is always a "constellation" of factors. A summary review of the data from the studies that have been previously cited presents a significant constellation:

Alcohol use/abuse—up to 30 percent of the general high school students were intoxicated once a month. As many as 70 percent of the students who attempted suicide had used alcohol or non-prescription drugs in collaboration with their attempt.

Family alcohol use/abuse—up to 22 percent of seniors reported their families had alcohol/drug problems.

Sexual abuse—among high school seniors, up to 19 percent of the females and 4 percent of the males reported they had been sexually abused. Fourteen percent of the high ability female students reported having been sexually assaulted.

Physical abuse—one in eight (12.5%) of the students reported they had been physically abused and one in seven (14.2%) reported they had witnessed physical abuse within their family.

Suicidal ideation—up to 62.9 percent of all high school students and 30.8 percent of the high achievers have expressed some suicidal ideation.

Suicide attempts—by their senior year, up to 23 percent of the females and 10 percent of the males have attempted suicide at least once in their lifetime.

Sought assistance for problems—approximately 3 percent of the students had sought any professional assistance for their concerns. They had usually confided in friends or waited for the problem to disappear.

This constellation is present in high school students. These factors are also very apparent within those students defined as high achievers. This group of high achievers becomes the group that is most highly recruited by colleges and universities as the basis for their freshman class. Colleges and universities need to understand that when they recruit these gifted youths there are a number of issues that require resolution.

In 1986, the American Association for Counseling and Development (AACD) (now known as the American Counseling Association [ACA]) devoted a special issue, *Counseling the Gifted and Talented* to addressing these concerns [31]. In this issue, Delisle defined four issues that confront these gifted persons: "perfectionism, societal expectations to achieve, differential development of intellectual and social gifts and impotence to affect real-world change" [32, p. 559].

There is also a significant effort to recruit gifted minority students. The data presented above demonstrate that these risk factors are also present in high ability minority students. For these students there are not only the four issues defined by Delisle but they have an additional set of issues. Lindstrom and Van Sant noted that minority students face the same unique issues of other gifted students but racial and cultural factors create a matrix of greater complexity for them [33]. The editors of this special issue stated that "this special issue is designed to caution counselors that gifted young people and adults need support to ensure healthy intellectual, emotional, and career development" [34, p. 547]. Their caution should be a caution to administrators, staff and faculty that there is more of an obligation to any student than simply to grant admission. Intellectual development and the acquisition of skills for a future career are an integral and important part of the tasks of the institution. However, if the institution cannot provide emotional support for the developmental tasks of the student body through counseling and other student services, it will fail in the totality of its tasks. If students' needs are not met, they have some alternatives. They can choose to leave the institution and seek another recourse. They can elect to remain and continue their studies in a less than satisfactory environment that will affect both their academic and their personal situations. And, they can exhibit a variety of suicidal behaviors beginning with low level ideation. They may also choose to attempt or commit suicide to relieve what they perceive as the numerous and intolerable pressures that are present.

Westefeld, Whitchard and Range asked "is there something inherent in the college experience that impacts the suicide rate? Or is there differential selection so that those predisposed to suicide are more or less likely to go to college in the first place?" [35, p. 466]. The first question will be dealt with later. However, from the portrait of prospective students that has been drawn here it would seem that the antecedents or predisposing conditions are in place.

It would be unreasonable to state that academic institutions could create circumstances where no suicidal behavior would take place. It is not unreasonable, however, to urge academic institutions to understand that they have a greater obligation to the student than simply to grant admission and provide academic resources. There is an obligation to provide resources for the complete development of the student—intellectually and emotionally.

REFERENCES

1. Prevention and Risk Reduction Unit, *Minnesota Student Survey, 1989-1992: Reflections of Social Change,* Minnesota Department of Education, St. Paul, Minnesota, 1992.
2. L. S. Wright, Suicidal Thoughts and their Relationship to Family Stress and Personal Problems among High School Seniors and College Undergraduates, *Adolescence, 20*:79, pp. 575-580, 1985.
3. M. Shafii, S. Carrigan, J. R. Whittinghill, and A. Derrick, Psychological Autopsy of Completed Suicide in Children and Adolescents, *American Journal of Psychiatry, 142*:2, pp. 1061-1064, 1985.
4. D. Robbins and N. E. Alessi, Depressive Symptoms and Suicidal Behavior in Adolescents, *American Journal of Psychiatry, 142*:5, pp. 588-592, 1985.
5. R. J. Kinkel, C. W. Bailey, and N. C. Josef, Correlates of Adolescent Suicide Attempts: Alienation, Drugs and Social Background, *Journal of Alcohol and Drug Abuse, 34*:3, pp. 85-96, 1988.
6. G. E. Murphy, Suicide and Substance Abuse, *Archives of General Psychiatry, 45*:6, pp. 593-594, 1988.
7. A. L. Berman, and R. H. Schwartz, Suicide Attempts Among Adolescent Drug Users, *American Journal of Disease of Children, 144*:3, pp. 310-314, 1990.
8. W. M. Felts, T. Chenier, and R. Barnes, Drug Use and Suicide Ideation and Behavior among North Carolina Public School Students, *American Journal of Public Health, 82*:6, pp. 870-872, 1992.
9. A. M. Downey, The Impact of Drug Abuse Upon Adolescent Suicide, *Omega, 22*:4, pp. 261-275, 1991.
10. R. F. Valois, M. L. Vincent, R. E. McKeown, C. Z. Garrison, and S. D. Kirby, Adolescent Risk Behaviors and the Potential for Violence: A Look at What's Coming to Campus, *Journal of American College Health, 41*:4, pp. 141-147, 1993.
11. J. E. Donovan and R. Jessor, Structure of Problem Behavior in Adolescence and Young Adulthood, *Journal of Consulting and Clinical Psychology, 53*:6, pp. 890-904, 1985.
12. C. R. Pfeffer, *The Suicidal Child,* Guilford Press, New York, 1986.

13. A. A. Leenars and S. Wenckstern, Suicide in the School Age Child and Adolescent, in *Life Span Perspectives of Suicide: Time-lines in the Suicide Process,* Leenars, A. A. (ed.), Plenum Press, New York, pp. 95-107, 1991.

14. E. R. Hall and P. J. Flannery, Prevalence and Correlates of Sexual Assault Experiences in Adolescents, *Victimology, 9*:3-4, pp. 398-406, 1984.

15. Many Boys, Girls Say Rape is OK, Herald, p. 1, Grand Forks, North Dakota, May 3, 1988.

16. S. Riggs, A. Alario, C. McHorney, J. DeChristopher, and P. Crombie, Abuse and Health Related Risk-taking Behaviors in High School Students who have Attempted Suicide, *Journal of Developmental and Behavioral Pediatrics, 73*:3, pp. 205-206, 1986.

17. R. I. Witchel, College-student Survivors of Incest and other Child Sexual Abuse, in *New Directions for Student Services: Dealing with students from dysfunctional families* (No. 54), Witchel, R. I. (ed.), Jossey-Bass, pp. 63-76, 1991.

18. J. Gagnon, Female Child Victims of Sexual Offense, *Social Problems, 13*:2, pp. 176-192, 1965.

19. K. Smith and S. Crawford, Suicidal Behavior among "Normal" High School Students, *Suicide and Life Threatening Behavior, 16*:3, pp. 313-325, 1986.

20. D. K. Curran, *Adolescent Suicidal Behavior,* Hemisphere, New York, 1987.

21. H. M. Hoberman and B. D. Garfinkel, Completed Suicide in Youth, *Canadian Journal of Psychiatry, 3*:6, pp. 494-503, 1988.

22. K. Shaunesey, J. L. Cohen, B. Plummer, and A. Berman, Suicidality in Hospitalized Adolescents: Relationship to Prior Abuse, *American Journal of Orthopsychiatry, 63*:1, pp. 113-119, 1993.

23. E. Y. Deykin, J. J. Alpert, and J. J. McNamarra, A Pilot Study of the Effect of Exposure to Child Abuse or Neglect on Adolescent Suicidal Behavior, *American Journal of Psychiatry, 142*:11, pp. 1299-1303, 1985.

24. Minnesota Extension Service, *Adolescent Health Survey Report,* University of Minnesota, Minneapolis, Minnesota, 1988.

25. J. M. Harkavy-Friedman, G. M. Asnis, M. Boeck, and J. DiFiore, Prevalence of Specific Suicidal Behaviors in a High School Sample, *American Journal of Psychiatry, 144*:9, pp. 1203-1206, 1987.

26. Who's Who Among American High School Students, *22nd Annual Survey of High Achievers,* Educational Communications, Inc. Forest Lake, Illinois, 1991.

27. Who's Who Among American High School Students, *23rd Annual Survey of High Achievers,* Educational Communications, Inc., Forest Lake, Illinois, 1992.

28. Public Health Service, A Public Health Service Progress Report on Healthy People 2000: Alcohol and Other Drugs, *Prevention Pipeline, 5*:6, pp. 80-81, 1992.

29. Fact File, This Year's Freshmen: A Statistical Profile, *The Chronicle of Higher Education, 39*:19, pp. A30, 1993.

30. D. Offer and R. P. Spiro, The Disturbed Adolescent Goes to College, *Journal of American College Health, 35*:5, pp. 209-214, 1987.

31. B. A. Kerr and J. Miller (eds.), Special Issue: Counseling the Gifted and Talented, *Journal of Counseling and Development, 64*:9, 1986.
32. J. R. Delisle, Death with Honors: Suicide among Gifted Adolescents, *Journal of Counseling and Development, 64*:9, pp. 558-560, 1986.
33. R. R. Lindstrom and S. Van Sant, Special Issues in Working with Gifted Minority Adolescents, *Journal of Counseling and Development, 6*:9, pp. 583-586, 1986.
34. B. A. Kerr and J. Miller, Introduction, *Journal of Counseling and Development, 64*:9, p. 547, 1986.
35. J. S. Westefeld, K. A. Whitchard, and L. M. Range, College and University Student Suicide: Trends and Implications, *The Counseling Psychologist, 18*:3, pp. 464-476, 1990.

CHAPTER 3

The Incidence of Suicide

> There is no longer doubt that suicide has come to represent a serious problem respecting community health and welfare. Its especial importance as affecting a group so highly selected as the college population, potentially so significant to society relative to later role and function, certainly is not to be gainsaid. [Raphael, Power and Berridge, 1, p. 1]

While this quotation is not from a recent publication, its content seems as clear and fresh as if it were written yesterday. The quotation is from an article, "The Question of Suicide as a Problem in College Mental Hygiene," written by Raphael, Power and Berridge in *The American Journal of Orthopsychiatry* in January 1937. Over fifty years ago, the issue of suicide on college campuses was considered to be a significant matter. These authors noted that the five suicides at the University of Michigan that year constituted one half of the total deaths on the campus. Unfortunately, their concern was again echoed by Reifler fifty-three years later.

> What about the other students needing care—well, now is the time to view with alarm. There is ample evidence that there is on campus a significant fraction of emotionally disturbed students whom we are not reaching. . . . The most dramatic and irreversible expression of our not having reached someone is suicide [2, p. 13].

Two more recent examples of the seriousness of suicide on campus were the reports in *The Chronicle of Higher Education* [3, 4]. In 1992 the University of Maryland—College Park reported that during the 1991-92 academic year eight students committed suicide out of a population of 35,000 students. This would equate to a rate of 22.9

suicides per 100,000 population, a significantly higher incidence than the rate for fifteen to twenty-four year olds (13.6/100,000 in 1990) in the general population. "That rate was three to six times the national average for college campuses, which the American College Health Association says is four to eight for every 100,000 students [3, p. A29]." For a campus that had no reported suicides the previous year this was a tragic change.

The second was a 1993 report from the University of Illinois where, between November and March, there had been two confirmed and three suspected suicides on the campus. This was a marked change on a campus that had averaged about one reported suicide per year since a suicide prevention program was put into effect in 1984. Two of these suicides were Korean students and all the suicides were males.

What do we know about suicide rates? How can we determine the rate of suicide for a college population? Where are the gaps in our knowledge? One of the most useful paradigms for gaining an understanding of our limitations is that of the iceberg paradigm [5]. The complete picture of suicidal behaviors is like the iceberg floating in the ocean, we see only a small portion of the reality. What we see are the recognized pseudo-accidents, suicide attempts, suicide completions. In this instance the word recognized is used very deliberately for there are many pseudo-accidents and suicide attempts that are not recognized for what they are. And many completed suicides will not be officially recognized. Below the surface, largely unseen, are the suicidal thoughts and the suicide threats. Jeanneret noted this is not a static condition, "whereas the inside of a real iceberg is frozen, the levels in the paradigm iceberg are obviously moving: starting from the thought to the equivalent, even to the attempt, as well as to the relapse" [5, p. 409]. Suicidal behavior, like the iceberg, conceals much from the discerning observer and even more from the general public.

To begin to reveal as much as possible of the epidemiological data, the statistics for the general population are a valuable starting point. Data from the National Center for Health Statistics revealed there were 30,810 suicides in the United States in 1991 for persons of all ages or a rate of 12.2/100,000 population [6]. This places suicide as the eighth leading cause of death. For the population in the age group fifteen to twenty-four years of age, the suicide rate was 13.1/100,000, a total of 4,751 suicides. For college age students, suicide was the second leading cause of death exceeded only by accidents. For the population in the age group twenty-five to thirty-four, the suicide rate was 15.2/100,000 (6,514 suicides). Stafford and Weisheit studied the changing age patterns of males and females in the United States between 1940 and 1980 and reported some important trends [7]. In this period, there was a 262 percent increase in suicides among young non-Caucasian males between the ages of fifteen and nineteen and a range from 97 percent to 182 percent among the twenty to thirty-four years of age group. This increase was larger than the suicide rates for young Caucasian males that had increased 232 percent and 12 percent to 116 percent respectively. Young non-Caucasian female suicide rates changed very little during this period. The changes in Caucasian female rates were much like that of Caucasian males. We encounter our first problem with the suicide rates at this point. These rates are minimum rates. There are many suicides that are not certified as suicides for various reasons including concern that the family will be stigmatized, that there will be a loss of insurance and the fact that there was no suicide note present. In addition, there are many suicides that are disguised, the most prominent being single car, single occupant automobile accidents. Farberow describes a number of self-destructive behaviors that may be suicidal and result in a death but will not be recorded as a suicide [8]. In the first chapter a student was quoted stating that he intended to drink himself to death because "my family can deal with a dead drunk they can't deal with a dead suicide." This is an example of what I would call a socially acceptable suicide. We may well know that the behavior was intended to cause death, yet we are able to define this death as an "accident" thus making it a more socially acceptable event. And yet, this self-destructive behavior may not always be socially acceptable. Flavin reported on three alcohol dependent individuals who were admitted to the same treatment program and who stated that they had actively sought to acquire AIDS as a means of committing suicide [9]. It is rather difficult to believe that these individuals sought AIDS as a means of suicide. However, self-destructive behaviors can proceed this far with the intent of suicide.

There are some important exclusions in the United States suicide data. Beginning in 1970, the government ceased counting non-resident aliens for inclusion in suicide and other statistics. The *Statistical Abstract of the United States 1991* reported that in 1989 there were approximately sixteen million non-resident aliens of which approximately 360,800 were students [10]. Given this number of non-resident aliens present in the country, as well as on college and university campuses, this is a significant exclusion. It provides yet another difficulty in determining the true number of suicides. Consequently, and unfortunately, it can be readily seen that accurate numbers are not possible. This significantly affects the accuracy and validity of statistics needed for the development of trends and the planning of human services to meet the needs of suicidal persons, their significant others and their survivors.

But, this is not a new problem. In 1977, Farberow, MacKinnon and Nelson wrote an article entitled "Suicide: Who's Counting?" [11]. They were particularly concerned with the certification of deaths and found a number of reasons for the variability in reporting. The first of these was with the determination of intent, a psychological state. The chaotic, risk-taking lives of some people made it difficult for even well trained coroner's staff "to determine whether the behavior that resulted in death was initiated with a conscious intent to die" [11, p. 223]. They also found that 28 percent of the coroners required more proof for a certification of suicide than for any other mode of death and 17 percent required a suicide note or a history of attempted suicide before they would certify the death as a suicide. The decisions of 34 percent of the coroners were affected by the prominence or reputation of the deceased or the family. While 76 percent of the coroners would order an autopsy in homicide deaths, only 30 percent of the coroners would order an autopsy if suicide was suspected. In general, coroners demanded significantly higher levels of evidence to certify a suicide than another mode of death. Consequently, "the validity of reported suicide rates may be seriously questioned" [11, p. 223].

Now, if we have difficulties in determining an accurate number of suicides in the United States each year we simply do not know the number of attempted suicides as there is no general reporting format. Even if there were, there are many attempts that are never treated physically or psychologically as the individual makes a very low level attempt in private and never mentions the action to anyone. Estimates have ranged from ten to 100 times the number of people who actually commit suicide. Perhaps the best indicators of the potential number of attempters for the college age population would come from data gathered by studies in the State of Minnesota [12], the Center for Disease Control [13] and *The Annual Survey of High Achievers* conducted by *Who's Who Among American High School Students* [14, 15].

The *Minnesota Student Survey Report* presented material developed from surveys administered to 91,175 students in grades six, nine and twelve from 390 of 433 public school districts [12]. One-fourth of the surveyed students reported that they had thought of suicide in the previous month. One in nine students indicated that they had attempted suicide. Of the twelfth grade students, 27 percent of the females and 21 percent of the males indicated that they had suicidal thoughts within the past month. Within this group, 16 percent of the females and 8 percent of the males indicated that they had made a suicide attempt. There were two interesting characteristics within this study. Physical or sexual abuse by a family member, an alcohol or drug problem in the family, or a combination of both experiences was reported by 63 percent of the suicide attempters. Of those adolescents who acknowledged a suicide attempt 43 percent received some form of professional treatment.

The Center for Disease Control's report on attempted suicide among high school students, surveyed 11,631 students in all fifty states, the District of Columbia, Puerto Rico, and the Virgin Islands and presented the following data [13]. In the twelve months preceding the survey, 27.3 percent of the students in grades nine to twelve reported they had serious suicidal ideation. Specific plans were developed by 16.3 percent and about half of this number (8.3%) reported actual attempts with 2.1 percent requiring medical attention as a result of their attempt. Previous studies indicated 9 percent to 14 percent of high school students had attempted suicide at some point in their life. Reports of suicidal ideation were more likely among female students (33.9%) than male students (20.5%) as was the reporting of the making of specific plans—females students (20.2%), male students (12.3%). Suicide attempts were more likely among females (10.3%) than males (6.2%).

This survey also provided information on differences between racial groups. Suicidal ideation was reported by 30.4 percent of the Hispanic, 28.1 percent of the Caucasian and 20.4 percent of the African American students. Specific suicide plans were reported by 19.6 percent of the Hispanic, 16.1 percent of the Caucasian and 13.5 percent of the African American students. Suicide attempts were reported by 12.0 percent of the Hispanic, 7.9 percent of the Caucasian and 6.5 percent of the African American students. It was noted that "Hispanic female students (12.9%) were significantly more likely to have attempted suicide during the 12 months preceding the survey than white females (10.1%) or black female students (8.2%)" [13, p. 11].

What do we know about suicide among the college and university student population? One of our first difficulties is determining who is a college student. With an ever increasing number of "non-traditional" students on the campuses, the old definition of a traditional four year plus graduate or professional school does not provide an accurate parameter. In addition, is the individual a student when she or he is a part-time student (calculated in terms of a full-time equivalency enrollment number)? Do institutions define full-time in credit hour terms, equivalencies or by some other method? If we use the standard government reporting age group, fifteen to twenty-four years of age, we are including a number of individuals in the fifteen, sixteen and seventeen year-old group who are not enrolled in colleges and universities as well as others in the age category who are not students. And given the increasing numbers of non-traditional students, using twenty-four years of age as the upper limit eliminates a number of students. This creates a significant difficulty when attempting to define the incidence of suicide on the campus and make comparisons with the general age group or non-student peers.

Determining the incidence of suicide on college and university campuses is also inhibited by the fact that many colleges and universities simply do not keep any statistics. In some institutions there is no one who is charged with this task. In other institutions, data are not maintained because it is viewed as negative information about the institution and there is a fear that the institution might become known as a "suicide school" and become the subject of a newspaper, radio or television exposé. In the competitive world of college recruitment, data often are not collected to avoid negative comparisons. So, given these difficulties, what do we know about college student suicide.

Initially, let's begin by stepping back from the behavior and looking at some of the most salient precursors to suicidal behavior. Depression, hopelessness, and helplessness have been recognized as integral parts of a continuum toward suicidal behavior. Depression has been a consistent mental health factor on campuses. While not the first study, Ross found depression was the most constant precursor to suicidal behavior in his University of Wisconsin study [16].

In an article for *Psychology Today,* "College Blues," Beck and Young stated that the leading psychiatric disorder on college campuses was depression where "as many as 78 percent of the 7,500,800 students enrolled in American colleges may suffer some symptoms of depression—roughly a quarter of the student population at any one time" [17, p. 80]. As depression has been shown to be a significant factor in suicide, it is important to our understanding of suicidal behavior to be aware of its incidence on the college campus. While there have been a number of studies exploring the connections between depression and suicidal behaviors, the focus here is on the college student. Consequently the studies cited will provide a brief summary of the incidence among college students.

DEPRESSION

Of course I feel down, doesn't everybody? I've just got a bad case of those "college blues" that all graduate students talk about. I just don't know that the world I see looks like the world that they see. I just feel like I'm always in a big black hole. I can see the light at the top I just can't get there no matter what I do. This past year things have just been getting worse. And, this past week I haven't gone to any classes, I just sat in my room and watched TV. I don't even remember what I saw, day or night. My friends told me I'm getting pretty strange and that I should talk to somebody about what's going on with me I just don't think I can handle grad work here. I feel so threatened by everything. Sometimes when I cry in my room I just want to lay down and sleep forever. That would be so peaceful.

—Wilma (graduate student)

Schotte and Clum studied students ($n = 96$; 47 males, 49 females) at Virginia Polytechnic Institute and State University who had reported suicidal ideation within the past month and compared them with seventy-nine nonideators [18]. The focus of the study was to determine if there was a relationship between negative life stress, cognitive rigidity and/or poor problem solving skills, and suicidal ideation and/or behavior. Their results indicated ideators were under higher levels of stress, were more hopeless and had higher levels of depression than nonideators. Depression was found to be a more important predictor with low level ideators while hopelessness was a more important predictor of suicidal intent. Hopelessness was shown to be a better predictor of suicidal intent than depression with both ideators and attempters.

Sherer engaged in a study of depression after a one month survey of clients ($n = 103$) at the Mississippi State University Counseling Center revealed that 39.9 percent of the clients were rated by clinicians as being depressed to the extent that it interfered with their optimal academic and social performance [19]. There was some risk of suicide in 15.5 percent of this client group. Sherer found that students in his study ($n = 149$; 68 males, 81 females) were more depressed than a general community sample. He then surveyed another 149 students and found that seventeen (11.4%) were depressed at the time of the survey and thirty-three (22.1%) reported that they believed that they had needed treatment for depression at some time. Within the past year, depression was reported 18 percent of the time by men and 26 percent of the time by women. Past suicidal ideation was reported by forty-nine students (32.9%) while fourteen (9.4%) had actually contemplated a specific means of suicide. A significant finding was that seventy-three (49%) of the students stated they had used alcohol or drugs to cope with their depression.

Vredenburg, O'Brien and Krames noted that despite the gravity of the problem of depression on college campuses, few studies had been devoted to investigation of depressed college students [20]. They developed a study to examine the nature of college student depression and its relationship to personality variables and experiences that are unique to college life. First year students at Erindale College,

University of Toronto (n = 74; 41 males, 33 females) completed a series of psychological tests. Thirty-five of these students were diagnosed as being depressed and thirty-nine were not depressed. Further testing indicated 74 percent of the depressed students had been depressed for more than three months and approximately one half of them had experienced suicidal ideation. Stressful situations, deficiencies in interpersonal skills, lack of self-control and coping skills as well as events unique to college life all contribute to varying levels of depression. This study as with the others cited, stated there is a necessity to undertake further research in this area.

Statistics indicate that there is a 2:1 female-to-male ratio for depression from adolescence through adulthood. However, other research had indicated that there were no gender differences in the level of depression among college women and men. Goodman and Koenig studied depression in high school and college women [21]. It appeared college women experienced better social support, fewer negative life events and a less traditional sex-role environment than did high school women. They suggested that the college environment may provide psychosocial advantages that protect women against depression.

Depression is a significant factor among college students. As it is a factor in the process of suicidal behavior it needs to be addressed as a mental health problem on the campus.

SUICIDAL IDEATION

A review of these few studies relating to depression indicates that depression often leads to suicidal ideation. Suicidal ideation is not a foreign concept either on the campus or in the general population. The concept of thinking about suicide can take place at any time and with varying levels of intensity. In fact, the universality of varying levels of suicidal ideation may preclude some individuals from engaging in intervention.

> When she told me that she was considering suicide I thought that I knew exactly what she was talking about since I had felt that way myself a couple of times. It never dawned on me that she was in a much worse place than I had ever been and that she was really serious about it.
>
> —Marcia (senior)

What do we know about college student ideation? In the studies cited above, the rate of suicidal ideation has ranged from 15 to 35 percent of the groups. Bonner and Rich recruited 186 volunteers (85 males, 101 females) to test a stress-vulnerability model of suicidal ideation [22]. Utilizing the Scale for Suicidal Ideation, they found a continuum of suicidal ideation among these students. Twenty-six percent reported no current suicidal ideation, 34 percent reported low-intent ideation, 15 percent reported moderate-intent ideation and 22 percent reported high-intent ideation. They found 74 percent of the students had some suicide ideation under the stress of midterms and that 40 percent had ideation that could be considered serious.

Rudd surveyed 737 students (287 males, 450 females) who ranged in age from sixteen to thirty. Of the total sample, 557 (75.75) had one year or less of college, seventy-five (10.2%) two years, fifty-two (7.1%) three years, thirty-seven (5.0%) four years, twelve (1.6%) five years and three (0.4%) had six or more years of college [23]. Racially, the group consisted of twenty-eight African-Americans (3.8%) seventy-three Hispanics (9.9%), 582 Caucasians (79.0%), fifty-three Asians (7.2%) and one unidentified (0.1%). Using the Suicidal Ideation Scale, he found 43.7 percent of the participating students had some level of suicidal ideation during the previous year. Of this group, 14.9 percent stated they had acted in some way on these thoughts. They had told others about their suicidal thoughts and some had come close to making an attempt. More seriously, 5.5 percent of the group stated they had made attempts. Males and females had experienced general suicidal ideation at approximately the same levels, 43.3 percent and 43.9 percent respectively. Likewise, serious suicidal ideation was reported by 13.59 percent of the males and 12.89 percent of the females. Males made fewer actual attempts (4.5%) than did females (6.2%). Rudd's work demonstrated that in this campus sample, 43.7 percent of the total students surveyed were ideators, 6.5 percent had taken some action relative to their ideation and 2.3 percent had made a suicide attempt.

Bertocci, Hirsch, Sommer and Williams conducted a mental health needs assessment at Columbia University [24]. They received responses from 344 students (return rate of 44%). Three-fourths of these students stated that depression was a concern for them "19% said it was crucial, 21% said it was very important, and 36% said it was fairly important" [24, p. 6]. More than one-fourth of the responding students reported suicidal and/or homicidal thoughts as a concern "6% said this was a crucial concern, 8% said it was a very important concern, and 12% said it was a fairly important concern" [24, p. 4]. The factors associated with suicidal and/or homicidal thoughts were representative of factors that were presented in the chapter relating to the portrait of a student body. These included (descending order) depression, personal use of drugs, experience with sexual assault or harassment and family problems including alcohol/drug use, physical/ emotional illness, and divorce/separation. If studies of this nature were conducted on campuses it would provide meaningful information for the development of mental health services for students.

SUICIDE ATTEMPTS

As previously noted, there is a substantial difficulty in the collection of this data. Students may make attempts which never come to the attention of anyone. Or their attempts may be known to some friends who attempt to console the person without any further action being taken. Sometimes student's attempts are managed in a community medical facility and are not reported to any campus staff. Due to privacy and other constraints or concerns, data may not be kept as a consistent record even if the student came to the college or university health service.

Schwartz and Reifler reviewed previous studies that had indicated suicide among college students was much higher than within the general population [25]. They concluded that claims that the rates were much higher than for comparable age persons could not be supported. They stated there was such an inaccuracy in the sample data and such uncertainty surrounding estimates that these obstacles prevented an assessment of the true incidence of student suicide. Schwartz noted that to have comparable data from institutions there would have to be a consensus as to when the individual was a student and when the individual's suicide would be considered a student suicide.

To begin to answer Schwartz's questions, there would have to be records that would enable researchers to study the phenomenon of college student suicide. Westefeld and Pattillo assessed institutional procedures for keeping records of suicides [26]. They received 147 responses to the questionnaires that were sent to Directors of Counseling Centers at 187 institutions. Twenty of the reporting institutions (13.6%) stated they had a systematic procedure for recording both attempters and completers, nine (6.1%) had a procedure for recording attempters, but not completers, and four (2.7%) had a procedure for recording completers but not attempters. This amounted to thirty-three institutions or 22.4% of the surveyed group. The remainder did not keep records. The major reasons given were the difficulty of compiling accurate data, confidentiality issues, "this is a political-controversial issue," "it's not necessary," "no one has been asked to do it," "no one has thought of it" and "too much trouble."

In a further effort to arrive at some determination of the rate of college student suicide, Schwartz and Reifler reviewed seven single institutions and nine multi-institution samples of student suicide at American colleges and universities [27]. They found that there was no evidence that college students had a higher rate of suicide than the general population within that age group. They noted that "for a very large campus (e.g., 45,000 full time students), one can anticipate about 5 suicides, 50 suicide attempts. . . ." [27, p. 58]. They also noted that when there are such infrequent events as suicides on campus it is difficult to determine rates.

If we can make the assumption that suicide rates among college students are equal to that of the general population, it is important to look at those rates. During the period 1960 to 1980 there was a significant increase in the rate of suicide among the fifteen to twenty-four year-old population. It rose from 5.2 to 12.3 (all rates given in terms of per 100,000 persons) in that 20 year period and then to 13.6 in 1990. The most recent data published in the *Statistical Abstract of the United States—1992* [28, p. 90] provides the following information for the year 1989.

Age Group — Male	White	Black
15-19	19.4	10.3
20-24	26.8	23.7
25-34	24.9	22.0
Age Group — Female		
15-19	4.5	2.3
20-24	4.3	3.4
25-34	5.9	3.7
Age Group Totals		
15-19	11.3	
20-24	15.3	
25-34	15.0	

Applying this data, Schwartz and Reifler's approximation of five student suicides on a campus of 45,000 students would be on target for the fifteen to nineteen years of age group and slightly low for the twenty to twenty-four years of age group (6.75 student suicides) and the twenty-five to thirty-four years of age group (6.9 student suicides) [27].

A significant summary of student suicide, trends and implications, has been done by Westefeld, Whitchard and Range [29]. They reviewed eleven studies reported between 1978 and 1988 and came to two conclusions. The first was that the gathering of accurate data was very difficult. Systematic and effective record keeping systems are not operational. The second was that the data that are being kept is inconsistent.

Given these two express difficulties does not mean, however, the studies should be accepted *carte blanche* or that they should be discarded as irrelevant due to their inconsistencies or methodological difficulties. Rather, efforts should be made to determine the actual rate of suicidal ideation, attempted and completed suicide among the students on any particular campus. This will be a major undertaking even on a small campus as it means that the administration of the institutions will have to accept this record keeping task. Then, while the major tracking effort will need to be assigned to a single office, all sectors of the institution will need to report suicide incidents that come to their attention. This may be a complex endeavor, particularly at a large institution. However, if we are to establish a baseline to ascertain trends and plan services for these students it is imperative that this work be undertaken immediately. Suicidal behavior is a problem on campuses throughout the nation. It will not disappear because we refuse to "count," take appropriate action to remedy the causes, to counsel the suicidal student and to support the survivors.

One specific group of students has been studied independently, medical school students. Schwartz, Swartzburg, Lieb and Slaby studied fifty-four medical school students who, if they had not entered the study of medicine would have been in a literary or artistic activity (A-L) or would have been in professional or scientific careers (P-S) [30]. In their pre-clinical years, there was no difference between the two groups. However, 29 percent A-L students expressed dissatisfaction or disillusionment with the choice of medicine which was twice the level of the P-S students. As the A-L group entered the clinical years, the percentage contemplating suicide doubled, going from 17 to 33 percent which was significantly higher than the P-S students (10%). Psychiatric treatment was sought by 37 percent of the clinical A-L students. It was felt that the A-L students were "more likely to appear in the ranks of the 'non-academic dropouts' and in the psychiatric treatment services of medical schools" [30, p. 185].

Pepitone-Arreola-Rockwell, Rockwell and Core surveyed all U.S. medical schools (96 of 116 responded [82.8%]) requesting a report on the number of suicides and attempted suicides among all students graduating or who would have been expected to graduate between 1974 and 1981 [31]. The annual rate of suicide (per 100,000) for men from 1974 to 1981 ranged from 7.7 to 31.2 with an average of 15.6. For women the range was from 0.0 to 64.3 with an average of 18.9. The rate for men was slightly below their agemates in the general population while the rate for women was two to three times the rate of their agemates in the general population. As with the study above, there was a clustering of suicide in the sophomore ("sophomore blues") and junior (beginning of clinical responsibility) years (66%). While November, December, and January are typically the period of lowest frequencies in the general population, 50 percent of the medical school student suicides took place at this time, almost exclusively sophomores. The authors noted they received reports of only fifty-four attempted suicides which seems to be a significant under reporting. It is possible students who made attempts did not seek treatment and/or avoided any reporting to the school for fear of dismissal.

The highly competitive and intensive environment of the medical school creates stress that leads to the types of life crises described by Gerstein and Russell—drug abuse, severe fatigue, loss of concentration, damage to personal relationships, and psychological disturbances [32]. Other studies are cited by Kaltreider who describes the powerful impact that a medical student's suicide has upon the survivors [33].

Perhaps their smaller numbers, a more closely supervised environment and the fact that a number of researchers are psychiatrists enable more definitive studies of medical students. Whatever the reason(s), there is more accurate information on medical students than any other group of students. These studies indicate that the rate of suicidal behavior among medical students is significant. This information could be utilized to develop various prevention and intervention strategies in medical schools. It would greatly assist efforts toward identification, prevention, intervention, and postvention if research were conducted on other student groups with the same degree of intensity.

DATA ON SPECIFIC POPULATIONS

If there is a difficulty in determining rates for the overall student population, there is even a greater difficulty in making determinations for specific populations on the campus. Again, this is an unfortunate circumstance as this makes the definition and accuracy of trends almost impossible. Often it is necessary to attempt to extrapolate from general population statistics to make some determinations to aid in the development of prevention, intervention, and postvention programs on the campus. There is, however, some data that can be utilized to assist in these programmatic efforts.

AFRICAN AMERICAN STUDENT POPULATION INCIDENCE

The U.S. Department of Education reported that in the fall of 1991:

- African American students comprised 9.3 percent of the total number of students in higher education.

- African American students comprised 9.9 percent of the under-graduate body, 5.4 percent of the graduate body and 6.0 percent of the professional school students.
- African American students comprised 9.3 percent of the total students in public institutions and 9.2 percent of students in private institutions.
- African American students comprised 8.7 percent of the total students in four year institutions and 10.2 percent of students in two year institutions.
- African American women accounted for 10.4 percent of the total women enrolled and 5.7 percent of the total student enrollment.
- African American men accounted for 8 percent of the total men enrolled and 3.6 percent of the total student enrollment [34].

While data are available and studies have been made of African American suicide rates, there has been no investigation of African American college student suicides to ascertain relevant data. It is known that African American suicides tend to occur predominately in young males (4 to 1 over females) with the majority of the suicides taking place between fifteen and thirty-four years-of-age and the peak range is twenty to thirty-four years-of-age [35]. Suicide is the third leading cause of death for young African American males. Combined with homicide, drug abuse, and accidents, these causes of death for African American youth under the age of twenty present a group at significant risk [36, 37]. From the general population data we can obtain a sense of what might be occurring on the campus. It needs to be understood that there is not a direct relationship between the suicidal behaviors of African Americans in colleges and universities and those in the general population. For example, we do not know the differences that exist in the hopelessness felt by an African American high school dropout who is unemployed and that felt by an African American student at a predominately Caucasian college where "if minority status were not challenge enough, the psychological needs and vulnerabilities characteristic of adolescence intensify these student's problems" [38, p. 292]. However, we do need some markers if we are to attempt to understand the issues and the problems.

Davis did a demographic analysis of suicide among African Americans [39, 40]. He noted the rate of suicide among young adult Black men "has risen over the past decade to the point where it approximates and sometimes surpasses that of their white male cohorts, which is well above average. The increase has been greatest among Black males aged 20-24 (15 percent) and 25-29 (42 percent)" [40, p. 179]. He noted that this increase in suicide among young African Americans began in the early 1960s. Suicide is predominately an issue among African American males as the African American female rate had declined somewhat during this same period. Davis also noted that the higher rates of suicide are in metropolitan areas.

Other researchers also have noted this increase. Houze, for instance, stated "not only have increases in Black youth suicide been significantly responsible for our over-all problem of American youth suicide, but for Blacks as a separate racial–cultural group, it as well represents a historical reversal" [41, p. 9]. Kirk noted that until recently "it was assumed, particularly by black persons, that suicide represented a white solution to white problems. In other words, black people believed that blacks did not commit suicide or that if they did, then the occurrence was very rare. The data indicate otherwise" [42, p. 1]. Gibbs pointed out that not only was the rate of suicide a significant problem and a cause for concern about African American youth but also "it has a disproportionate impact on the black population, which is a youthful population with a median age of 25.8 years" [43, p. 75].

Miles [44] and Bush [45] both make specific references to suicide among African American females. Both commented on the recent increase in suicide among this group. They noted that although African American females, particularly in the age group fourteen to thirty years of age, have the lowest rates, there has been a rapid rise in their suicide rate. Among eight metropolitan areas, Miles found that suicide had decreased by 46 percent in the Los Angeles/Long Beach area while there was an increase of 87.9 percent in the Cincinnati area.

Berman and Jobes compared suicide rates for the years 1960 and 1987 [46]. This was a period of significant increase in suicide rates for the population in the fifteen to twenty-four years of age group and African American youth reflected the same trend. In the age group fifteen to nineteen years of age, the rate of suicide for African American males increased 206 percent from 2.9 to 8.9 (all rates given per 100,000) and females increased by 145 percent from 1.1 to 2.7. In the age group twenty to twenty-four years of age, males increased by 196 percent from 5.8 to 17.2 and females by 60 percent from 1.5 to 2.4.

The *Statistical Abstract of the United States: 1992* provides the following data for 1989 (rates per 100,000) (p. 90) for African Americans [28]:

	Males	Females
10-14 years of age	1.7	0.1
15-19 years of age	10.3	2.3
20-24 years of age	23.7	3.4

In the two year period from 1987 to 1989, there has been an increase in the rate of suicide for males, particularly in the twenty to twenty-four years of age group where the rate rose from 17.2 to 23.7.

Ellis and Range used the Reasons for Living Inventory to determine differences between African Americans and Caucasians, men and women in an undergraduate population at a predominately Caucasian university [47]. They found African Americans and women endorsed stronger reasons for living. Even with the difficulty of being a small minority in a predominately Caucasian institution there was a statistically significant difference between African Americans and Caucasians. Ellis and Range noted further research is needed to explore "our understanding of suicide and the advantages of being Black in terms of reasons for living" [47, p. 346].

Contrasting with Ellis and Range's conclusions that African Americans presented stronger reasons for living, would be Durkheim's theory that suicides may occur when an individual finds difficulty in adjusting to social change and/or loses contact with his society [48]. Davis draws particular attention to this issue, noting that social mobility may result in isolation and the disruption of contacts with primary and secondary relationships [40, 49]. This is certainly a possibility that young African Americans enrolled in primarily Caucasian institutions may find it difficult to establish extensive ties with Caucasian students due to a reluctance on their part to treat them as an equal. Like other upwardly mobile groups, they "must choose between abandoning hope of translating his occupational success into social acceptance by a more prestigious group and sacrificing valued social ties and customs in an effort to gain such acceptance" [50, p. 290]. Davis believed that the lack of supports, particularly within the African American community was very important

> As a caring and protective system is likely to be less available to young, upwardly mobile Black males. When these young Black males, because of racial differences, envy, personal crises, and the like, begin to experience recurrent stressful social situations, they must do so without access to stable, positive social networks within the Black community [40, pp. 194-195].

While Davis' work was with African American males it would seem reasonable to assume that similar circumstances could be experienced by African American females.

The psychosocial dynamics of African American adolescent suicide were examined by Smith and Carter [51]. They stated that "black suicide is particularly baffling and seems inconsistent with historical reports of black coping styles, culture, and religion. In fact, the suicide rate among young blacks has risen to a level that is as high as that of their white peers" [51, p. 1061]. They noted that the suicide rates were highest in the North and West regions and lowest in the South. Drug overdose was speculated to be the most common form of suicide with young African American men (15-24 years of age) attempting suicide about twice as often as young African American women. The African American men also "have a stronger tendency toward alcoholism and drug abuse" [51, p. 1062].

One study that provided some information that may be relevant to African Americans in colleges and universities was conducted by Davis [52]. He found immigration had a consequence for suicide.

> Thus, the current increase in Black suicide can be attributed, at least in part, to young upwardly mobile Blacks who are isolated from their families, communities, and social institutions. The Black community, in effect, does not function as a substitute society for these individuals [52, p. 23].

While Davis did not specifically speak of college students, his description is similar to that of African American students who enroll at colleges and universities that are distant from their homes and other support systems.

Whatever the case, it is particularly important to note that young African Americans, particularly males are at high risk. A recent report by the Group for the Advancement of Psychiatry placed a focus on the key concept of hopelessness as an integral part of suicidal behavior among African Americans and noted "it is unfortunate that the hopelessness of the Black population is being borne by the young, those who would seem to merit most the chance to achieve their dreams" [53, p. 28]. Even without highly specific data relating to the collegiate experience, the potential precipitators and risks for the incidence of suicide within the African American group merits the attention of all individuals within the educational community.

ASIAN STUDENT POPULATION INCIDENCE

Asian Americans are the fastest growing minority group constituting approximately 3 percent of the population according to the 1990 census. The U.S. Department of Education reported that in the fall of 1991:

- Asian American students comprised 4.4 percent of the total number of students in higher education.
- Asian American students comprised 4.5 percent of the undergraduate body, 3.5 percent of the graduate body and 7.5 percent of the professional school students.
- Asian American students comprised 4.6 percent of the total students in public institutions and 4 percent of the students in private institutions.
- Asian American students comprised 4.4 percent of the students in four year institutions and 4.5 percent of the students in two year institutions.
- Asian American men accounted for 5 percent of the total enrolled and 2.3 percent of the total student enrollment.
- Asian American women accounted for 4 percent of the total women enrolled and 2.2 percent of the total student enrollment [34].

Unfortunately, the definition of Asian American that is being used in this book, confounds an issue of consequence—the demographic and ethnic diversity of the Asian American population. Magner has pointed out that this has raised complex questions for educational institutions [54].

> Colleges find it difficult to deal with the varying needs of a population that includes refugees, recent immigrants, and native-born Americans and that encompasses more than two dozen ethnic subgroups from places as distinct as China, Japan, Vietnam and India" [54, p. A32].

The complexity of defining and understanding the incidence of suicide among various groups of Asian Americans is a problem that will not be resolved here. It is, however, an issue that needs to be addressed both in the gathering of statistical information as well as in understanding the possible variations in data.

The scarcity of information and research on Asian American suicide is illustrated by the fact that the work by Yu, Chang, Liu and Fernandez as part of the U.S. Department of Health and Human Services' *Report of the Secretary's Task Force on Youth Suicide* was characterized as:

> perhaps one of the very first efforts at exploring the National Center for Health Statistics' archival death files to analyze the inter-ethnic differences among Asian American youth. . . . we have

barely scratched the tip of the iceberg on Asian American suicide at the national level [55, pp. 3-163].

Studies of Chinese and Japanese Americans' suicides have been the major focus of previous research. However, there are now forty Asian American subgroups enumerated in the census. The large number of new Asian immigrants since approximately 1970 has created greater diversity in many areas of the nation. Many of these individuals are classified as non-resident aliens. Since 1970, suicide data on non-resident aliens has not been maintained. This also creates a significant void in the study of suicide for these individuals are not included. In Yu et al.'s work, only statistics for Japanese and Chinese Americans were presented "for reasons of availability and confidence in the quality of the data" [55, pp. 3-159]. The current college population has considerable numbers of Koreans, Laotians, Vietnamese, Cambodians, Hmong, and other Asian peoples for whom, unfortunately, there are no accurate data readily available. This represents a significant gap in the literature related to college students.

In the survey of high achievers which was reported in chapter one, Asian American high school students represented the highest percentage (44%) of individuals who had considered suicide [15]. This was considered a significant finding in this study as ideation was considered to be predominately a Caucasian phenomenon. Also of significance was the fact that Asian American high school students were among the highest percentage (8%) for racial group members who had attempted suicide. Thirty-four percent of the Asian American high school students gave school pressure as a reason for considering suicide. This percentage was more than double that of other racial groups.

Yu et al. noted:

> In interview after interview with Asian American high achievers, the public learned from the media that the children explained their drive to excel in terms of the shame that can befall their parents should they fail, and the glory they bring to their parents when they succeed. It comes as no surprise that we have a cohort of high-achieving Asian American parents who are putting tremendous pressure on their children to become even more successful than they are [55, pp. 3-163-3-164].

Another stress factor presented by Yu et al. is that Asian Americans born in the United States are perceived to be "foreigners" by the general society and as non-traditional by their parents since many of them do not speak their parents' native language [55]. The foreign born

Asian American faces "perhaps even more inner turmoil because of the inevitable clash of values held by their immigrant parents and the larger society, especially their American peers" [55, p. 3-164]. These young adults are caught between two worlds, attempting to belong to both and perhaps perceiving they are not firmly grounded in either. Lack of support from either or both could lead to significant emotional trauma as they attempt to develop their own self identity.

Yu et al. found in the 15-24 years of age groups, the rates of suicide (per 100,000) were (1980 data) [55].

	Japanese American	Chinese American
Foreign	14.3	7.1
Native born	8.1	5.2
Males	14.1	8.1
Females	4.5	4.6

Suicide among Asian American youth accounts for a larger proportion of deaths than among their Caucasian counterparts. Yu et al. reported that among males:

> suicide represents 21.3 percent of all deaths for Japanese Americans, 15.1 percent for Chinese Americans and only 12.9 percent for white Americans. Among females, it constitutes 20.8 percent for Chinese Americans, 14 percent for Japanese Americans, and 8.8 percent for white Americans [55, p. 3-161].

We are only beginning to understand the problem of suicide among Asian American youth. We need more research to explore the various ethnic groups and to provide appropriate base data. We need to determine what dynamics are present within the individual's culture that may create the belief they (and maybe their society) would be better if they were dead. It is apparent that suicidal behavior is a significant issue for young Asian American men and women. Our knowledge is very incomplete and consequently our efforts may be patchwork at best. These students deserve better.

CAUCASIAN STUDENT POPULATION INCIDENCE

The U.S. Department of Education reported that in the fall of 1991:

- Caucasian students comprised 76.5 percent of the total number of students in higher education in the fall of 1991.

- Caucasian students comprised 76.4 percent of the undergraduate body, 76.8 percent of the graduate body and 79.1 percent of the professional school students.
- Caucasian students comprised 76.2 percent of the total students in public institutions and 77.6 percent of the students in private institutions.
- Caucasian students comprised 78 percent of the total students in four year institutions and 74.3 percent of students in two year institutions.
- Caucasian women accounted for 76.7 percent of the total women enrolled and 42 percent of the total student enrollment.
- Caucasian men accounted for 76.3 percent of the total men enrolled and 34.6 percent of the total student enrollment [34].

Suicide by Caucasians constitutes the majority of the suicides in the United States and Caucasian males commit the greatest number of suicides. Data from the National Center for Health Statistics clearly demonstrate this [56]. In 1990, the suicide rate (per 100,000) for Caucasians was 13.2, for males it was 22.0 and for females it was 5.3, clearly demonstrating that the male/female ratio for completed suicide is 4:1. Caucasians committed 90.9 percent (28,086) of the total suicides (30,906) with Caucasian males committing 72.6 percent (22,448) of the total suicides and 90.8 percent of the total male suicides (24,724). For Caucasian males, suicide is the seventh leading cause of death. Caucasian females committed 18.2 percent (5,638) of the total suicides and 91.2 percent of the total female suicides (6,182).

For Caucasians in the fifteen to twenty-four years of age group, suicide was the second leading cause of death with a rate of 15.2/100,000. In 1990, suicide accounted for 4,869 deaths or 18.1 percent of the total deaths for this Caucasian age group.

It is apparent Caucasians may most closely fit the statistical data on suicide as they currently account for the vast majority of suicides. This is more true for Caucasian males. It is still important to remember that changes have been occurring. Some questions remain to be answered such as, is the increase in young African American male suicide within the college population identical to or close to the current rate for all fifteen to twenty-four years of age African American males? If as Davis noted, the differences between suicide rates for the African American and Caucasian male fifteen to twenty-four years of age cohorts is becoming almost nonexistent it will have a significant impact [40]. There will be an even stronger need for all racial suicide rates to be separated by race and by age group if we are to know exactly what is happening among various groups.

HISPANIC STUDENT POPULATION INCIDENCE

The U.S. Department of Education reported that in the fall of 1991:

- Hispanic students comprised 6 percent of the total number of students in higher education.
- Hispanic students comprised 6.5 percent of the undergraduate body, 3.1 percent of the graduate body and 3.9 percent of the professional school students.
- Hispanic students comprised 6.6 percent of the total students in public institutions and 4.1 percent of students in private institutions.
- Hispanic students comprised 4.4 percent of the total students in four year institutions and 8.6 percent of students in two year institutions.
- Hispanic women accounted for 6.1 percent of the total women enrolled and 3.3 percent of the total student enrollment.
- Hispanic men accounted for 4.9 percent of the total men enrolled and 2.7 percent of the total student enrollment [34].

Data on suicide rates for the general Hispanic population is difficult to obtain. Until approximately 1985, the National Center for Health Statistics tended to report data in terms of white and non-white or white, black, and other. Likewise studies of Hispanic college student suicides have not been undertaken and any data are included in non-white or other categories. Consequently, it is necessary to review some available data on the general Hispanic population to have any base for information.

The Hispanic suicide rate is also difficult to study because of the low number of Hispanics enrolled in institutions of higher education. Santiago and Feinberg noted that in 1981, Hispanics comprised 3.5 percent of the undergraduate populations and 2.2 percent of the graduate population in colleges and universities [57]. They also noted that over one half of the Hispanics who matriculated failed to earn a bachelor's degree. Most of the drop-outs were for financial reasons. Of particular note to the study of suicide, they reported that Hispanic students encountered a series of stressful life events that can become precipitators for mental health problems including suicidal behaviors.

Seven years later, Fields reported Hispanics still accounted for only 4.3 percent of the total college enrollment while they comprised 8.2 percent of the eighteen to twenty-four years of age population [58]. She further noted the rate of high school graduation for Hispanics was 62.9 percent compared with Anglo-Americans (83.6%) and African Americans (75.6%). Hispanics accounted for 3.1 percent of the enrollment at four year institutions and 6.4 percent at two year colleges (54.4% of all Hispanic students were enrolled in community colleges). Hispanics earned 2.7 percent of all bachelor's degrees awarded in 1985, men earned 2.1 percent and women earned 2.9 percent of master's degrees, men earned 2.0 percent and women earned 2.2 percent of doctoral degrees. While 20.6 percent of non-Hispanics earn bachelor's degrees by the age of twenty-five, 8.6 percent of Hispanics earn these degrees by age twenty-five. Fields also chose to examine differences within Hispanic subgroup populations and their completion of four years or more of college and found the following: Cubans comprise 5 percent of the population with a 17.1 percent rate of completion; Central/South Americans comprise 11 percent of the population with a 12.2 percent rate of completion; Puerto Ricans comprise 12 percent of the population with a 8 percent rate of completion; and Mexican Americans comprise 63 percent of the population with a 5.8 percent rate of completion. Fields attributes these variations to varying levels of poverty and English proficiency among other factors.

Domino noted there were several studies that reported "the suicide rates for Mexican Americans are lower than for Anglos, but are accelerating quite rapidly" [59, p. 385] and that the dominant incidence was for males in their twenties. Smith, Mercy, and Warren studied Hispanic suicide in five southwestern U.S. states (Arizona, California, Colorado, New Mexico, and Texas) where more than 60 percent of the Hispanic population resided in 1980 [60]. The found suicide was predominately a youthful phenomenon among Hispanics. During the 1976-1980 period, the suicide rate for persons in the fifteen to nineteen years of age category was 14.8 (per 100,000) for males and 3.4 for females. In the twenty to twenty-four years of age category, the suicide rate was 33.1 for males and 5.4 for females.

Sorenson and Golding studied the lifetime prevalence of suicidal ideation and attempts of Hispanics in the Los Angeles area [61]. They also found suicidal behavior occurred most frequently in the twenty to twenty-nine years of age group. The age group that they reported was eighteen to twenty-four years of age. The rate of suicidal ideation within this group was 14.3 (per 100,000) for males and 15.6 for females. The attempt rate was 1.1 for males and 6.0 for females.

In their 1989 report on suicide and ethnicity, the Group for the Advancement of Psychiatry noted there was a relative paucity of information on suicide among the diversity of Hispanic populations of the United States. They found, with limited data, that there appeared to be a greater increase in the suicide rates among Puerto Ricans in the United States than those in Puerto Rico. They believed migration created stresses on the mainland not found on the island. The same stresses seemed apparent between Mexican Americans and Mexicans living in Mexico. As with African Americans and Native Americans, the peaks were found in young males. "Young adult males seem to be particularly strongly affected by the stress of acculturation, as reflected in their inordinately high suicide rates" [53, p. 92]. The acculturation issue would seem to apply to those students who are the first-in-family to attend an institution of higher education. This factor needs attention by all members of the academic community.

While it is difficult to ascertain an accurate rate of suicide for Hispanics, suicidal behaviors need the attention of all college personnel. The Hispanic population is increasing. "Just after the year 2000, the minority will become the majority of the people in the Southwest under age 30. They will become the majority of the Southwest total population shortly thereafter" [58, p. 27]. Even if a worst case scenario is that the current low percentage rate of enrollment indicated by statistics continues, Hispanic students will be matriculating at an ever increasing overall number. These students will require services to meet their special needs. The first of these is that "Mexican American students are not part of an educational pipeline for which the goal is to deposit them at the door of some institution of higher education" [62, p. 137]. If that were not enough of a disadvantage, Fiske poses a second unfavorable potential.

> For many Hispanic students the most serious problems are not those confronting getting into college but those they face once they get there. The problems range from the anxiety of breaking close family ties to the loneliness and tensions inherent in finding their way in institutions built around an alien culture [63, p. 29].

These students will encounter subtle or not so subtle discrimination, they will have to cope with cultural differences perhaps even culture shock and for some of them, this will be the first time that they will be identified as a member of a minority group. These are clearly stressful life events that require solid support systems. Family and other usual support systems probably are not available in this new setting. Consequently, these students become at risk and need the attention of the collegiate community.

NATIVE AMERICAN STUDENT
POPULATION INCIDENCE

The U.S. Department of Education reported that in the fall of 1991:

* Native American students comprised 4.8 percent of the total number of students in higher education.
* Native American students comprised 0.85 percent of the undergraduate body, 0.43 percent of the graduate body and 0.36 percent of the professional school students.
* Native American students comprised 0.9 percent of the total students in public institutions and 0.5 percent of students in private institutions.
* Native American students comprised 0.59 percent of the total students in four year institutions and 1.1 percent of students in two year institutions.
* Native American women accounted for 0.84 percent of the total women enrolled and 0.46 percent of the total student enrollment.
* Native American men accounted for 0.74 percent of the total men enrolled and 0.33 percent of the total student enrollment [34].

Determining the incidence of suicide among Native American college students is also difficult. First, they comprise the smallest racial group on the campus and the data relating to Native Americans are usually relegated to the category, "other." Second, the rate of suicide differs dramatically between tribes and pueblos which could affect the rate of Native American suicide on campuses in different areas. Shore [64], McIntosh and Santos [65] and Berlin [66] have all noted the rates vary from as low as eight to as high as 100 per 100,000 depending upon the tribe or pueblo. Shore states emphatically "the stereotype of the 'suicidal Indian' is inaccurate" [64, p. 63]. Other factors that may have an effect on the incidence of suicide could be related to whether the individual is from a reservation or residing in an urban area and the distance between the individual and members of his or her tribe or pueblo.

The high rate of suicide among young Native American men has been well established. The Indian Health Service reported that from 1986 to 1988 in the fifteen to twenty-four years of age group the rate (per 100,000) for men was 62.7, for women 8.7 [67].

> Nationwide, young Native American men are committing suicide at a rate more than twice the average for their age group. . . . For example, Native Americans comprise 15% of the population of Alaska, yet the suicide rate among men between 20 and 24 years of age is more than 10 times the national mean [68, p. 39].

Even with these high rates there is a strong belief they are underestimates and conservative. Berlin has stated

> in addition to the clearly recognized suicides, about 3/4 of the adolescents killed while driving alone in a car are believed to be suicides. Since auto fatalities and other accidents, often related to drinking or taking of drugs, are the most important causes of death in adolescents, it means the suicide problem is a very serious one [69, p. 2].

Again, it is necessary to attempt to gain an understanding of the potential risk factors involved rather than a total reliance on statistics, which is probably what should be done anyway to provide adequate support and mental health services to these or any students.

The Indian Health Service has estimated that, compared with other ethnic groups, fewer Native American teenagers will graduate from high school (55.4% vs. 66.5%) and that only 7.4 percent will graduate from college (vs. 16.2%) [70]. A recent report on Native American youth health indicated that even among those students who did succeed there was a prevailing sense of hopelessness that was particularly reflected in the female self-injurious behaviors increasing between the seventh and twelfth grades [71].

Why this pervasive sense of hopelessness exists and what factors may be inherent in the development of suicide risk needs to be attended to within a collegiate setting. Dizmang, Watson, May and Bopp have determined from postmortem interviews on southwestern Native American youth suicides the following important factors (contrasted with non-suicide controls):

- Seventy percent of the suicides had more than one primary caregiver before age fifteen (controls = 15%).
- Forty percent of these primary caretakers have five or more arrests (controls = 7.5%),
- Fifty percent of the suicides had experienced two or more losses (divorce or desertion) (controls = 10%).
- Eighty percent of the suicides had one or more arrests in the year before the suicide (controls = 25.5%).

- Seventy percent of the suicides had been arrested by age fifteen (controls = 20%),
- Sixty percent of the suicides had attended a boarding school prior to the ninth grade (controls = 27.55) [72].

The suicidal youths in this study experienced a greater degree of individual and familial disruption. A significant number of disruptions and stresses are antecedents to suicidal behaviors.

Native American students are the smallest racial population on the majority of campuses. In addition, these students are very likely to be separated from their families and Native American communities who would provide support during disruptive periods in their lives. Isolation from their primary group and a lesser degree of integration into any secondary group(s) creates a discontinuity in their lives that may precipitate a crisis. A Native American student may also find the same difficulties which Blau described for other upwardly mobile persons [50]. Isolation and lack of a support system are antecedents to possible suicidal behavior. Even without a definitive accounting of the rate of Native American suicide on the campus, the risk factors indicate that this is a group of students who deserve attention to preclude suicide among this group.

INTERNATIONAL STUDENT POPULATION INCIDENCE

The U.S. Department of Education reported that in the fall of 1991:

- International students comprise 2.9 percent of the total number of students in higher education.
- International students comprise 1.9 percent of the undergraduate body.
- International students comprise 11 percent of the graduate body.
- International students comprise 2.1 percent of the professional school students.
- International students comprise 2.4 percent of the total students in public institution and 4.6 percent of students in private institutions, 3.9 percent of the total students in four year institutions and 4.6 percent of the students in two year institutions.
- International male students accounted for 4 percent of the total men enrolled and 1.8 percent of the total student enrollment.
- International female students accounted for 2 percent of the total women enrolled and 1.1 percent of the total student enrollment [34].

In the academic year 1991-92, *The Chronicle of Higher Education* reported that the international student enrollment at U.S. colleges and universities was at an all time high with 419,585 students in residence [3]. Of this number, 8,270 were classified as refugees. International students, however, still comprised less than 3 percent of the total student population. As in the previous five years, the largest number of students came from Asia (58.7%). The remaining students came from Europe (12.8%), Latin America (10.4%), the Middle East (7.3%), Africa (5.2%), North America (4.7%) and Oceania (0.9%). In addition, *The Chronicle of Higher Education,* December 9, 1992 reported that there were 62,148 foreign scholars who were teaching or doing research [3]. Forty-seven percent of these scholars came from Asia, slightly over 33 percent came from Europe and the remaining 20 percent mainly came from Latin American and Middle Eastern nations. The largest number of scholars came from China (16.0%), followed by Japan (7.0%) and India (5.4%).

The incidence of suicide in this group is probably close to totally unknown. Some individual institutions may maintain records of incidents on their campus. As previously noted, since 1970, the U.S. Government does not keep data on internationals or resident aliens. Given the stresses of adapting to a new culture, coping with a new language of instruction and the pressure of desiring to succeed in an academic institution where there are probably few supports, it is certain that there are incidents of suicidal behaviors such as that of two Korean men reported in *the Chronicle of Higher Education* [73]. In addition, from my personal experience while working in residence halls, most international students do not wish to reveal their psychological problems out of fear that they will be deported. This further exacerbates an already stressful situation for even if they wanted to seek counseling assistance, they would probably not do so as they do not trust the concept of counseling confidentiality. While there is no data base, it is important for institutions to recognize the potential for significant precipitating factors and to work to maintain an open, positive stance that will permit these individuals to discuss their stresses and, where appropriate, to seek assistance.

GAY, LESBIAN AND BISEXUAL STUDENT POPULATION INCIDENCE

Gays, lesbians, and bisexuals can constitute a significant invisible minority within a college population, including persons from all racial and ethnic groups. There are no clear data as to the number of young people within this group. However, it is clearly a group that is at risk because they are young and face the prospect of total rejection by family and friends if they reveal their sexual orientation. In addition, on the college campus there is the distinct possibility they will face harassment and physical assaults. Improving the campus climate for gay, lesbian, and bisexual students is a distinct challenge as "this is a group that people will hate without knowing them" [74, p. A24]. In the *Report of the Secretary's Task Force on Youth Suicide,* Gibson's summary stated:

> a majority of suicide attempts by homosexuals occur during their youth, and gay youth are 2 to 3 times more likely to attempt suicide than other young people. They may comprise up to 30 percent of completed youth suicides annually [75, p. 110].

Three major studies from the 1970s still provide the majority of the data relating to gay, lesbian, and bisexual suicide. These studies "are further hampered because the two factors we are attempting to isolate—homosexuality and suicide—are both difficult to assess in a population" [76, p. 16]. Suicide is regarded as immoral and brands the individual as a "failure." Homosexuality is regarded as immoral and brands the individual as a "sinner." Both stigmatize the individual. Consequently, these studies are of individuals who are self-identified as homosexual or bisexual. There may be significant differences in attitudes toward suicide and rates of suicide between individuals who have identified themselves as gay, lesbian, and bisexual and those individuals who remain unidentified or "closeted" in current jargon. Since there are no studies on the latter group, the former group provides the data for interpretation and assessment.

The first study was done by Saghir and Robins [77]. This study was largely middle class and upper middle class persons who belonged to gay and lesbian organizations. They found 7 percent (*n* = 6) of the gay men had attempted suicide and one had made two attempts. These attempts were made by wrist slashing and ingestion of non-prescription drugs (considered mild attempts). By contrast, none of the heterosexual male controls had attempted suicide. Five of the six men attempted suicide before they reached the age of twenty, "when conflict at home and with one's self concerning homosexuality was quite intense" [77, p. 118]. Twelve percent (*n* = 3) of the lesbians and 5 percent (*n* = 1) of the heterosexual women had attempted suicide. Their attempts were regarded as being more serious than for gay males, utilizing slashing and prescription medications (usually tranquilizers).

The second study was done by Bell and Weinberg [78]. Beginning with over 5,000 participants, their final sample (*n* = 979) consisted of

575 Caucasian gay males, 111 African American gay males, 229 Caucasian lesbians and sixty-four African American lesbians. They were matched with a heterosexual population. Thirty-seven percent of the Caucasian gay males had either seriously considered (19%) or attempted suicide at least once (18%) compared with 13 percent of the Caucasian heterosexual males who had either seriously considered (10%) or attempted suicide at least once (3%). Twenty-four percent of the African American gay males had either seriously considered (4%) or attempted suicide at least once (20%) compared with the African American heterosexual males where 3 percent attempted suicide at least once. Forty-one percent of the Caucasian lesbians had either seriously considered (16%) or attempted suicide at least once (25%) compared with 26 percent of their heterosexual counterparts (16% seriously considered, 10% attempted). Twenty-five percent of the African American lesbians had seriously considered (8%) or attempted suicide at least once (17%) compared with 19 percent of their heterosexual counterparts (3% seriously considered, 16% attempted). Significantly, the first attempt at suicide by 16 percent of the Caucasian gay males, 9 percent of the African American gay males, 4 percent of the Caucasian lesbians and 9 percent of the African American lesbians took place when they acknowledged their homosexuality. Fifty-two percent (n = 105) of the Caucasian and 59 percent (n = 22) of the African American gay males first attempted suicide by age twenty. In addition, 27 percent of the Caucasian group and 23 percent of the African American group made attempts between the ages of twenty-one and twenty-five. Thus, 79 percent of the Caucasian and 82 percent of the African American gay males had attempted suicide by age twenty-five. Forty-two percent of the Caucasian and 52 percent of the African American lesbian first attempted suicide by age twenty. In addition, 29 percent of the Caucasian group and 27 percent of the African American group made attempts between the ages of twenty-one and twenty-five. Thus, 71 percent of the Caucasian and 79 percent of the African American lesbians had attempted suicide by age twenty-five. These figures are significantly higher than those reported by Saghir and Robins [77]. However, the most important factor is that lesbians and gay men were making their first attempts before age twenty-five. It is impossible to know from this study what percentage of the subjects were college students. A significant percentage of gay males and lesbians within this study were within the age parameters of a college population. Regardless of the actual numbers, the risk factors for attempted suicide are clearly present in a group that is resident among the college and university population.

A third major study was by Jay and Young [79]. This was a very comprehensive study of over 4,400 gay men and 1,000 lesbians in the United States and Canada who were between the ages of eighteen and eighty-two. This was predominately a Caucasian group (over 90%) with African Americans being represented by 2 percent of the gay males and 1 percent of the lesbians. Native Americans and Asian Americans accounted for less than 1 percent of the group. Gay Hispanic males made up 1 percent and lesbian Hispanics constituted 1.6 percent of the group. Overall, 40 percent of the gay males and 39 percent of the lesbians stated that they had seriously considered or attempted suicide. Fifty-three percent of the gay males and 33 percent of the lesbians stated their suicide attempts were related to their homosexuality. Jay and Young noted it is more than just the suicidal experiences of the individual gay male or lesbian that affects their lives. "In addition to their own experiences seriously contemplating or attempting suicide, many gay people live with the specter of suicide and suicide attempts involving friends, lovers and acquaintances" [79, p. 728]. Consequently, in addition to having a significant risk factor of their own, for gay, lesbian, and bisexual youth "suicide or suicidal behavior of relatives and friends appears to be a significant factor in influencing a vulnerable young person to commit suicide" [80, p. 1064].

In a recent investigation, Remafedi, Farrow and Deisher studied both the rate of suicidal behavior and the risk factors associated with gay and bisexual male youth who were between fourteen and twenty-one years of age [81]. Of this group ($n = 137$), 88 percent described themselves as gay and 12 percent as bisexual. Eighty-two percent of the group was Caucasian, 13 percent African American, 4 percent Hispanic and 1 percent Asian American. Thirty percent of the men ($n = 41$) reported at least one suicide attempt and 44 percent of this number ($n = 18$) had made more than one attempt. The attempters were 20 percent Catholic, 24 percent Protestant, 29 percent listed other faiths or religiosity and 27 percent stated that they had no religion. Ingestion and laceration accounted for 80 percent of the suicidal actions. Approximately 75 percent of the attempts received no medical or mental health intervention. The percentage of attempts following initial self-acknowledgment of sexual orientation was considerably higher than that reported in the Bell and Weinberg study [78]. Seventy-five percent of the first attempts reported in this study took place at this time. The difference may be that this is a group of young males who are at a different development stage. The lethality of the attempt by 54 percent of the attempters was judged to be moderate to high lethality. The authors noted that the "rate of completed suicide among homosexual attempters is unknown as is the relative contribution of homosexual adolescents to total youth suicides" [81, p. 875]. Suicide attempters were more likely than nonattempters to be victims of sexual abuse, have undergone chemical dependency treatment, used or were in possession of illicit drugs, or engaged in theft. Peer conflicts, depression and relationship problems were also present.

This corresponds directly with findings by Saunders and Valente who reviewed suicide risk among gay men and lesbians [82]. Alcohol abuse, drug abuse and interrupted social ties were major risk factors found in their study.

Directly related to college suicide rates is the Schneider, Farberow and Kruks study of 108 gay male college students in the Los Angeles area [83]. They found 55 percent of the gay men reported a history of suicidal ideation. Ideation was associated with a family background history of alcoholism and physical abuse, social supports rejecting of homosexuality and no religious association. Suicide attempts were made by 20.4 percent of the men. The authors noted there was an overrepresentation of Hispanic gay men with greater suicidal ideation. They argued for a cautious interpretation of this information due to the small sample of Hispanics. "In general, however, being a stigmatized 'minority within a minority' may contribute to suicidality" [83, p. 391].

As noted by Jay and Young, "there is no doubt that suicide and attempted suicide are frequent responses of gay people to the difficulties of the gay experience in a hostile environment" [80, pp. 728-729].

The impact of AIDS among gay, lesbian, and bisexual students is unknown. With the establishment of gay, lesbian and bisexual student groups on the campuses it appears certain that students will be acquainted with persons who are HIV+ or have AIDS. It is also certain that there will be HIV+ persons and persons with AIDS (PWAs) on campuses. There appear to be no studies of persons with AIDS on a campus at this time. However, it is known that there is an increased risk of suicide when there is a diagnosis of HIV+ or AIDS. Marzuk, Tierney, Tardiff, Gross, Morgan, Hsu, and Mann reported the relative risk of suicide in men with AIDS was 36.3 times that of men aged twenty to fifty-nine without this diagnosis and 66.15 times that of the general population [84]. The issue of AIDS and suicide will need to be a priority item for college students, staff and faculty if there is to be the development of any proactive efforts. Otherwise, institutions will once again be handling a major issue in a reactive manner that is not the most productive effort.

REFERENCES

1. T. Raphael, S. H. Power, and W. L. Berridge, The Question of Suicide as a Problem in College Mental Health, *The American Journal of Orthopsychiatry, 7*:1, pp. 1-14, 1937.
2. C. B. Reifler, "Clements Fry, If You Could See Us Now"—The Robert L. Arnstein Retirement Lecture, *Journal of College Student Psychotherapy, 5*:1, pp. 3-18, 1990.
3. *The Chronicle of Higher Education, 38*:45, p. A29, July 15, 1992.
4. *The Chronicle of Higher Education, 39*:26, p. A5, March 3, 1993.
5. O. Jeanneret, A Tentative Epidemiological Approach to Suicide Prevention in Adolescence, *Journal of Adolescent Health, 13*:5, pp. 409-414, 1992.
6. National Center for Health Statistics, *Advance Report of Final Mortality Statistics 1991*, Hyatsville, Maryland: Public Health Service, Monthly Vital Statistics Report *42*:2 Public Health Service, Hyattsville, Maryland, 1993.
7. M. C. Stafford and R. A. Weisheit, Changing Age Patterns of U.S. Male and Female Suicide Rates, 1934-1983, *Suicide and Life Threatening Behavior, 18*:2, pp. 149-163, 1988.
8. N. L. Farberow (ed.), *The Many Faces of Suicide: Indirect Self-destructive Behavior*, McGraw-Hill, New York, 1980.
9. D. Flavin, Alcohol Abuse, Suicidal Behavior and AIDS, in *Acquired Immune Deficiency Syndrome and Chemical Dependency*, Petrakis, P. (ed.), National Institute on Alcohol Abuse and Alcoholism, Rockville, Maryland, pp. 67-73, 1987.
10. Bureau of the Census, *Statistical Abstract of the United States: 1991 (111th Edition)*, Superintendent of Documents, Government Printing Office, Washington, DC, 1991.
11. N. L. Farberow, D. R. MacKinnon, and F. L. Nelson, Suicide: Who's Counting? *Public Health Reports, 92*:3, pp. 223-232, 1977.
12. Minnesota Department of Education, *Minnesota Student Survey Report—1989*, Learner Support Systems, St. Paul, Minnesota, 1989.
13. Center for Disease Control, Attempted Suicide Among High School Students—United States, 1990, *Journal of the American Medical Association, 266*:14, pp. 1911-1912, 1991.
14. Who's Who Among American High School Students, *22nd Annual Survey of High Achievers*, Educational Communications, Inc., Forest Lake, Illinois, 1991.
15. Who's Who Among Americans High School Students, *23rd Annual Survey of High Achievers*, Educational Communications, Inc., Forest Lake, Illinois, 1992.
16. M. Ross, Suicide among College Students, *American Journal of Psychiatry, 126*:2, pp. 220-225, 1969.
17. A. T. Beck and J. E. Young, College Blues, *Psychology Today, 12*:4, pp. 80-92, 1978.

18. D. E. Schotte and G. A. Clum, Suicidal Ideation in a College Population: A Test of a Model, *Journal of Consulting and Clinical Psychology, 50*:5, pp. 690-696, 1982.

19. M. Sherer, Depression and Suicidal Ideation in College Students, *Psychological Reports, 57*:3, pt. 2, pp. 1061-1062, 1985.

20. K. Vredenburg, E. O'Brien, and L. Krames, Depression in College Students: Personality and Experiential Factors, *Journal of Counseling Psychology, 35*:4, pp. 419-425, 1988.

21. T. R. Goodman and L. J. Koenig, *Sex Differences in Depression: Explaining the Absence in College Populations,* paper presented at the American Psychological Association annual meeting, Washington, D.C., August 1992.

22. R. L. Bonner and A. R. Rich, A Prospective Investigation of Suicidal Ideation in College Students: A Test of a Model, *Suicide and Life Threatening Behavior, 18*:3, pp. 245-258, 1988.

23. M. D. Rudd, The Prevalence of Suicidal Ideation among College Students, *Suicide and Life Threatening Behavior, 19*:2, pp. 173-183, 1989.

24. D. Bertocci, E. Hirsch, W. Sommer, and A. Williams, Student Mental Health Needs: Survey Results and Implications for Service, *Journal of American College Health, 41*:1, pp. 3-10, 1992.

25. A. J. Schwartz and C. B. Reifler, Suicide among American College and University Students from 1970-71 through 1975-76, *Journal of the American College Health Association, 28*:4, pp. 205-210, 1980.

26. J. S. Westefeld and C. M. Pattillo, College Student Suicide: The Case for a National Clearinghouse, *Journal of College Student Personnel, 28*:1, pp. 34-38, 1987.

27. A. J. Schwartz and C. B. Reifler, College Student Suicide in the United States: Incidence Data and Prospects for Demonstrating the Efficacy of Preventative Programs, *Journal of American College Health, 37*:2, pp. 53-59, 1988.

28. Bureau of the Census, *Statistical Abstract of the United States 1992 (112th Edition),* Superintendent of Documents, Government Printing Office, Washington, DC, 1992.

29. J. S. Westefeld, K. A. Whitchard, and L. M. Range, College and University Student Suicides: Trends and Implications, *The Counseling Psychologist, 18*:3, pp. 464-476, 1990.

30. A. H. Schwartz, M. Swartzburg, J. Lieb, and A. E. Slaby, Medical School and the Process of Disillusionment, *Medical Education, 12*:3, pp. 182-185, 1978,

31. F. Pepitone-Arreola-Rockwell, D. Rockwell, and N. Core, Fifty-two Medical Student Suicides, *American Journal of Psychiatry, 138*:2, pp. 98-201, 1981.

32. L. H. Gerstein and N. Russell, The Experience of Medical School: A Major Life Crisis, *College Student Journal, 24*:2, pp. 128-138, 1990.

33. N. B. Kaltreider, The Impact of a Medical Student's Suicide, *Suicide and Life Threatening Behavior, 20*:3, pp. 195-205, 1990.

34. J. Evangelauf, College Enrollment by Racial and Ethnic Group, Fall 1991, *The Chronicle of Higher Education, 39*:20, pp. A30-A31, January 20, 1993.
35. E. Spaights and G. Simpson, Some Unique Causes of Black Suicide, *Psychology, 23*:1, pp. 1-5, 1986.
36. R. Staples, *Black Masculinity,* Black Scholar Press, San Francisco, 1982.
37. T. A. Parham and R. J. McDavis, Black Men, an Endangered Species: Who's Really Pulling the Trigger?, *Journal of Counseling and Development, 66*:1, pp. 24-27, 1987.
38. J. Fleming, Special Needs of Blacks and Other Minorities, in *The Modern American College,* A. W. Chickering and Associates, Jossey Bass, San Francisco, pp. 279-295, 1981.
39. R. Davis, Black Suicide in the Seventies: Current Trends, *Suicide and Life Threatening Behavior, 9*:3, pp. 131-140, 1979.
40. R. Davis, A Demographic Analysis of Suicide, in *Black Men,* L. E. Gary (ed.), Sage Publications, Beverly Hills, California, 1981.
41. B. Houze, *Black Youth Suicide: Individual Psychological and Socio-historical Components,* paper presented at the National Symposium on Black Suicide, University of Chicago, Chicago, Illinois, April 1980.
42. A. R. Kirk, *Psycho-social Modes of Adaptation and Suicide among Blacks,* National Institute of Mental Health paper, February 1986.
43. J. T. Gibbs, Conceptual, Methodological, and Sociocultural Issues in Black Youth Suicide, *Suicide and Life Threatening Behavior, 18*:1, pp. 73-89, 1988.
44. D. E. Miles, *Suicide among Black Females: A Theoretical Perspective,* paper presented at the National Symposium on Black Suicide, Howard University, Washington, DC, May 1981.
45. J. A. Bush, *Conceptual Frameworks for Viewing and Intervening in Suicide Among Blacks,* National Institute of Mental Health paper, February 1986.
46. A. L. Berman and D. A. Jobes, *Adolescent Suicide: Assessment and Intervention,* American Psychological Association, Washington, DC, 1991.
47. J. B. Ellis and L. M. Range, Differences between Blacks and Whites, Women and Men, in Reasons for Living, *Journal of Black Studies, 21*:3, pp. 341-347, 1991.
48. E. Durkheim, *Suicide,* Free Press, Glencoe, Illinois, 1951. (Originally published in 1897 as *Le Suicide.*)
49. R. Davis, Suicide among Young Blacks: Trends and Perspectives, *Phylon, 41*:3, pp. 223-229, 1980.
50. P. M. Blau, Social Mobility and Interpersonal Relations, *American Sociological Review, 21*:3, pp. 290-295, 1956.
51. J. A. Smith and J. H. Carter, Suicide and Black Adolescents: A Medical Dilemma, *Journal of the National Medical Association, 78*:11, pp. 1061-1064, 1986.
52. R. Davis, *Black Suicide and the Relational System: Theoretical and Empirical Implications in Communal and Family Ties,* Discussion paper presented at the Institute for Research on Poverty. University of Wisconsin, Madison, Wisconsin, 1978.

53. Group for the Advancement of Psychiatry, *Suicide and Ethnicity in the United States* (Report No. 128), Brunner/Mazel, New York, 1989.
54. D. K. Magner, Colleges Faulted for not Considering Differences in Asian-American Groups, *The Chronicle of Higher Education, 39*:23, pp. A32-A34, February 10, 1993.
55. E. Yu, C-F. Chang, W. T. Liu, and M. Fernandez, Suicide among Asian American Youth, in Alcohol, Drug Abuse, and Mental Health Administration, *Report of the Secretary's Task Force on Youth Suicide, Vol. 3, Prevention and Intervention in Youth Suicide,* DHHS Pub. No. (ADM)89-1623. Superintendent of Documents, Government Printing Office, 3-157-3-176, Washington, DC, 1989.
56. National Center for Health Statistics, *Advance Report of Final Mortality Statistics 1990, Public Health Service, Monthly Vital Statistics Report, 41,* Hyatsville, Maryland, 1993.
57. R. L. Santiago and R. C. Feinberg, The Status of Education for Hispanics, *Educational Leadership, 38*:4, pp. 292-297, 1981.
58. C. Fields, The Hispanic Pipeline: Narrow, Leaking and Needing Repair, *Change, 20*:3, pp. 20-27, 1988.
59. G. Domino, Attitudes toward Suicide among Mexican American and Anglo Youth, *Hispanic Journal of Behavioral Science, 3*:4, pp. 385-395, 1981.
60. J. C. III, Smith, J. A. Mercy, and C. W. Warren, Comparison of Suicides among Anglos and Hispanics in Five Southwestern States, *Suicide and Life Threatening Behavior, 15*:1, pp. 14-26, 1985.
61. S. B. Sorenson and J. M. Golding, Suicide Ideation and Attempts in Hispanics and Non-Hispanic Whites: Demographic and Psychiatric Disorder Issues, *Suicide and Life Threatening Behavior, 18*:3, pp. 205-218, 1988.
62. P. C. Kavanaugh, and P. M. Retish, The Mexican American Ready for College, *Journal of Multicultural Counseling and Development, 19*:3, pp. 137-144, 1991.
63. E. B. Fiske, The Undergraduate Hispanic Experience, *Change, 20*:3, pp. 29-33, 1988.
64. J. H. Shore, Psychiatric Epidemiology among American Indians, *Psychiatric Annals, 4*:11, pp. 56-66, 1974.
65. J. L. McIntosh and J. F. Santos, Suicide among Native Americans: A Compilation of Findings, *Omega, 11*:4, pp. 303-316, 1981.
66. I. N. Berlin, Suicide among American Indian Adolescents: An Overview, *Suicide and Life Threatening Behavior, 17*:3, pp. 218-232, 1987.
67. Indian Health Service, *Trends in Indian Health 1992,* U.S. Department of Health and Human Services, Public Health Service, Rockville, Maryland, 1992.
68. R. D. Herring, Seeking a New Paradigm: Counseling Native Americans, *Journal of Multicultural Counseling and Development, 20*:1, pp. 35-43, 1992.
69. I. N. Berlin, *Suicide among American Indian Adolescents,* Linkages Project, Native American Indian Court Judges Association, Washington, DC, 1984.

70. Indian Health Service, *Trends in Indian Health 1990,* U.S. Department of Health and Human Services, Public Health Service, Rockville, Maryland, 1990.

71. R. W. Blum, B. Harmon, L. Harris, L. Bergeisen, and M. D. Resnick, American Indian—Alaskan Native Youth Health, *Journal of the American Medical Association, 267*:12, pp. 1637-1644, 1992.

72. L. H. Dizmang, J. Watson, P. A. May, and J. Bopp, Adolescent Suicide at an Indian Reservation, *American Journal of Orthopsychiatry, 44*:1, pp. 43-49, 1974.

73. Rise in Suicides Alarms Campus, *The Chronicle of Higher Education,* p. A5, March 3, 1993.

74. Openly Gay Students Face Harassment and Physical Assaults on Some Campuses, *The Chronicle of Higher Education, 39*:27, pp. A22-A24, March 1993.

75. P. Gibson, Gay Male and Lesbian Youth Suicide, Alcohol, Drug Abuse, and Mental Health Administration, *Report of the Secretary's Task Force on Youth Suicide, Vol. 3: Prevention and Interventions in Youth Suicide,* DHHS Pub. No. (ADM)89-1623, Supt. of Docs., U.S. Government Printing Office, Washington, DC, 1989.

76. E. E. Rofes, *"I Thought People Like That Killed Themselves" Lesbians, Gay Men and Suicide,* Grey Fox Press, San Francisco, 1983.

77. M. T. Saghir and E. Robins, *Male and Female Homosexuality: A Comprehensive Investigation,* Williams and Wilkins, Baltimore, Maryland, 1973.

78. A. Bell and M. Weinberg, *Homosexualities: A Study of Diversity Among Men and Women,* Simon and Schuster, New York, New York, 1978.

79. K. Jay and A. Young (eds.), *The Gay Report: Lesbians and Gay Men Speak Out about their Sexual Experiences and Lifestyles,* Simon and Schuster, New York, 1979.

80. M. Shafii, S. Carrigan, J. Whittinghill, J. Russell, and A. Derrick, Psychological Autopsy of Completed Suicide in Children and Adolescents, *American Journal of Psychiatry, 142*:9, pp. 1061-1064, 1985.

81. J. Remafedi, J. A. Farrow, and R. W. Deisher, Risk Factors for Attempted Suicide in Gay and Bisexual Youth, *Pediatrics, 87*:6, pp. 869-875, 1991.

82. J. M. Saunders and S. M. Valente, Suicide Risk among Gay Men and Lesbians: A Review, *Death Studies, 11*:1, pp. 1-23, 1987.

83. S. G. Schneider, N. L. Farberow, and G. N. Kruks, Suicidal Behavior in Adolescent and Young Adult Gay Men, *Suicide and Life Threatening Behavior, 19*:4, pp. 381-394, 1989.

84. P. M. Marzuk, H. Tierney, K. Tardiff, E. M. Gross, E. B. Morgan, M. Hsu, and J. J. Mann, Increased Risk of Suicide in Persons with AIDS, *Journal of the American Medical Association, 259*:9, pp. 1333-1337, 1988.

CHAPTER 4

The Mythology of Suicide

> You would know the secret of death. But how shall you find it
> unless you seek it in the heart of life? . . . If you would indeed
> behold the spirit of death, open your heart wide unto the body of
> life. For life and death are one, Even as the river and the sea are
> one [Gibran, 1, p. 80].

College students find writers like Gibran to be fascinating. The mysticism relating to life and death provides them with an intellectual focus on these issues. Yet, while college students may intellectually accept the fact of death as a part of life, the actual intrusion of death into their lives continues to be viewed as an anathema. For this is a time when life is emphasized, change and growth are anticipated in body, mind and soul. Life is exciting! Students look forward to the day when they will graduate and enter into an adult world that is filled with hopes, desires, and the anticipated personal power of a youthful oriented society. Magazine, newspaper, television, and radio advertising images are formulated with the concept of either being or maintaining the images of youth. Aging is to be avoided. Instant gratification is the code word for avoiding all pain, physical or mental. Having been raised in an age when science and technology seem to know no boundaries, students consider all problems solvable, perhaps even their mortality. Relationships are changing. The concepts of dependence, independence, and inter-dependence are creating significant shifts in the relationships between student and parent, student and student and student and significant other. New forms of relationships are evolving in all areas of their lives. There is no time for death. It is ignored or denied during this period of seeming immortality and invulnerability. Yet, vulnerability coexists with these denials—a paradox.

> The young adult, at the peak of physical strength and attractiveness, emancipated from the constraints of family, finds it easy to
> avoid or deny the subject of death. Indeed, young males often take
> chances that seem to suggest a belief in their own immortality [2, p. 6].

Indeed, students may view themselves as invulnerable and immortal. Yet as Gordon noted, the cloak of immortality has already begun to be somewhat tattered [3].

College students are continually reminded of the possibility of the presence of death on the campus, even amidst their peers. The majority of students are aware of individuals who have attempted or committed suicide including fellow students on the campus. One way to cope with this intrusion is through the use of euphemisms. The euphemism is used as "the substitution of an inoffensive term for one considered offensively explicit" [4, p. 452].

There are two major areas of life where euphemisms are used extensively—issues of human sexuality and dying and death. In issues of human sexuality it would appear that more often than not the euphemisms are more offensively explicit than the correct terminology. However, one specific word consistently appears—"IT." Everything seems to revolve around doing "it" and variations on that theme. In issues of dying and death, the euphemisms are soft and comforting. No one dies! People "meet their maker," "pass on," or, in the case of suicide, "hurt themselves."

However, particularly in the case of suicide, we have developed over time an entire panoply of sanctions and myths. There is a reason for the use of the word "panoply" because it refers to "the complete armor and weapons of a warrior . . . any magnificent shining array that covers or protects" [4, p. 948]. Myths and sanctions do cover our discomfort like a suit of armor and protect us from those matters which we find offensive or do not wish to discuss. Mythology may enable us to develop some equilibrium from the disequilibrium resulting from a suicidal action, particularly when that person is known to us.

Our discomfort with discussing suicide or attempting to cope with the aftermath of a suicide has long and tenacious roots. It may have begun 4,000 years ago in Egypt when a man wrote this part of the earliest written reference to suicide:

> Lo, my name reeks
> Lo, more than carrion smell
> On summer days of burning sky. . . .
>
> Death is before me today
> Like a man's longing to see his home
> When he has spent many years in captivity.

As this ancient Egyptian contemplated his suicide his writings make it clear that the emotions and characterizations of himself were powerful negative images. His name reeked, more than carrion under the hot desert sun. The images of stench are powerful and create an image of a man that no one would want to come near, much less touch. These images create powerful impressions of suicidal persons as "untouchable" or "unreachable."

It may have begun with the traditional Jewish interpretation of Genesis 9:5: "Surely the blood of your lives will I require; at the hand of every beast will I require it, and at the hand of man; by the hand of every man's brother, I shall require the life of man" [5, p. 7]. Rabbinical literature cites this passage as a specific prohibition of suicide or destroying oneself wittingly. Rosner also notes "the Talmud is replete with stories concerning suicide and martyrdom as well as discussions relating to the laws of burial and mourning for the deceased" [6, p. 321].

Or it may have begun as we read of the suicides of Saul (I Samuel 31:4), Achitophel (II Samuel 17:23), Zimri (I Kings 16:18) Abimelech (Judges 9:54) or Samson (Judges 16:18) in the *Old Testament,* Ptolemeus Macron (II Maccabees 10:13), or Razis (II Maccabees 14:37) in *The Apocrypha* or of Judas Iscariot (Matthew 25:5) in the *New Testament.* However, these suicides were reported without negative comment. Indeed, Samson's suicide is regarded as being exemplary in that he destroyed his enemies who had blinded and tormented him.

Or it may have begun as we read of the suicide of Socrates by hemlock in 399 B.C. Socrates has been lauded for adamantly adhering to his philosophy of life that was not accepted by the Greek authorities. Or, it may have begun forty years later as Aristotle taught that suicide should be illegal because it offended the state, depriving the state of that individual's services.

More likely, at least within traditional western society this need to impose some order out of chaos, some comfort out of the discomforting, some reason out of the seemingly unreasonable began with St. Augustine writing *The City of God* in 466 A.D. For the first time suicide was proclaimed to be a sin and the Catholic Church through a series of councils developed sanctions against those who would attempt or commit suicide. In 563, the Council of Braga declared that funeral rites were denied and burial rites were denied by the Council of Hereford (673) to a suicide. In 693, the Council of Toledo declared the suicide attempter should be excommunicated. The bodies of suicides, now being denied Christian burials, were often dragged outside the city, a stake driven through the heart and rocks placed upon the body to prevent the "evil spirit" from returning to the city or house from which it came. Suicide became a crime in several countries, oddly enough often a capital offense like murder or treason for which a person could be put to death. Indeed, it was not until Parliament passed the "Suicide Act" in 1961, that punishment for attempting suicide was abolished in England.

John Donne, the Dean of St. Paul's Cathedral in London, wrote a book entitled, *Biathanatos,* which was not published until after his death (1644). Donne argued that suicide was precipitated by a variety of reasons and that it was the *intent* of the act that determined whether it was sinful or not. Alvarez devoted a chapter to a discussion of the background of the experience of suicide and humankind's reactions [7]. While these sanctions were intended to codify a moral stance relating to suicide, their result was to create a climate in which the discussion of suicide became impossible for the person who wished to seek help. Suicide was indeed anathema to both God and man. As a result, what has occurred is we have a background which contains ecclesiastical sanctions, legal sanctions, moral condemnation and a fear that those individuals who commit suicide are in some way evil.

It was not until 1763 that another viewpoint would be heard. Merian stated that suicide resulted from emotional illness [8]. This was followed by Freud's *Mourning and Melancholia* which made a substantial contribution to the concepts relating to suicide [9]. In this work, the concept of *thanatos,* the death instinct, and other intrapsychic reasons were developed to explain suicide. Included was the concept that suicide was murder in the 180th degree. That is to say that the anger which is felt toward an external object (however, murder cannot take place) is turned inward resulting in a self-murder.

However, this is only one spectrum, a western, basically Judaeo-Christian point of view. There are other points of view that are frequently overlooked that affect various individuals' concepts of and rationale toward suicidal behavior. The ethical and moral issues that are present in the religious or spiritual tenets of non-western, non-Judaeo-Christian persons must certainly be considered given this large population of individuals who are resident in or come to the United States to study. Their reactions to suicide are based on different philosophies and it is important to understand that many people do not subscribe to the majority view. To do otherwise would do a great disservice to these individuals and disrespect their presence on the campus. The following is not intended to provide a complete review of non-Western philosophies. Rather, it will hopefully provide a basis for reminding ourselves that the students in educational institutions are multicultural and we need to respect them and determine their belief system. Otherwise we will lose their respect and will probably fail in our interventions.

For Muslims, self-mutilation and suicide are sins. There is an unconditional prohibition against individuals interfering with their destiny as preordained by Allah. However, the prohibition of suicide is not clearly stated in Islam's holy book, *Qur'an.* Rather it is defined in the

Sunna which is a record of the sayings, actions and approvals of the Holy Prophet Muhammad and his followers. This work is popularly known as the *Hadith* (literally a saying). Ali (undated) translated the most comprehensive and authentic of the *Hadith* literature known as *Sahih Bukhari,* written by Muhammad Ismail al-Bukhari [10]. In the section on the burial service, there is a clear proscription against suicide. "Abu Huraira said, The Prophet, peace and blessings of Allah be on him, said: 'Whoever strangles himself strangles himself into fire, and whoever stabs himself with a spear stabs himself into fire (Bukhari 23:83)" [10, pp. 200-201]. Ali states that suicides are not to be deprived of a burial service. In one *Hadith* the Holy Prophet did not lead a burial service of a suicide but his companions held a service. Masse noted "whether this prayer should be made over the dead who have committed suicide has not yet been settled" [11, p. 149]. The prospect of casting oneself into the "fire" probably has inhibited some suicides. It also may have fostered situations where individuals have resorted to various contrivances (including martyrdom) to avoid shame and stigma.

For Buddhists, life within this world is a transitory state that is filled with human suffering. Self denial enables individuals to achieve the knowledge that would facilitate their movement to a higher plane. The avoidance of suffering and stress through the action of suicide would mean that the individual lacked the moral fortitude to survive in this world. As the body is only a container for the soul in this world, the body must also act (i.e., the human must act) to prepare the soul to move onward after the death of the body into Nirvana. The rule, *Dharma,* prohibited suicide as it is an act of self-consciousness and vanity. While there is compassion towards the suicide, there is also the understanding that the complete preparation for the soul's journey has not been fulfilled. The sanction for suicide follows in the afterlife. The soul of a person who commits suicide will spend a hundred years in a form of hell. Perhaps most importantly, there is no hope of reincarnation. The soul of the suicide thus remains in limbo forever. Nevertheless it would appear that there may be some "loopholes" in the doctrine. As with other religions, it appears that suicide for a worthy cause may allay the sanctions. A case in point is the self-immolation of several Buddhist priests and nuns in protest against the South Vietnamese government in the late 1960's and early 1970's. Colt noted "if a person acquits himself well at the moment of death, offenses committed during his early life are forgiven. In some cases suicide can be the most exquisite death of all" [12, p. 137].

Within the traditional Hindu religion, the concept of *Karma,* cosmic justice, occupies a central position. Life does not end with death. Rather, death opens a passage into a new life (reincarnation) which is determined by the manner in which a person previously lived. Suicide is viewed from a normal point of view in the *Dharmashastra*. Rao stated that suicides by ascetics, those suffering from incurable diseases and religious suicides were not condemned [13]. Other suicides were regarded as cardinal sins and "Kautilya, the ancient lawgiver of India, prescribed severe penalties to the bodies of suicides, and also to their relations if they performed the last rites" [13, p. 232]. One form of suicide had an honored place within Indian society. This was the custom of *suttee* or *sati* (which originally was a law designed to prevent a wife from poisoning her husband). Women were expected to engage in self-immolation upon their husband's funeral pyre. The purpose was to act as a propitiation for their husband's sins and enable him to gain heavenly paradise. Failure to do so would result in condemnation and ostracization of the wife by the local populace. In some instances, wives were forcibly thrown onto the funeral pyres. The British outlawed the practice in 1829. However Colt reported an instance of *suttee* took place in 1987 and the village celebrated the woman's memory [12].

Best noted that westerners assumed both Buddhism and Hinduism were "life-negating religions. This, of course, is a huge oversimplification. Both have contributed positively to great civilizations and neither takes a positive view of suicide" [14, p. 97].

Rituals are as important as religions in considering attitudes toward suicide. Ritual suicide that is a part of a cultural tradition is an important aspect in the individual's development of attitude toward suicide. The most notable is that of *seppuku*, the ritual disembowelment that was developed by the Japanese samurai. The code of honor of the samurai considered loyalty to the sovereign and dying with honor as the ultimate discipline of the samurai class. Ritual suicide was sometimes voluntary and at other times demanded by a ruler as a result of impropriety by a subject. Colt outlined the extensive special vocabulary that was developed in Japan for describing various types of suicides [12]. While obligatory *seppuku* was outlawed in 1873, ritual suicides to atone for errors, family dishonors and extreme criticism continue. Among students, the failure to pass examinations that permit admission to high educational levels continues to be a significant source of suicide. The ritual *seppuku* has been replaced by ingestion of medications, hanging, and other methods. There have been changes in the attitude toward ritual suicide as illustrated by Yukio Mishima's *seppuku* in 1970. Having failed to rouse the Japanese Defense Force to return to the pre-World War II military stance, Mishima committed ritual suicide. With a few exceptions his action was seen as the act of a miserable person, not a hero. However, the vestiges of the past are clearly present in contemporary Japan and among contemporary Japanese.

It is not possible to cover all possible religions or spiritual views towards suicide. However, some comments on the attitudes towards suicide among Native American pueblos and tribes are important given the number of Native American students on the campus. There is a considerable variation of spiritual practices among Native American tribes and pueblos and only a few will be noted here. As with any other religious or spiritual group it is important to ascertain that group's beliefs relating to suicide and then determine if the individual's belief system corresponds [15].

Navajos are the largest tribe in the United States and there have been a number of studies of this tribe unlike many other tribes and pueblos. In 1945, Wyman and Thorne investigated the Navajo's beliefs concerning the spirits of suicides [16]. It appeared suicide was not sanctioned in Navajo mythology. Their Navajo informants "had a rather casual attitude towards suicide. A victim is merely an unfortunate person who could have lived longer if he had done the right thing. The act is not condoned, neither is it greatly condemned" [16, p. 284]. Their traditional culture has appeared to condemn suicide because it was seen as an escape from the responsibilities of life. The Navajo also noted that the spirits of suicides do not go where other dead people go. This occurs because suicides must carry with them the lethal implement (e.g., a rock, gun, knife) and as a result the other dead would be afraid of them. The Navajo accorded the suicide the same burial rites as preparation for the afterworld and as a precaution against the ghost returning. "In summary, the idea pattern is that the spirit of a suicide goes to the afterworld and can return thence as a ghost, but while there it may not live with nor be in the same place as the spirits of other mortals" [16, p. 286]. A study by Levy, found that the condemnation resulted from the Navajo fear of ghosts of the dead [17]. Suicides are regarded as unnatural deaths where the soul does not leave the body. Then as a ghost they "will cause any individual who comes into contact with it to become sick in some manner. The ghosts of witches and suicides are thought to be especially pernicious for they live apart in the afterworld" [17, p. 314]. Webb and Willard noted "any Navajo finding the body of a suicide is likely to suffer some misfortune, and if the suicide is a family member that danger is compounded" [18, p. 29]. Consequently, it is not that suicide is an abominable act in and of itself, rather its potential for catastrophic effect upon the living is what causes the condemnation.

Wyman and Thorne noted the Hidatsa had similar belief patterns to the Navajo, but the Iroquois believed that suicides remained earth bound and were excluded from the land of the dead [16].

Another southeastern tribe, the Hopi, has somewhat similar attitudes. They also believe that death brings pollution and there is a fear of death and the dead person. For the Hopi, the spirit becomes a depersonalized entity that is not Hopi and does not have the characteristics of the deceased. The deceased are to be quickly forgotten and a normal life pattern continued. "The Hopi go to great lengths to make sure that the dichotomy of quick and dead is sharp and clear. Many rites having to do with spirits conclude with a ritual device which breaks off contact between mortals and spirits" [19, p. 202].

Among the Inuit from Greenland to Alaska some forms of suicide were supported by cultural values. Leighton and Hughes found that suicide was generally non-ritualized, varied in method and was usually the result of sickness, suffering or feelings of uselessness [20]. A Netsilik Inuit stated,

> For our custom up here is that all old people who can do no more, and whom death will not take, help death to take them. And they did this not merely to be rid of a life that is no longer a pleasure, but also to relieve their nearest relations of the trouble they would give them [20, p. 328].

There was an important belief that the souls of suicides occupied the best place in the afterworld together with those who had been murdered or died in another violent manner. The person intending to commit suicide would ask relatives to kill him or her or assist in the suicide. There was a ritual request that the suicide not happen but if the request was again made, the suicide would take place. Once the request was made, a retraction was very difficult and required a significant sacrifice to the deity.

This practice still continues. At an American Association of Suicidology conference a few years ago, the following was recounted by a mental health professional who worked in Alaska with native peoples. An elderly Inuit man decided he was a burden to his family and decided to commit suicide by walking out into the frozen winter land. It appeared that somewhere on his walk he changed his mind and returned to the village. This became a significant problem as they viewed him as "dead" and would not associate with him in any manner. Traditional methods of social control play an important role in suicide among these peoples.

Among the Native Americans of the Pacific Northwest, tribal mores opposed suicide. The Group for the Advancement of Psychiatry reported that among the Tlinglit, suicide was a method of revenge, to harass and burden others [21]. Both the Nootka and the Bella Coola believed that a suicide would not rest with the other dead and consequently the victim was not buried with the other dead. Among the Plains tribes, suicide was generally viewed as spiritual death although there were suicides among older Mandans because of behaviors that were not appropriate to their age. Some Boreal forest tribes institutionalized suicide as an appropriate response to the loss of a loved one or for insolvable marital problems.

These brief comments on suicide among native peoples merely serve to illustrate the point that the belief system of a group of people can have profound impact upon their view of suicide and we need to be cognizant of these variations. Otherwise we will not only do a disservice to the suicidal person but also perpetuate a very ethnocentric view of suicide.

Quite aside from all of this, there is also the realization that suicide is within the grasp of any person. Given certain circumstances, it is possible that any individual could conceivably move through the continuum of suicidal behavior from ideation to attempt to completion. For most individuals, this is a frightening idea and one that is avoided in thought, word and deed.

Particularly in thought (I can't even think about it!), word (I can't talk about it!) and deed (I can't do anything about it!), we find the mythology of suicide to be highly protective. Whether we refer to these concepts as fallacies [7], as idols [22], or as just plain myths, the results are still the same. I believe there are nine reasons for accepting the mythology of suicide. Although there is some overlapping of issues such as detachment and avoidance, they constitute separate entities from which we pick and choose to attempt to avoid our emotional and physical involvement.

First, by believing the mythology we can detach ourselves from a potentially traumatic situation. We do not have to become involved in any discussion of the value of human life or make any other significant commitment about our own beliefs relating to the issues of life and death. Somehow we hope to bring some order out of the chaos of suicide and to pretend that we believe we know what is happening is "out there" beyond our realm of comprehension.

Second, by believing the mythology we shift the responsibility to someone or something else. As we are very quick to want to blame and to assign guilt, we have to have a target. So, our targets become heredity, individual circumstances, the phase of the moon or whatever else we may conjure. We want to make very certain that this suicidal behavior is not the fault of our friend, co-worker, lover, spouse, or roommate. We want to make very certain that we are in no way to blame, be blamed, feel guilty, or be made to feel guilty. Someone, something else that is totally beyond control is responsible because we may have such a limited understanding of what occurred in the suicidal person's life.

Third, by believing the mythology of suicide we place ourselves in the posture that "nothing can be done." After all, we have a very limited understanding, we don't want to talk about suicide and it is out of our control. If indeed, then nothing can be done, we propel ourselves into the fourth myth.

Fourth, by believing the mythology we absolve ourselves of taking any action and avoid contact with the suicidal person. After all, the unfortunate individual is beyond assistance or we simply are not knowledgeable enough to effectively intervene. Or, the only individuals who can intervene are highly trained psychologists or psychiatrists leaving everyone else "off the hook."

Fifth, by believing the mythology of suicide we can maintain the taboos and avoid conversations about the suicidal person (except in the most gossipy fashion). The longer we maintain the taboos, the longer we can remain protected from any significant encounter with the suicidal person.

Sixth, by believing the mythology of suicide we not only maintain the taboos, we draw very significant boundaries for ourselves and others. By believing the mythology we are able to maintain significant distances so that we can "protect our guts." Usually, we are not desirous of putting ourselves in situations where we can be hurt, we usually avoid masochistic behaviors. So, if we can avoid any involvement with a suicidal person we assume we can avoid the pain.

Seventh, by believing the mythology of suicide we can maintain those religious, legal, moral, philosophical sanctions, and condemnations that work to exacerbate the psychological pain which the suicide person experiences. And, in the process, we can believe that we have done "what is right."

Eighth, by believing the mythology of suicide we can create for ourselves some illusion that everything is all right. We can accept, for instance, that people who talk about suicide don't take suicidal actions. They are "OK" if they are willing to talk about feeling suicidal. If they are "OK" we are "OK" in not taking any action because everyone's "OK."

Ninth, by believing the mythology and believing that we are helpless to intervene, we avoid the possibility of becoming a "survivor." We may never fully avoid the pain and frustration following an attempted or a completed suicide, but the distancing may permit some lesser degree of grief. This may be the ultimate protection that we are seeking.

The mythology of suicide, as with all mythologies, may contain some slight piece of truth. Misinformation and inaccurate information are more likely the hallmark of the myth. What are the myths? What are the facts? The following myths and facts were synthesized from works by Blimling and Miltenberger [23], Resnick [24], Resnick and Hawthorne [25], Shneidman and Farberow [26], and Stillion, McDowell and May [27].

Myth: People who talk about suicide rarely attempt or commit suicide.

Fact: At least 70 to 75 percent of the people who attempt or commit suicide have given some verbal or non-verbal clue of their intentions. It is not that depressed or suicidal persons do not talk about their mental state, rather it is that we would prefer not to hear what they have to say. The insulation of "not hearing" provides a method of avoiding confrontation or intervention. The responses that college students (among others) have often made is, "You wouldn't do anything like that." or, "Things can't be that bad." Indeed, they would and their circumstances can be that difficult. Our denial system operates immediately in these situations.

Myth: The tendency toward suicide is inherited.

Fact: Suicide has no characteristic genetic quality. There may be factors contributing to the suicidal behavior such as schizophrenia that does have some genetic characteristics. However, suicidal patterns in a family are more likely the result of other factors such as social learning. If there is a pattern of maladaptive solutions such as suicide within a family there is a strong possibility that this will be seen as an appropriate solution. There may also be a pattern of the "family secret." Everyone knows that Uncle Ed committed suicide. However, no one directly talks about the event and yet everyone who wants to know, knows what has happened. For the vulnerable person this tacit acknowledgment and acceptance may present a solution to their life crisis. Again, this myth perpetuates the concept that there is nothing that can be done. It's an inevitable phenomenon that has been created as the individual was developing in the womb.

Myth: The suicidal person wants to die.

Fact: Ambivalence is the greatest suicide prevention factor that exists. The suicidal person does not want to die. They simply cannot determine how they can live with their intense psychological pain. If all suicidal persons really wanted to die there would be no clues, there would be no statements about "not wanting to be here." The "cry for help" would be a non-existent entity. The myth however, does give us an excuse for not acting to intervene. After all the individual is responsible for his or her own actions and if they want to die it is their choice.

Besides, there's nothing I can do. If they really want to die, they'll succeed. So, why bother?

Myth: All suicidal persons are depressed.

Fact: Depression is often associated with suicidal feelings. But not all persons who attempt or commit suicide are depressed. A number of other emotional factors may be involved. The escape "clause" is depression. After all, only a mental health professional is qualified to work with a depressed person. Consequently, without this training and understanding, we would only make things worse. Again, it is a safe response. Becoming involved with a depressed and/or suicidal person may not only be extensively time consuming but it may also be very emotionally draining. These two factors may be beyond our coping mechanisms. So, instead of intervening and facilitating the person's movement toward professional help, we give ourselves an excuse and bow out.

Myth: Suicidal persons are mentally ill.

Fact: Many persons who have attempted or committed suicide would not have been diagnosed as mentally ill. This myth works in the same way as the depression myth, but perhaps even more forcefully since the term, mental illness, carries a much stronger impact.

Myth: Once a person has attempted suicide, she or he will always be suicidal.

Fact: After a suicide attempt, and particularly if professional assistance is secured, a person may be able to manage his or her life appropriately and engage in no further suicidal action. Some of the data previously presented indicates that a single suicidal action is commonplace. Certainly, there are individuals who do make a number of attempts and there are those individuals who are regarded as living a chronic suicidal lifestyle. However, they are not the majority. Rather, this myth permits us to avoid the suicidal person after an attempt. This enables us to avoid discussion of suicide or the painful events that led to the suicidal action. We avoid any confrontation and we surely don't have to be concerned about someone who is going to attempt repeatedly until they succeed.

Myth: Suicide is more common in lower socio-economic groups.

Fact: Suicide knows no artificial boundaries. Sometimes suicide has been called the "curse of the poor" and sometimes it has been called the "disease of the rich." At other times it is called the "affliction of the elderly" or the "destroyer of youth." The myth, however, allows us to draw some boundaries, to speak of the "unfortunates" with which we have little contact. Protectionism is at its worst here for it speaks of classism, racism, ageism, and a sense of "those less fortunate."

Myth: "Good circumstances" prevent suicide.

Fact: Frequently, quite the opposite is true. Physicians, psychiatrists, and dentists, as a group, have high rates of suicide. This myth is really a double edged sword. For if we are going to relegate suicide to only those persons who are in "bad circumstances" (whatever that may mean—and like in Wonderland, it probably means exactly what *I* want it to mean, nothing more and nothing less) what happens when suicide happens to someone with whom we have an intimate relationship, someone we may regard as in "good circumstances?" This myth may allow us to "pity the poor person" and stand at some distance, avoiding involvement. However, it can also draw some boundaries that make life very difficult for us if we suddenly find ourselves as survivors of a person in "good circumstances" for we then have to search for another myth to maintain our avoidance.

Myth: Suicidal persons rarely seek medical help.

Fact: Medical assistance has been sought within the six months prior to their suicidal action by approximately 50 percent of the people who have committed suicide. The attending physician may simply not have been attending to all the information presented by the patient. But, as mythology goes, it reinforces the concept that nothing can be done, so why try.

Myth: Suicide is related to weather phenomenon.

Fact: It appears that neither suicide nor attempted suicide is significantly related to weather phenomenon. Instead, the myth enables us to attribute the action to something well beyond our control. It may make it easier to accept the suicide if we can find a way to attribute the cause to something other than the person. This may be particularly true as our relationship with the suicidal person becomes more intimate.

Myth: Asking "Are you thinking about committing suicide?" will lead the person to consider suicide.

Fact: Asking a direct, caring question will often minimize the anxiety and act as a deterrent to suicidal behavior. Indeed, the suicidal person has most likely been looking for someone who would ask, who would care, who would become involved. The myth is for our protection. If we don't know (i.e., ask), we don't have to do anything. If a suicide occurs, we are not at fault because we didn't have any information. It is probably the most devastating myth in the repertoire of suicide mythology. It is the myth that should be eliminated as it is the greatest deterrent to proactive suicide prevention and intervention.

Myth: Improvement in a suicidal person means the danger is over.

Fact: If a person has been very depressed and suddenly seems quite relieved and happy, it is time to *watch out*. This usually means that the person is no longer ambivalent. They have made the decision to die and they are greatly relieved. Improvement of a real sort can occur during hospitalization or other treatment. There is a significant danger within the first ninety days after a suicidal person has been released from a hospital. They are vulnerable and perceived problems can create a dangerous situation. Whereas they may not have had the physical or mental strength to make an attempt while they were in treatment, it may be that now they have the strength. Many students have remarked, "I never want to feel that badly again!" just before making another attempt. The myth permits us to create the illusion that everything is now all right.

Myth: Only a mental health professional can prevent suicide.

Fact: If this were true, the suicide prevention work by lay persons working in crisis centers and on telephone hot lines would not be the important part of suicide prevention that they are today. Remember, we are talking about prevention, the intervention by a caring person to prevent a suicidal behavior. We are not talking about a psychological course of treatment or hospitalization or medication. We are talking about asking the caring question, responding in a caring manner and referring the person to a place where they can obtain professional assistance. The myth again permits us to place the responsibility somewhere else.

There are, however, some specialized myths relating specifically to college and university students that are prevalent on campuses and which are equally detrimental to the student population.

Myth: High ability students have little or no need for support services. They are intelligent, can take care of themselves, have few problems and are at little risk for suicide.

Fact: Quite to the contrary, these students are often the very students who either impose upon themselves or have imposed on them, very high expectations. These expectations can be from parents, siblings, faculty (high school and college), peers, and themselves. They find coping with "failure" to be very difficult and highly stressful. One senior class student reported that his grades were very bad and as a consequence he would not be able to enter a law school as he (and his father) wished to have him do. When he revealed his "bad grades," he acknowledged a "B" in one class. He acknowledged that during his entire college career it was the only class in which he did not receive an "A." The real issue was that he could never satisfy his father and a "B" was an absolute failure. We want to believe that a successful academic career indicates that the student has absolutely everything under control. We may, in fact, contribute to the imposition of even greater expectations and stress by this attitude. However, this is also a protectionist myth supposedly giving us a reason not to be concerned about the mental health of these high risk students.

As previously noted, Kerr and Miller edited a special issue of the *Journal of Counseling and Development* devoted to the special issues of counseling the gifted and talented [28]. The entire volume is well worth reading, but specifically the article by Delisle related to suicide among gifted adolescents [29]. Delisle noted some characteristics that are common to the gifted population that may serve as contributing factors to suicidal behaviors among people from fifteen to twenty-four years of age. They are:

1. The perception of failure may be far different than among average students (the "B" equals an "F" concept in the quest for perfection).
2. Perfectionism may be the most influential, yet most overlooked trait among gifted persons,
3. The societal expectations placed upon these "future leaders" may result in goals that appear unattainable to these young men and women.
4. The constant "you are so lucky to be so bright" becomes an "embarrassment of riches" [29, p. 559].
5. Social, physical, and emotional states may not equal the physical state. There is a need for a peer group that has a common ground.
6. An understanding of adult and world situations but an impotence to effect change contributes to a powerlessness and frustration that is a definite emotional concern.

Delisle concluded that,

> today's gifted adolescents are enmeshed (as is everyone) in a world that often seems uncaring and uncomprising. With the support of significant adults and peers, these troubled adolescents may come to see options as less severe and less definitive than suicide [29, p. 560].

Myth: Graduate and professional school students likewise have it "all together or they wouldn't be in graduate school." So, they have little need for support services.

Fact: In a study of suicide in the Big Ten Schools from 1980-81 to 1984-85, Bessai reported while graduate students composed 25 percent of the total student body, they accounted for 32 percent of the suicides [30]. In their study of medical school students, Pepitone-Arreola-Rockwell, Rockwell and Core found male medical students had a suicide rate that was comparable to their agemates in the general population [31]. Female medical students had a rate of suicide equal to male medical students, but two to three times the rate of their female agemates.

Then, there are a couple of institutional myths relating to suicide that significantly affects how the institution engages in the prevention of and responds to suicidal behaviors on the campus.

Myth: Programming on issues of suicide means that "we have a problem."

Fact: Whenever programming is attempted on a topic that is considered "sensitive" it implies that the institution has a problem. This applies to programming in the areas of human sexuality, sexually transmitted diseases and dying and death to name a few. The institution may indeed have a problem if this programming is not done. The point is missed that education is an excellent preventive action that can provide accurate information and dispel myths.

Myth: If we keep data and permit these data to be in the public domain, we are at risk of being labeled a "suicide school."

Fact: If anything, the maintenance of secrecy about a topic that is reasonably well known within the institution and the community may well cause speculation about "what are you trying to hide and what else is there?" This myth enables individuals to engage in denial. If we don't have the information, we can't answer the questions. If there are no answers, then there is the possibility that "it" doesn't exist. Confidentiality issues can become a denial smoke screen. It is not necessary to name the students who commit suicide, but the data can be used to determine what remedial actions may need to be taken. Unfortunately, a public television production may well have contributed to this myth. *College Can Be Killing* compared the suicide rates between two Big Ten institutions [32]. While there was a considerable amount of excellent information in this TV production, the main impression was that one school was the "bad guys" and the other school was the "good guys." This was an unfortunate outcome of a serious effort to bring the issues of suicide on campus to the public's attention. More regrettably, it also created a fear in the mind of administrators who could see their reputations being placed "on the line" should a similar production be made about their school.

Neuringer noted "truthful inquiries into the meaning of life, death, and suicide must be made in order to gain understanding that will aid in the effort to convince individuals yearning to embrace death that they ought to seek life" [33, p. 160]. Truthful inquiry means the dispelling of the mythology. The dispelling of myths means a more pro-active stance in suicide prevention and intervention.

The dispelling of myths is a very important issue in working with college students. Assumptions may be made that this high achieving group will have the intellect to discern the differences between myth and fact. However, McIntosh, Hubbard, and Santos conducted a study with 271 college students (171 females, 100 males, average age 22.1 years) to determine to what extent a number of traditional myths were believed or accepted [34]. They found that generally students' "information levels regarding suicide were poor with most groups scoring within chance levels" [34, p. 270], with the average score on the thirty-two item test being 18.9 (59.1%). Fortunately, 97 percent of the group knew that a direct question about suicide would not lead to an attempt, 90 percent knew that intervention was possible with someone who had decided to commit suicide and 85 percent knew that the suicidal person does not clearly want to die.

Rogers conducted a similar study with 171 students [35]. In this case, the community had an extensive history of involvement in and dedication to suicide prevention through a variety of programs. Among these students, 87.1 percent knew that a direct question would not encourage suicide and 50.3 percent knew that the suicidal person did not want to die. A number of particularly salient factors were recognized as being myths (i.e., suicidal people are mentally ill; suicide is basically a problem of the young; when a depression lifts, there is no longer any danger of suicide; and suicide is a spontaneous activity that occurs without warning) by over 80 percent of the students. Fifty percent of the students were able to recognize thirteen of the sixteen statements as false. Rogers stated "that this suggests a relatively high level of awareness of issues related to suicide" [35, p. 4]. However, Rogers noted that there were some significant items (i.e, all suicidal people are obviously depressed; if someone attempts suicide, he/she will always entertain thoughts of suicide, and suicidal people rarely seek medical attention) which were accepted by large percentages of the students.

For purposes of both education and training it is clear that efforts need to be made to combat the persistence of the mythology.

The mythology of suicide is very pervasive and enduring. It is pervasive because there is a desire to avoid involvement. It endures because myths have a very lengthy, healthy life span providing a protective haven when we don't understand something. It is important that we work to dispel the myths and provide information that can assist in the prevention, intervention, and postvention activities on all campuses.

REFERENCES

1. K. Gibran, *The Prophet,* Knopf, New York, 1968.
2. J. S. Stephenson, Death and the Campus Community: Organizational Realities and Personal Tragedies, in *Coping with Death on Campus,* E. S. Zinner (ed.), Jossey-Bass Publishers, San Francisco, pp. 5-13, 1985.
3. A. K. Gordon, The Tattered Cloak of Immortality, in *Adolescence and Death,* C. A. Corr and J. N. McNeil (eds.), Springer Publishing Company, New York, pp. 16-31, 1986.
4. W. Morris (ed.), *The American Heritage Dictionary of the English Language,* American Heritage, Boston, 1969.
5. *Bible, The (Revised Standard Version)* American Bible Society, New York, 1952.
6. F. Rosner, Suicide in Jewish Law, in *Jewish Bioethics,* F. Rosner and J. D. Bleich (eds.), Sanhedrin Press (Hebrew Publishing Company) New York, 1979.
7. A. Alvarez, *The Savage God: A Study of Suicide,* Random House, New York, 1971.
8. J. Merian, Sur la crainte de la mort, sur le mepris de la mort, sur le suicide, memoire. (About the Fear of Death, about Contempt for Death, about Suicide, Recollection.), *Histoire de l'Academie Royale des Sciences et Belle-Lettres de Berlin, Volume 19,* Berlin, 1763.
9. S. Freud, Mourning and Melancholia, in *The Standard Edition of the Complete Psychological Works of Sigmund Freud,* J. Strachey (ed. and trans.). (originally published in 1923), Hogarth Press, London, 1961.
10. M. M. Ali, *A manual of Hadith,* The Ahmadiyya Anjun Ishaat-I-Islam, Lahore, Pakistan, undated.
11. H. Masse, *Islam,* Khayats Book, Beirut, Lebanon, 1966.
12. G. H. Colt, *The Enigma of Suicide,* Summit Books, New York, 1991.
13. A. V. Rao, Suicide in India, in *Suicide in Different Cultures,* N. L. Farberow (ed.), University Park Press, Baltimore, Maryland, pp. 231-238, 1975.
14. E. E. Best, Suicide: Ethical and Moral Issues from a Theological Perspective, *Canadian Journal of Psychiatry, 31*:2, pp. 97-100, 1986.
15. R. L. V. Rickgarn, Risk Assessment of the Suicidal Religious Person, *Counseling and Values, 35*:1, pp. 73-76, 1990.
16. L. C. Wyman and B. Thorne, Notes on Navajo Suicide, *American Anthropologist, 47*:2, pp. 278-288, 1945.
17. J. E. Levy, Navajo Suicide, *Human Organization, 24*:2, pp. 308-318, 1965.
18. J. A. Webb and W. Willard, Six American Indian Patterns of Suicide, in *Suicide in Different Cultures,* N. L. Farberow (ed.), University Park Press, Baltimore, pp. 17-34, 1975.
19. D. G. Mandelbaum, Social Uses of Funeral Rites, in *The Meaning of Death,* H. Feifel (ed.), McGraw-Hill, New York, 1959.
20. A. H. Leighton and C. C. Hughes, Notes on Eskimo Patterns of Suicide, *Southwestern Journal of Anthropology, 11*:4, pp. 327-338, 1955.
21. Group for the Advancement of Psychiatry, *Suicide and Ethnicity in the U.S.* (Report No. 128), Brunner/Mazel, New York, 1989.

22. E. Shneidman, *Definition of Suicide*, John Wiley & Sons, New York, 1985.
23. G. S. Blimling and L. J. Miltenberger, *The Resident Assistant: Working with College Students in Residence Halls*, Kendall/Hunt Publishing Company, Dubuque, Iowa, 1970.
24. H. L. P. Resnik (ed.), *Suicidal Behaviors: Diagnosis and Management*, Little-Brown & Company, Boston, 1968.
25. H. L. P. Resnik and B. C. Hawthorne (eds.), *Suicide Prevention in the 70's*, NIMH Center for Studies of Suicide Prevention, Rockville, Maryland, 1973.
26. E. S. Shneidman and N. L. Farberow (eds.), *Clues to Suicide*, McGraw-Hill, New York, 1957.
27. J. M. Stillion, E. E. McDowell, and J. H. May, *Suicide across the Life Span—Premature Exits*. Hemisphere, New York, 1989.
28. B. A. Kerr and J. Miller, Counseling the Gifted and Talented (Special Issue), *Journal of Counseling and Development, 64*:9, 1986.
29. J. R. Delisle, Death with Honors: Suicide among Gifted Adolescents, *Journal of Counseling and Development, 64*:9, pp. 558-560, 1986.
30. J. L. Bessai, *College Student Suicide: A Demographic Profile*, paper presented at the American Psychological Association Convention, Washington, DC, August 1986.
31. F. Pepitone-Arreola-Rockwell, D. Rockwell, and N. Core, Fifty-two Medical School Student Suicides, *American Journal of Psychiatry, 138*:2, pp. 198-201, 1981.
32. WTTW, *College Can Be Killing*, PBS Documentary, Chicago, 1978.
33. C. Neuringer, The Meaning Behind Popular Myths about Suicide, *Omega, 18*:2, pp. 155-162, 1987.
34. J. L. McIntosh, R. W. Hubbard and J. F. Santos, Suicide Facts and Myths: A Study of Prevalence, *Death Studies, 9*:3-4, pp. 267-281, 1985.
35. J. R. Rogers, *Adherence to Suicide Myths in a College Population*, paper presented at the 23rd Annual Conference of the American Association of Suicidology, New Orleans, Louisiana, April 1990.

CHAPTER 5

The Etiology of Suicide

The study of the causes, origins and reasons for suicidal behavior is an attempt to answer the question, "Why?" Our search begins with a significant difficulty. The individual who has committed suicide can no longer inform anyone of his or her reasons for this action. Even if there is a suicide note (and this occurs in approximately 25% of the suicides), it probably offers little to explain the action and much is left to speculation. Psychological autopsies gather retrospective material from people who knew the person, if they are willing to discuss their involvement and understanding of the person.

And yet, there is a great desire to attempt to understand what happens between the moment when the fleeting thought of suicide slips through the mental processes of an individual to that moment when he or she may take an irrevocable action. The information that we have on the etiology of suicide has been derived in various ways. Information has been given by those individuals who have attempted suicide, have not died, and are willing to discuss the causal factors in their lives. Information also has been derived from a few individuals who took a very lethal action with no intention of being rescued and yet there was an intervention that precluded their death. Retrospective studies and psychological autopsies have also provided further information.

The etiology of suicide in college students needs to be understood to generate effective prevention, intervention, and postvention activities on a campus. Without this information, the development of effective strategies will be significantly inhibited.

One of the most significant factors that works against an understanding of the etiology of suicide is the supposition that there is a single causative factor that produces suicidal behavior. For example, the statement, "he killed himself because he broke up with his girl friend," may be heard in conversations among students. Or a college newspaper may have a headline "student commits suicide—academic dismissal blamed." Similar simplistic statements that attribute the suicidal death of a single factor are heard consistently in the aftermath of an attempted or completed suicide on the campus and elsewhere.

A great part of our difficulty in understanding suicidal behaviors is that suicide is not a single, unconnected action. There is usually a history, a constellation of issues which eventually precipitates the action. As Beck, Resnick and Lettieri stated, "Suicide is the end result of a process, not the process itself. . . . In suicide, all we usually have is the end result, arrived at by a variety of paths. Unraveling the causes after the fact is well nigh impossible" [1, p. 4].

Research has failed to isolate any single causative factor. Rather what has been discovered is that there are a number of factors that enter into this behavior and which may work to propel the individual along the path from ideation to pronouncement to gesture to action (and not always in that precise order). A number of researchers have defined various contributing factors. Among them are:

Adam, Lohrenz, Harper and Streiner—a history of early parental loss (before age 16), with loss of a father or both parents being more significant than the loss of a mother, plus the subsequent disruption of the home life [2].

Allen—family problems; no friends or conflicts with friends; loss or lack of a confidant; acceptance of suicide; mobility and rootlessness; depression; external locus of control and hopelessness [3].

Bernard and Bernard—social problems including love relationships, dating and friends and family problems [4].

Carson and Johnson—inability or lack of resources to cope with stressful life events [5].

de Jong—lowest security of attachment and least degree of individuation in current relationship with parents; rating parents and mothers as emotionally absent in childhood; family instability [6].

deWilde, Kienhorst, Diekstra and Wolters—more turmoil in families; more often sexually abused; social instability; changes in residence; and having to repeat a class [7].

Domino, Gibson, Poling and Westlake—one's attitude toward suicide [8].

Greenberg—birth trauma (complications at or before birth) [9].

Grob, Klein, and Eisen—family problems including divorce, conflict, alcoholism, suicide of a family member, loss of job by parent, mental illness and high parental expectations [10].

Hawton, Crowle, Simkin, and Bancroft—concern about examinations, work problems, difficulties in a relationship with a boy/girlfriend [11].

Hoberman and Garfinkel—arguments, relationship breakups (with males 5 times as likely to have experienced a relationship breakup in the 3 days before a suicide) and problems with police [12].

Knott—social and psychological isolation; early loss of a father through death or physical absence; impoverished interpersonal relationships; and an intense competitive atmosphere [13].

Kraft—increase in economic pressure on students to succeed; anxiety about the usefulness of a university degree [14].

Kaczmarek, Backlund, and Biemer—loss of a romantic relationship particularly if ended suddenly as opposed to being anticipated and the relationship was regarded as closer than any other they had previously experienced [15].

Leonard—physical disequilibrium and control problems [16].

Levy and Deykin—major depression and substance abuse (alcohol, drugs, or both), with substance abuse having a particularly deleterious effect on men; a prolonged desire to be dead being a high risk factor for attempted suicide [17].

Lopez, Campbell, and Watkins—conflicted, angry and resentful exchanges between student and parents as parents fail to adapt to the student's separation from the family [18].

Mehyar, Hekmat, and Khajavi—interpersonal difficulties; social withdrawal and aloofness; social nonconformity [19].

Murphy—alcoholism and substance abuse [20].

Nelson, Nielsen, and Checkettes—less social involvement; lower levels of tolerance for others [21].

Peck and Bharadwaj—personal stress of a college experience including rapid changes in role relationships and uncertainty which may contribute to feelings of helplessness and a fatalistic response [22].

Ray and Johnson—depression; loss of a parent; alienation from the family; blurring of sex roles creating identity problems; and a magical or mystical concept of death [23].

Reynolds—depression; hopelessness; a history of suicide attempts; and self-esteem [24].

Strang and Orlofsky—an absence or disruption of interpersonal attachments; a conviction of personal helplessness; and a sense of hopelessness regarding the future [25].

Sundberg—a pervasive sense of loneliness among college freshmen, more among women than men and more among Caucasian students than African American students even though African American students felt more isolated [26].

Towbes and Cohen—chronic stress [27].

Westefeld and Furr—loneliness; hopelessness; girl/boyfriend problems; helplessness; grades; parental and money problems [28].

Wright—parents having conflicts with each other; a poor parental relationship; parents who are angry or depressed much of the time; and students perceiving themselves as having a drinking or drug abuse problem [29].

Wright, Snodgrass, and Emmons—inner turmoil; poor self concept; decreased life satisfaction; self reported drug abuse and drinking problems; delinquency; and a history of family problems [30].

Between these precipitating factors and the actual suicidal behavior there is a continuum of interaction among three major identified constituent components of suicidal behavior. They are depression, hopelessness and an external locus of control. Although the continuum functions in a serial fashion, for individuals there will be variations on the intensity felt and the time spent within each component as well as movement back and forth between the components. The interaction among the three components of the continuum functions is presented in a narrative form to illustrate the connections between them.

A complex number of individual
issues (a multidimensionality)
which results in

|

A depressed individual who is unable
to adequately cope with the
given situation leading him/her
to develop

|

A sense of hopelessness that s/he
will be able to do anything
to influence

|

The loss of control s/he feels as
his/her sense of control becomes
more and more external
leading to

|

Suicidal ideation and other
suicidal behaviors including
attempted and/or completed suicide.

There have been extensive studies on each of these components. Many of these have related specifically to a single component and others have examined the relationship of one component to another. Some researchers have focused specifically on the effect within the college population. A review of the findings from a number of studies will illustrate how individuals progress through this continuum and the linkage between them.

DEPRESSION

Following from the contributing factors, depression becomes one of the most commonly cited factors in any discussion of suicidal behavior. Volumes have been written about depression describing it as ranging from a brief, mild state to a severe clinical disorder. Beck discussed depression in terms of cognitive distortions and having a negative view of the self, the world and the future [31]. Seligman discussed depression in terms of the development of feelings of helplessness [32]. Miller stated that depression was the most common emotion felt by a suicidal person [33]. Coleman, Butcher, and Carson stated that approximately 8 to 10 percent of the American population will have a major depressive episode at some time in their lives [34]. Edwards, Cangemi, and Kowalski found that depression was a strong, common contributing factor in college dropouts [35]. These students also were not likely to seek help. What happened to these students after they left college is not known. They do resemble suicidal students in that they are not recognized as having problems and they chose to move away from a stressful situation. Perhaps this is a more positive adaptation to depression that enables them to continue living. However, clearly not all depressed persons commit suicide and there are differences between non-suicidal and suicidal depressed persons that can be determined. Waters, Sendbuehler, Kincel, Boodoosingh and Marchenko examined suicidal depressed persons a few days following their suicidal action [36]. They found the emotional state of these persons exhibited greater ego sensitivity, low self esteem and confidence and a fragile sense of sexual identity. Hendin believed that "depression is actually a form of protective deadness and may even make suicide unnecessary for some" [37, p. 113]. In "College Blues," Beck and Young stated depression was considered to be the leading psychiatric disorder on college and university campuses [38]. Teuting, Koslow and Hirschfeld found depression to be a contributing factor in most suicides [39].

Depression can be both normal for an individual or it can become an abnormal function. Blatt, D'Afflitti and Quinlan studied normal depression in college students as they believed there was a continuum of depression from normality to severity [40]. They found there were three major variables that contributed to varying levels of depression: 1) a sense of dependency—students were in need of help and support from others; 2) a sense of self-criticism—students had an exaggerated tendency to criticize their faults and to self-devaluate; and 3) inefficacy—students had a sense that things were "out of control" of their own efforts and actions. Blatt et al. believed that it is necessary to continue research in both clinical and nonclinical populations. "The study of these experiences in nonclinical samples may provide leads into dimensions that are important in the predisposition to depression and are not readily apparent in the severe symptomatology of the clinical state" [40, p. 389].

Depression becomes a significant factor when students' coping mechanisms begin to fail and their view of the world and of themselves becomes significantly negative. While depression alone may be an impetus for a suicidal action, from the literature there is a consensus that depression is definitely a part of a continuum toward suicide with hopelessness and locus of control being the other two components.

There has been at least one dissenter on this viewpoint. Leonard believed the relationship between depression and suicide had not been adequately clarified [16]. She noted depression occurs widely among persons who do not commit suicide. "The depression reported in committed suicides may also be due to observer bias, since depression is expected and may thus be read in retrospectively" [16, p. 98]. Leonard found depression and suicidality were multidimensional and relatively independent factors. She discovered psychological disequilibrium and difficulties with control/being out of control were found more often in suicidal individuals than feelings of hopelessness and despondency. While a dissenting viewpoint, there is one particular point which she made that is salient in counseling with suicidal college students. Efforts need to be made to ascertain what is present and not what is expected to be present.

The multidimensionality of depression and suicide also has been noted by Hendin who saw a more integrated set of factors in his studies of seriously suicidal students [41]. Hendin found depression, suicide, and death as a life style. That is to say, for these students, death had become an actual way of life, an integrated, continuing effort in their adaptation towards emotional extinction. While a strong viewpoint, Hendin stated that "suicide for such students was the radical answer to radical emotions" [41, p. 218].

The extent of incidence of depression on college campuses is illustrated in three studies. The first of these was conducted by Sherer [42].

He studied sixty-eight men and eighty-one women and found that 11.4 percent reported depression at the time of the survey and 33 percent believed that they had needed treatment for depression at some time. Within the past year, the men reported that they had been depressed 18 percent of the time while women reported depression 26 percent of the time. Forty-nine percent of the students admitted to the use of alcohol or drugs to cope with their depression. Suicidal ideation was reported by 32.9 percent of the students while 9.4 percent actually contemplated a specific means of suicide. Sherer found no significant differences between men and women in their responses.

A second study was done by Westfeld and Furr [28]. They surveyed 962 students in three institutions through a random survey. Eighty-one percent of the students stated they had experienced depression since entering college. Furthermore, 32 percent of the students had experienced suicidal ideation while 4.5 percent had attempted suicide. A highly significant finding in this study was that students who attended a "small, predominately female college experienced many more problems in the areas of depression and suicide than did students at the two larger coeducational institutions" [28, p. 122]. Loneliness and hopelessness were predominate factors in the lives of the suicide attempters (particularly at the small college).

A third study was conducted by Vredenburg, O'Brien and Krames who studied thirty-five depressed and thirty-nine non-depressed college students [43]. They found "the results of the study demonstrated that the depressions that college students experience, though relatively mild in severity, are more than simple, transient mood swings" [43, p. 422]. However, this mild level of intensity was deceiving. A serious problem existed as three-fourths of the depressed students reported that they had been depressed for over three months. Half of these depressed students reported that they had contemplated suicide.

Vobejda reported that in 1988 more than 10 percent of freshmen reported frequently feeling depressed compared with 8.2 percent in 1985 [44]. She reported that college freshmen were reporting more stress and "overwhelmed by all I have to do" [44, p. A1]. Alexander Astin, director of the survey, stated "things are beginning to change in an alarming direction" [44, p. A1] and this increasing level of stress should be a red flag for institutions.

Researchers will continue to study depression in all of its manifested forms and it is very unlikely one single theory will evolve which can successfully encompass the multidimensional concept of depression. As Evans and Farberow have noted, "certainly not all severely depressed persons commit suicide; nor do all those who kill themselves suffer from depression. But depression is a warning sign that cannot be ignored" [45, p. 87]. While the issue of why some depressed individuals commit suicide and others do not continues to be researched, the preponderance of the present evidence indicates that depression is a definite factor in suicide and a significant component in the continuum of suicidal behavior.

HOPELESSNESS

The next factor in the continuum is hopelessness. Minkoff, Bergman, Beck and Beck identified hopelessness as "one factor in the syndrome of depression—the cognitive factor of negative evaluation of the future pessimism or hopelessness" [46, p. 458]. Their research and that of others [16, 47-56] has demonstrated that hopelessness is not only the stronger factor, but a major predictor of suicidal behavior, a key variable linking depression to suicide.

Minkoff et al. stated there was a paucity of systematic research that would "test and explore these clinical observations of the relationship between hopelessness and suicide" [46, p. 453]. They hypothesized the reason for this striking deficit was that most clinical research had explored the relationship between depression and suicide. Their research found significant correlations between what was called "negative expectancies" (or hopelessness) and the seriousness of attempts made by individuals. "Seriousness of intent of suicidal attempts is more closely related to hopelessness than to the syndrome of depression in general" [46, p. 456]. While they had pointed out this relationship, they felt that there needed to be more research to define how hopelessness led to suicidal behavior.

Farber however, states quite categorically that "it is when life outlook is of despairing hopelessness that suicide occurs" [57, p. 12].

Crumley offered some perspectives on this linkage in his research on individuals in the fifteen to nineteen years of age range [58]. In his research, Crumley found adolescents who felt they had been let down by someone or had a significant object loss experienced strong feelings of hopelessness. These feelings were part of an escalation of stressful events that often preceded a suicide attempt.

Other issues of hopelessness were summarized by Schotte and Clum [54]. They found individuals who were unprepared to cope with high levels of life stresses, due to almost any causal factor, are likely to become hopeless as they cannot engage in effective problem solving behaviors. This produces a high risk suicidal individual as "hopelessness becomes an increasing salient factor in predicting suicide intent, relative to depression, as the level of intent increases" [54, p. 694]. For our purposes, it is important to note that whereas other researchers have focused on a general population, Schotte and Clum's work was done with a group of college student suicide ideators. They found the difference between the ideators and non-ideators, was the ideators were under higher levels of negative life stress, had higher levels of depression and were more hopeless. Their conclusion relating to depression and hopelessness was that "at the highest level of intent, hopelessness gains in importance as a predictor of suicide intent, whereas depression is more important in low intent ideators" [54, p. 695].

Four other recent studies of hopelessness have focused directly on the college student population. Cole chose to research the concepts of hopelessness and social desirability (an inclination to respond in a socially acceptable manner) which might constrain suicidal behavior [59]. Cole found the social desirability factor did not override the hopelessness factor among parasuicides (non-lethal attempters).

Bonner and Rich tested a stress-vulnerability model of suicidal ideation and found, among other things, that "more complex theories and methodologies are needed to unravel such a complex, multidimensional process as suicide" [60, p. 256]. They agreed with other researchers that hopelessness was the best predictor of more lethal forms of suicide. They believed it was particularly important to determine why some individuals become "vulnerable to the development of hopelessness, as well as the ways in which hopelessness transforms passive suicidal ideation to more active suicidal planning and actions" [60, p. 256].

Dixon, Heppner, and Anderson stated "suicide can be conceptualized as an inability to adapt to life's demands" [61, p. 54]. They conducted two studies involving over 1,600 students. They suggested that a difficulty in adjusting to the demands of life situations by students was a function of both their negative life events and their perceived inability to engage in effective problem solving. This produced individuals who are at risk for suicidal behavior. Individuals who reported higher levels of stress and ineffective problem solving skills "reported significantly more hopelessness and suicidal thoughts than individuals under lower levels of stress" [61, p. 54].

Continuing this research, Dixon, Rumford, Heppner and Lips explored different sources of stress to predict hopelessness and suicide ideation in a college population [62]. They surveyed 3,393 students in their two studies. In addition to negative life events, they predicted hassles that are encountered by college students would be a significant predictor of hopelessness. For this purpose they used the *Hassles Scale* which assesses the demands of everyday transactions some of which could certainly relate to group living situations (i.e., troublesome neighbors, too much noise and losing things) [63]. Hassels were found to contribute to the hopelessness effect. This was particularly true when negative life events and hassles were joined (i.e., loss of a student job [negative event] would lead to concerns about finances on almost a daily basis [hassles]). "In addition, the relation between negative life events and hassles may be reciprocal so that the occurrence of either can begin a vicious downward cycle" [62, p. 347].

Consistently researchers note a need for more research on hopelessness and its relationship to depression, stress, and suicidal behavior. However, the research that has been done to this point clearly indicates that hopelessness is a significant and integral part of the continuum toward suicide.

LOCUS OF CONTROL

The final factor to be considered in the continuum is the locus of control, or perhaps more precisely, the perception of the loss of control and the movement toward the externality end of the locus of control scale. A number of researchers have linked hopelessness to a loss of control [16, 52-54, 64-66], or view the loss of control as the final determinant in the decision making process to commit suicide [21, 67-70].

Cellini and Kantorowski found a number of phenomena on the campus to support the concept of students continuing to become more externalized [68]. Among these were the increases in membership in fundamentalist religious groups indicating a sense of powerlessness and having someone else take control and a sense of powerlessness in their influence over the environment. They also looked at society at large and stated "it is also possible that some of the reported changes in locus of control orientation are more a reflection of societal changes than they are of personality changes in the individual" [70, p. 234]. Regardless of the source, the change in students to a more external locus of control contributed to a feeling of powerlessness.

Clum, Patsiokas, and Luscomb found the literature relating to the locus of control and parasuicide was non-definitive, with significant disagreements whether suicidal behavior was precipitated by a shift in the locus of control or even which end of the locus of control scale related to parasuicide [71]. They did not find a clear relationship between external issues of control and parasuicide. However, they did find that individuals whom they defined as "congruent externals" (i.e., individuals who believe their reinforcements are not contingent upon their own behavior and whose behavior reflects this belief) and who had high stress "were more likely to be found in a group of parasuicides than in a control group of psychiatric patients" [71, p. 939].

Goldney found suicidal subjects as a group tended to score in a more external manner than comparison groups which was consistent with the previous clinical reports he cited [52]. "It is of note that, for the suicidal subjects, those who made suicide attempts with the greatest risk to life tended to score in a more external manner than those whose attempts involved no threat to life" [52, p. 200]. Goldney felt there was a higher correlation between locus of control and hopelessness than between locus of control and depression.

Peck viewed fatalism as a form of external locus of control and found it was a definite factor in youthful suicide [72]. Adam et al reviewed issues of locus of control and used the instability of early parental loss as an example of external locus of control issues that are related to youthful suicide [2]. Goldney concurred with this point of view stating "affectively significant events in childhood tend to lead to an external locus of control orientation" [52, p. 201].

Strang and Orlofsky studied 191 college students who were twenty-one years of age or less [25]. Some suicidal ideation was reported by 60.7 percent of the students, 21 percent reported moderate or high levels of ideation and 6.2 percent reported prior suicide attempts. Three factors related to suicidal behavior were considered with this group: an absence or disruption of interpersonal attachments; a conviction of personal helplessness (regarding family and academic achievement); and a sense of hopelessness. Individuals who identified with these factors were found to accept a sense that their lives were controlled by external events. Security of attachment to parents was a more important factor for women than men. However, this "may be an important factor underlying suicidal ideation of both sexes" [25, p. 51].

Lester, Castromayor, and Icli compared issues of locus of control among American, Philippine, and Turkish students in their three respective countries [73]. Their analysis showed that external locus of control was associated with suicidal ideation among Turkish students and with attempted suicide among both Filipino and American students.

The predominant point of view from these research studies is that the locus of control is a significant factor in the continuum towards suicide. Indeed, following depression and hopelessness, the individual who accepts the belief everything is out of his or her control severely restricts his or her options and alternatives. At the negative extreme of these factors, the individual no longer perceives the broad range of options and alternatives that may be available. Instead the individual is faced with two alternatives: living or dying. The intensity of this choice making is then reflected in their suicidal behavior.

This process began with any number of contributing factors and has moved through the continuum to some form of suicidal behavior. Even within the last component, locus of control, there is a continuum ranging from ideation to gesture to attempt to completion. The etiology of suicide is complex and for each individual there will be significant variations. Individuals may move partly through this continuum and then find a way to move back towards a solution of the contributing factors. Most often they will search for someone who is willing to intervene and facilitate their movement away from suicide. It is not that they want to die. It is that they simply cannot find a way to live with the acute psychological pain that is endemic to their movement on this continuum towards a suicidal action. It is necessary to be aware of the factors within this continuum to begin the process of prevention and intervention and to assess more clearly the risk of suicide during this process.

REFERENCES

1. A. T. Beck, H. L. P. Resnick, and D. J. Lettieri (eds), *The Prediction of Suicide*, Charles Press, Bowie, Maryland, 1974.
2. K. S. Adam, J. G. Lohrenz, D. Harper, and B. Streiner, Early Parental Loss and Suicidal Ideation in University Students, *Canadian Journal of Psychiatry, 27*:6, pp. 275-281, 1982.
3. B. P. Allen, Youth Suicide, *Adolescence, 22*:86, pp. 271-290, 1987.
4. J. L. Bernard and M. L. Bernard, Factors Related to Suicide Behavior among College Students and the Impact of the Institutional Response, *Journal of College Student Personnel, 23*:5, pp. 409-413, 1982.
5. N. D. Carson and R. E. Johnson, Suicidal Thoughts and Problem-Solving Preparation among College Students, *Journal of College Student Personnel, 26*:6, pp. 484-487, 1985.
6. M. L. de Jong, Attachment, Individuation and Risk of Suicide in Late Adolescence, *Journal of Youth and Adolescence, 21*:3, pp. 357-373, 1992.
7. E. J. de Wilde, I. C. W. M. Kienhorst, R. F. W. Diekstra, and W. H. G. Wolters, The Relationship between Adolescent Suicidal Behavior and Life Events in Childhood and Adolescence, *American Journal of Psychiatry, 149*:1, pp. 45-51, 1992.
8. G. Domino, L. Gibson, S. Poling, and L. Westlake, Student's Attitudes toward Suicide, *Social Psychology, 15*:3, pp. 127-130, 1980.
9. J. Greenberg, Birth Trauma Linked to Adolescent Suicide, *Science News, 127*:12, p. 183, 1985.
10. M. Grob, A. Klein, and S. Eisen, The Role of the High School Professional in Identifying and Managing Adolescent Suicidal Behavior, *Journal of Youth and Adolescence, 12*:2, pp. 163-173, 1983.

11. K. Hawton, J. Crowle, S. Simkin, and J. Bancroft, Attempted Suicide and Suicide among Oxford University Students, *British Journal of Psychiatry, 132*, pp. 506-509, 1978.
12. H. M. Hoberman and B. D. Garfinkel, Completed Suicide in Youth, *Canadian Journal of Psychiatry, 33*:6, pp. 494-504, 1988.
13. J. E. Knott, Campus Suicide in America, *Omega, 4*:1, pp. 65-71, 1973.
14. D. P. Kraft, Student Suicide During a Twenty-year Period at a State University Campus, *Journal of the American College Health Association, 28*:6, pp. 258-262, 1980.
15. P. Kaczmarek, B. Backlund, and P. Biemer, The Dynamics of Ending a Romantic Relationship: An Empirical Assessment of Grief in College Students, *Journal of College Student Development, 31*:4, pp. 319-324, 1990.
16. C. V. Leonard, Depression and Suicidality, *Journal of Consulting and Clinical Psychology, 42*:1, pp. 98-104, 1974.
17. J. C. Levy and E. Y. Deykin, Suicidality, Depression and Substance Abuse in Adolescence, *American Journal of Psychiatry, 146*:11, pp. 1462-1467, 1989.
18. F. G. Lopez, V. L. Campbell, and E. E. Jr. Watkins, Construction of Current Family Functioning among Depressed and Nondepressed College Students, *Journal of College Student Development, 30*:3, pp. 221-228, 1989.
19. A. H. Mehyar, H. Hekmat, and F. Khajavi, Some Personality Correlates of Contemplated Suicide, *Psychological Reports, 40*:3, pt. 2, pp. 1291-1294, 1977.
20. G. E. Murphy, Suicide and Substance Abuse, *Archives of General Psychiatry, 45*:6, pp. 593-594, 1988.
21. V. L. Nelson, E. C. Nielsen, and K. T. Checkettes, Interpersonal Attitudes of Suicidal Individuals, *Psychological Reports, 40*:3, pt. 1, pp. 983-989, 1977.
22. D. L. Peck and L. K. Bharadwaj, Personal Stress and Fatalism as Factors in College Suicide, *Social Science, 55*:1, pp. 19-24, 1980.
23. L. Y. Ray and N. Johnson, Adolescent Suicide, *Personnel and Guidance Journal, 62*:3, pp. 131-135, 1983.
24. W. M. Reynolds, Psychometric Characteristics of the Adult Suicide Ideation Questionnaire in College Students, *Journal of Personality Assessment, 56*:2, pp. 289-307, 1991.
25. S. P. Strang and J. L. Orlofsky, Factors Underlying Suicidal Ideation among College Students: A Test of Teichner and Jacob's Model, *Journal of Adolescence, 13*:1, pp. 39-52, 1990.
26. C. P. Sundberg, Loneliness: Sexual and Racial Differences in College Freshmen, *Journal of College Student Development, 29*:4, pp. 298-305, 1988.
27. L. C. Towbes and L. H. Cohen, *Chronic Stress in the Lives of College Students: Scale Development and Prospective Prediction of Distress,* paper presented at the American Psychological Association, Washington, DC, August 1992.

28. J. S. Westefeld and S. R. Furr, Suicide and Depression among College Students, *Professional Psychology: Research and Practice, 18*:2, pp. 119-123, 1987.
29. L. S. Wright, Suicidal Thoughts and Their Relationship to Family Stress and Personal Problems among High School Seniors and College Undergraduates, *Adolescence, 10*:79, pp. 275-281, 1985.
30. L. S. Wright, G. Snodgrass, and J. Emmons, Variables Related to Serious Suicidal Thoughts Among College Students, *NASPA Journal, 22*:1, pp. 57-64, 1984.
31. A. T. Beck, *Depression: Clinical, Experimental and Theoretical Aspects,* Harper & Row, New York, 1967.
32. M. E. P. Seligman, *Helplessness: On Depression, Development and Death,* W. H. Freeman, New York, 1975.
33. J. Miller, Suicide and Adolescence, *Adolescence, 10*:37, pp. 11-24, 1975.
34. J. C. Coleman, J. N. Butcher, and R. C. Carson, *Abnormal Psychology and Modern Life,* Scott, Foresman & Company, Glenview, Illinois, 1980.
35. M. Edwards, J. P. Cangemi, and C. J. Kowalski, The College Dropout and Institutional Responsibility, *Education, 111*:1, pp. 107-111, 1990.
36. B. G. H. Waters, J. M. Sendbuehler, R. L. Kincel, L. A. Boodoosingh, and I. Marchenko, The use of the MMPI for the Differentiation of Suicidal and Non-Suicidal Depressions, *Canadian Journal of Psychiatry, 27*:8, pp. 663-667, 1982.
37. H. Hendin, Suicide: The Psychosocial Dimension, *Suicide and Life-Threatening Behavior, 8*:2, pp. 99-117, 1978.
38. A. T. Beck and J. E. Young, College Blues, *Psychology Today, 27*:9, pp. 275-281, 1978.
39. P. Teuting, S. H. Koslow, and R. M. A. Hirschfeld, *Special Report of Depression Research,* National Institute of Mental Health, Rockville, Maryland, 1981.
40. S. J. Blatt, J. P. D'Afflitti, and D. M. Quinlan, Expression of Depression in Normal Young Adults, *Journal of Abnormal Psychology, 85*:4, pp. 383-389, 1976.
41. H. Hendin, Student Suicide: Death as a Life Style, *The Journal of Nervous and Mental Disease, 160*:3, pp. 204-219, 1975.
42. M. Sherer, Depression and Suicidal Ideation in College Students, *Psychological Reports, 57*:3, pt. 2, pp. 1061-1062, 1985.
43. K. Vredenburg, E. O'Brien, and L. Krames, Depression in College Students: Personality and Experiential Factors, *Journal of Counseling Psychology, 35*:4, pp. 419-425, 1988.
44. B. Vobejda, Freshman Reporting More Stress, *The Washington Post,* pp. A1, A 18, January 9, 1993.
45. G. Evans and N. L. Farberow, *The Encyclopedia of Suicide,* Facts on File, New York, 1988.
46. K. Minkoff, E. Bergman, A. T. Beck, and R. Beck, Hopelessness, Depression and Attempted Suicide, *American Journal of Psychiatry, 130*:4, pp. 455-459, 1973.

47. A. T. Beck, G. Brown, R. J. Berchick, B. L. Stewart, and R. A. Steer, Relationship between Hopelessness and Ultimate Suicide: A Replication with Psychiatric Outpatients, *American Journal of Psychiatry, 147*:2, pp. 190-195, 1990.

48. A. T. Beck, M. Kovacs, and A. Weissman, Hopelessness and Suicidal Behavior, *The Journal of the American Medical Association, 234*:11, pp. 1146-1149, 1975.

49. A. T. Beck, M. Kovacs, and A. Weissman, Assessment of Suicidal Intention: The Scale for Suicide Ideation, *Journal of Consulting and Clinical Psychology, 47*:2, pp. 343-352, 1979.

50. A. T. Beck, R. A. Steer, M. Kovacs, and B. Garrison, Hopelessness and Eventual Suicide: A 10-year Prospective Study of Patients Hospitalized with Suicidal Ideation, *American Journal of Psychiatry, 142*:5, pp. 559-563, 1985.

51. J. A. T. Dyer and N. Kreitman, Hopelessness, Depression and Suicidal Intent in Parasuicide, *British Journal of Psychiatry, 144,* pp. 127-133, 1984.

52. R. D. Goldney, Locus of Control in Young Women Who have Attempted Suicide, *Journal of Nervous and Mental Disease, 170*:4, pp. 198-201, 1982.

53. T. J. Prociuk, L. J. Breen, and R. J. Lussier, Hopelessness, Internal-external Locus of Control and Depression, *Journal of Clinical Psychology, 32*:2, pp. 299-300, 1976.

54. D. E. Schotte and G. A. Clum, Suicide Ideation in a College Population: A Test of a Model, *Journal of Consulting and Clinical Psychology, 50*:5, pp. 690-696, 1982.

55. R. D. Wetzel, Hopelessness, Depression and Suicide Intent, *Archives of General Psychiatry, 33,* pp. 1096-1073, 1976.

56. R. D. Wetzel, T. Margulies, R. Davis, and E. Karam, Hopelessness, Depression and Suicide Intent, *Journal of Clinical Psychiatry, 41*:5, pp. 159-160, 1980.

57. M. L. Farber, *Theory of Suicide,* Arno Press, New York, 1977.

58. F. E. Crumley, The Adolescent Suicide Attempt: A Cardinal Symptom of Serious Psychiatric Disorder, *American Journal of Psychotherapy, 36*:2, pp. 158-165, 1982.

59. D. A. Cole, Hopelessness, Social Desirability, Depression, and Parasuicide in Two College Samples, *Journal of Consulting and Clinical Psychology, 56*:1, pp. 131-136, 1988.

60. R. L. Bonner and A. R. Rich, *A Longitudinal Study of Suicide Ideation: Support for a Stress-vulnerability Model,* paper presented at the American Association of Suicidology conference, San Francisco, California, May 1987.

61. W. A. Dixon, P. P. Heppner, and W. P. Anderson, Problem-solving Appraisal, Stress, Hopelessness and Suicide Ideation in a College Population, *Journal of Counseling Psychology, 38*:1, pp. 51-56, 1991.

62. W. A. Dixon, K. G. Rumford, P. P. Heppner, and B. Lips, Use of Different Sources of Stress to Predict Hopelessness and Suicide Ideation in a

College Population, *Journal of Counseling Psychology, 39*:3, pp. 342-349, 1992.

63. A. D. Kanner, J. C. Coyne, C. Schaefer, and R. S. Lazarus, Comparison of Two Modes of Stress Measurement: Daily Hassles and Uplifts Versus Major Life Events, *Journal of Behavioral Medicine, 4*:1, pp. 1-39, 1981.

64. M. Boor, Relationship of Internal-external Control and National Suicide Rates, *Journal of Social Psychology, 100* (1st half), pp. 143-144, 1976.

65. M. Boor, Relationship of Internal-external Control and United States Suicide Rates, 1966-1973, *Journal of Clinical Psychology, 32*:4, pp. 795-797, 1976.

66. P. Topol and M. Reznikoff, Perceived Peer and Family Relationships, Hopelessness and Locus of Control as Factors in Adolescent Suicide Attempts, *Suicide and Life Threatening Behaviors, 12*:3, pp. 141-150, 1982.

67. G. N. Braucht, International Analysis of Suicidal Behavior, *Journal of Consulting and Clinical Psychology, 47*:4, pp. 653-669, 1979.

68. V. Cellini and L. A. Kantorowski, Internal-external Locus of Control: New Normative Data, *Psychological Reports, 51*:1, pp. 231-235, 1982.

69. L. Diamant and G. Windholz, Loneliness in College Students: Some Theoretical, Empirical and Therapeutic Considerations, *Journal of College Student Personnel, 22*:6, pp. 515-522, 1981.

70. S. Thurber and D. P. Torbet, On the Word Preferences of Suicidal versus Nonsuicidal College Students, *Journal of Consulting and Clinical Psychology, 46*:2, pp. 362-363, 1978.

71. G. A. Clum, A. T. Patsiokas, and R. L. Luscomb, Empirically Based Comprehensive Treatment Program for Parasuicide, *Journal of Consulting and Clinical Psychology, 47*:5, pp. 937-945, 1979.

72. D. L. Peck, Towards a Theory of Suicide: The Case for Modern Fatalism, *Omega, 11*:1, pp. 1-14, 1980.

73. D. Lester, I. J. Castromayor, and T. Icli, Locus of Control, Depression and Suicidal Ideation among American, Philippine and Turkish Students, *Journal of Social Psychology, 131*:3, pp. 447-449, 1991.

CHAPTER 6

Prevention and Awareness

> Hey, I've got an attitude and you better damn well know it! And my attitude is that you don't have any right to tell me anything or do anything to stop me if I want to commit suicide. I know that you and a lot of others are all concerned about me but you don't have to live for me. So if I want to die, I'll decide when and how and you stay the hell out of my way. I don't need any "do-gooders." Dying is up to me. That's my right!
>
> —Ellen (graduate student)

This is one student's attitude toward suicide and the efforts of anyone wanting to intervene in her affairs. Is it reflective of other students' attitudes or is it an anomaly? What do we know about college student's attitudes toward suicide? And, what difference does it make? If effective prevention efforts are to be made on the campus it would seem important to know what are the attitudes of the students who are the targets of the interventions. The most obvious reason for this is that it may have an effect on how suicide prevention programs are developed and where the focus is targeted.

Then what programs can be developed to assist in suicide awareness? The use of the newer term, suicide awareness, is an understanding that any prevention efforts have to begin with an awareness of the issues of suicide. When individuals become aware of the dynamics of the process of suicide and their ability to intervene early in the process, we can truly have both an awareness and a prevention program.

Domino, Gibson, Poling and Westlake explored college student attitudes using the Suicide Opinion Questionnaire (SOQ) [1]. The SOQ is a one-hundred item instrument that asks respondents to respond to statements using a five point scale ranging from strongly agree to strongly disagree. The SOQ tests the knowledge of the respondent about suicide through questions such as "a suicide attempt is essentially a 'cry for help'." The SOQ also inquires about personal attitudes toward suicide. The study involved 800 college students (400 males, 400 females), freshmen to seniors, from various size institutions throughout the United States. A number of findings from this study relate to suicide prevention activities. The foremost was "suicide is intimately related to religion, personal values, one's views toward mental illness, and a person's very self-concept. Despite the obviousness of such a conclusion, it is worth repeating since we often seek unitary explanations to complex phenomenon" [1, p. 130]. In support of prevention efforts, 72 percent of the students believed there should be interference if someone wished to commit suicide. Forty-seven percent "see suicide as a very serious moral transgression, and 54% see suicide as against the laws of God and/or nature" [1, p. 130]. Other responses supported the need for education as prevention tactic. Thirteen percent believed that suicide happens without warning (the myth appears) and only 20 percent agreed that suicide is a leading cause of death (it being the 8th leading cause of death overall and the 2nd for college age persons).

Minear and Brush explored many of the same beliefs and values among 394 students (153 males, 141 females) in schools in New England [2]. They found a majority of the students had liberal attitudes toward suicide including agreeing that it was *not* morally wrong to commit suicide. However, the majority did not perceive suicide as a personal option. There was a small group who had positive and accepting attitudes toward their own suicide. "The research gives evidence that students with weak or non-existent religious ties have the most favorable, most accepting attitudes toward suicide both for others and for themselves" [2, p. 324].

In chapter two it was noted there were a significant number of students entering college who had either considered or attempted suicide. In chapter three the incidence of suicide among college students (or college age persons) was presented. It is clear there are a number of students who have suicidal behavior histories. Are there differences in their attitudes toward suicide and what implications does this have for suicide programs? Limbacher and Domino explored this issue utilizing the SOQ with 236 male and 413 female under-graduates [3]. In this group there were thirty-five attempters, 131 ideators and 483 persons who had no history of either ideation or attempts. Some of the results were as follows:

- suicide ideators and attempters are more accepting of suicide than those students who had no suicidal ideation or behavior.
- attempters were more likely than ideators to believe that suicidal persons wish to die.
- those who had no suicidal behavior believed that suicide attempts are manipulative behavior.

- those who had no suicidal behavior saw attempters as out of control with little acceptance or tolerance of their behavior.
- males were more accepting of suicide than females.
- males believed that the attempter really wants to die.

These differences are important to consider not only in developing programs but also when intervening with a suicidal person.

Gordon, Range and Edwards assessed generational differences to adolescent suicide [4]. Fifty-six college students and their parents ($n = 112$) were asked to respond to a fictitious report of an adolescent's suicidal or non-suicidal death. Both groups expressed more negative reaction to the suicidal death. However, college students viewed the suicidal adolescent as less psychologically disturbed than did their parents. Parents were more emotionally supportive toward survivors. College students expected to feel tension and have trouble expressing sympathy towards the survivors. The latter two findings have implications that will be explored in the chapter on postvention.

Does the age and/or the manner of death of the person make a difference in students' attitudes? Range and Goggin found it did [5]. They found undergraduate students responded more negatively to both the victim and the family if death was by suicide than by illness. The students perceived the individual who commits suicide and his/her family as more psychologically disturbed. The students also expected the families of suicides to be sadder and more depressed if the individual was between eighteen and thirty years of age than if the suicide was older.

Does the reason for wanting to commit suicide make a difference to students? In 1982, Droogas, Siiter and O'Connell investigated the proposition that an undergraduates' attitude would be affected by the individual's personal characteristics and the nature of the situation [6]. Would there be situations that would be deemed more "justifiable" than others? Various students ($n = 80$; 20 males, 60 females) were presented with four of the sixteen fictional suicide case histories and asked to make judgments using such word pairs as justified/not justified, moral/immoral, and selfish/unselfish. They were also asked if they were the person's physician and were asked for a drug that would create a painless suicide would they do so. And, if they came upon a person in the act of suicide would they try to stop him (all cases presented were males, researchers noting that this type of study needed to be conducted using female examples). They found the students accepted suicide as a rational act under certain or extenuating circumstances. While there was a tolerance for severe physical pain being a cause for suicidal behavior, students viewed mental anguish as transient and less justifiable. If there were either severe mental or physical deterioration (loss of function), suicide would be more acceptable. However, mental deterioration again had a slightly lesser acceptance. The same concepts held when students were asked if they would supply drugs or attempt to stop the suicide. Again physical pain would be a greater reason than psychological pain for supplying drugs or not attempting to stop the person from suicide. Students did not find the concept of social utility (i.e., some have greater value, convict versus biochemist) as significant. "The findings seem to indicate that many college students are sensitive to quality of life as an important factor and are disinclined to see life as incontrovertibly sacred under all circumstances" [6, p. 139]. The students were also debriefed after the survey and it was found that proximity or intimate relationships would make a difference. It was noted that "tolerance for suicide will decrease markedly when emotional attachments are involved and the loss of a loved one has a direct impact on the individual" [6, p.142].

DeLuty conducted a study with 455 students (175 males, 280 females) with five scenarios in which a forty-five year old man was suffering from severe, chronic depression (differing descriptions) [7]. In the sixth, he has severe physical pain and in the seventh, terminal bone cancer. Again, suicide as a result of physical illness was viewed more favorably than psychological illness with terminal illness viewed most positively. DeLuty also noted that further research needed to be done with a female example as well as males and females of differing ages to determine if age of the suicidal person would make a difference.

Ellis, Meade, and Bjornstad presented 150 college students with five different scenarios involving persons who wanted to commit suicide [8]. Students expressed greater understanding and sympathy for those persons who were on life support, had cancer or AIDS or who were shot in a robbery and wished to commit suicide. There was less understanding and sympathy for those persons who were injured while involved in a robbery or for a suicide resulting from depression. There were no differences in responses between traditional and non-traditional (those over 30, married or having children) students.

Lester and Bean conducted a small study to determine attitudes toward preventing versus assisting suicide [9]. Sixty-four students (11 males, 53 females) took part in this study. Students stated they were more willing to prevent than assist suicide. However, an interesting outcome of the study was that "91% supported the prevention of suicide in general, but only 39% would demonstrate in public for this cause; in contrast, 52% supported the right of people to kill themselves, but only 11% would demonstrate in public for this cause" [9, p. 126]. For suicide prevention efforts, this would seem to indicate that students are less likely to publicly demonstrate their support for prevention. However, this does not mean that these students wouldn't intervene with their peers. Apparently there is a difference between what will be done in public (demonstrate) than what will be done in a one-on-one situation (intervene).

The respondents in most of these studies were predominantly Caucasian. A study involving both Mexican Americans and Anglos was conducted with mostly high school juniors and seniors using the Suicide Opinion Questionnaire [10]. Ninety-three percent of the students reported they were Catholics. Forty-two percent of the Mexican Americans were born in Mexico. This study offers some other viewpoints that reflect the complexity of attitudes. Mexican Americans believed that there was a significant link between religious values and suicide. Suicides were regarded as less religious, as having committed a moral transgression and suicidal acts were not to be condoned. Suicides were also regarded as more depressed, lonelier, irrational, and psychically more distressed. Mexican Americans find suicide unacceptable, cowardly and a way to get attention. It was noted that Mexican Americans believed a suicide would be shameful to the family. There was a denial that suicide rates were a problem in minority groups that may "reflect a denial of suicide as a problem among Chicanos rather than factual knowledge of incidence" [10, p. 393]. This is illustrated by one contact I had with a young Hispanic male, Roberto, whom I had met in a residence hall. A year after he left the residence hall, he came to my office and asked if he could talk with me about a problem. A close friend of Roberto's had died in an accident.

> My friends and me are all having some problems. You see, we all really know what happened. It wasn't an accident. He had talked about dying when he was drinking and we all knew things weren't going so well for him. Then we heard he died in this accident. Well, we didn't know what to say. His family—they'd never accept a suicide because—well we're all Catholic and to commit suicide is to sin and go to hell. So, we've just left it as an accident. But, we all know better. I think even the priest knows, but he buried him without any questions. But, now what do we do? We all are just hurting and yet to talk about it is to admit that he's a bad person. He's not, but that's the way it would seem.
>
> —Roberto (senior)

Domino noted that trans-cultural differences need to be understood in order to assist these individuals. This also was emphasized by the Latino Task Force on Community Mental Health that presented cultural conflicts, oppression and the Latino psychic structure as the key factors of Latino mental health needing recognition by mental health professionals [11].

These transcultural differences were succinctly presented in the Group for the Advancement of Psychiatry's (GAP) book, *Psychotherapy With College Students* [12]. In a chapter on working with special student populations, GAP presented the transcultural issues which face African American, Native American, Asian American, and Hispanic students while they are enrolled in colleges and universities. These issues included isolation, loss of individuality, lack of same race counseling staff, stereotyping, questions relating to assimilation within the general college population, harassment and other issues contributing to personal, social and intellectual difficulties.

GAP also included in this special population group students who are the first in their family to attend a college or university. These students do not have "the almost automatic backing and understanding found in families whose members have been to college and know about the experience" [12, p. 101]. These students may find themselves becoming increasingly alienated from their families as they develop greater personal and intellectual understanding. This creates an unanticipated tension. While this phenomenon has impact for any family, students coming from groups with little tradition of college attendance may find this tension creates even more difficulties. The GAP reported noted this may be particularly true for Native American and Hispanic students. The report also notes as special populations the very young and the older student. Attention to the needs of all of these groups is important if we are to satisfy their needs, intercept them and facilitate their ability to cope with frustrations and anxieties. This is a task for the entire academic community that has special importance in the reduction of stress and depression, important components in a suicide prevention program.

The major emphasis of suicide programs over the past several years has been the development of suicide prevention programs. This has resulted in the establishment of suicide hot lines, crisis centers, and suicide prevention centers. Focusing on these programs has facilitated the development of a mentality that there is not much that can be done about suicide until an individual reaches a point where she or he either talks about or engages in a suicidal action. At that point, the hot lines, the crisis centers, and other similar establishments are used if the individual chooses to contact them or if there is an intervention by another person. However, that point in time may be too late for some suicidal persons such as the young man who committed suicide and left the following note: "To whom it may concern. Seeing that I am unable to find a plausible reason for living and having never experienced death I thought I would give it a try" [13, p. 122].

The integration of prevention and intervention has been demonstrated in Pruett and Brown's *New Directions for Student Services: Crisis Intervention and Prevention* [14]. This book focused on crisis intervention and prevention as a campus-as-community mental health model. Some of the data that are reported in this volume indicated that counseling centers will have to work with students with more psychiatric histories than ever before. Astin, Green, Korn, Schalit and Berz had earlier discovered "10.5 percent of entering freshmen in the fall of 1988 reported feeling depressed frequently, and 21.5 percent reported feeling overwhelmed. These figures are the highest ever reported in the twenty-three years that the survey has been conducted" [15, p. 77]. This combined with a 17 percent increase in hospitalizations between 1986 and 1987, provides sufficient evidence that there is a definite need for a mental health model for prevention and intervention.

Our concept of prevention is basically drawn from the standard definition of the word "prevention" which is to keep someone from doing something, to hinder, or impede them. There is however a definition listed as "obsolete." That definition is "to anticipate or counter in advance" [16, p. 1038]. This is a definition that should not be considered as obsolete as concepts and programs for suicide awareness are developed. If anything, we may need to completely revamp our thinking pattern. If we did, then the obsolete definition of anticipating in advance would become the thrust of our suicide awareness programs and the idea of impeding individuals would be the link between prevention and intervention. Indeed, the concepts of prevention, intervention, and postvention have often been considered as three separate and distinct entities. They are not! These concepts overlap each other and are interdependent. They can interact in a circular manner. For example, a prevention effort that encourages an open and honest discussion of depression and suicide should enable a depressed person to discuss his or her problems thereby becoming an intervention as the "listener" becomes a facilitator for action to assist in the resolution of the problems. While an effective intervention can impede or prevent a suicidal behavior, it can also become part of postvention activities as there is a need to resolve issues relating to the suicidal behavior within the suicidal person's immediate community. If a completed suicide occurs, the postvention efforts not only are needed to enable the survivors to process their bereavement, grief, and mourning. Rather, beyond this, postvention efforts should become awareness and prevention efforts with suicide and its consequences being discussed openly Then there needs to be a clear invitation for those who also are feeling depressed and suicidal to search out assistance to resolve their issues. By this action, postvention efforts extend into intervention activities. Each entity is essential and integral to the others not only as a resource but as a collaboration between individual and individual, individual and society, and society and the individual. As this is a broad sequence of related entities effecting a total approach to the issues of suicide, it becomes a full spectrum approach.

The full spectrum approach to the issues of suicide is essential so that depressed and suicidal individuals may feel free to discuss their psychological pain. It is important to emphasize that suicidal persons need extensive permission to discuss their pain. Once their pain is expressed, they can obtain support and assistance from a broad range of care givers who can be peers, friends, teachers, health professionals (mental and physical), clergy, or any other individuals who are willing to become involved. This will not be an easy task for either the individual or the potential helper because suicide is not a neutral word, it is not a neutral behavior. It is a unique word. By itself it often evokes apprehension and creates a desire to avoid any discussion of this historically proscribed activity. Likewise, suicide is not a neutral behavior. As a behavior it evokes powerful emotional reactions regardless of the outcome. Fear, anxiety, disbelief, and anger are but a few of the emotions that are connected with this behavior. These emotions can create a negative atmosphere that effectively precludes effective discussion or involvement in the issues of suicide.

Overcoming indifference or fear resulting from emotional reactions or inadequate or incorrect information may be difficult, as was illustrated in the discussion of the mythology of suicide. Integrated information and the creation of realistic expectancies may alleviate or supplant avoidance and indifference with positive actions and reactions.

Suicide is a traumatic event for the individual involved and for all persons who have some connection to him or her. The trauma will only be increased if myths and inaction become the indications of our concern. Shneidman stated "human understanding is the most effective weapon against suicide. The greatest need is to deepen the awareness and sensitivity of people to their fellow men" [17, pp. 108-109].

Awareness and prevention are both anticipatory states of mind and action as well as a means of impeding the process of suicide. Again, it is important to point out that suicide is not just the occurrence, the act. It is the process through which the individual moves beginning with a fleeting thought and potentially culminating in a lethal action. A number of persons active in the field of suicidology have referred to education and awareness as the quintessential process to begin prevention efforts. This is not intended to be simply the process of increasing awareness of suicide as a major issue on the college campus. Rather it is the development of effectively educated individuals and groups who will undertake both educational endeavors and be willing to act. Grollman stated "the educational process must be extended to the 'gatekeepers'—the physicians, nurse, social worker, clergyman, and others who are most likely to hear hints that a person may take his life" [18, p. 126]. The gatekeepers on a college campus can include everyone—students, staff, and faculty. The importance of educating the potential campus gatekeepers can be illustrated by an event that occurred one evening as I was waiting to board the bus at a campus bus stop. A campus food service director, Bob, approached me and told me that he had an unusual experience just before he left work. It was payday and Jack, a student employee, had just told Bob to give his check to Margo as she needed the money and he wouldn't be needing it and he left. As Bob said this the busses arrived. I asked him to call me immediately when he got home as it seemed to me that this student was about to commit suicide. We talked over the phone and I quickly gave Bob a short course in intervention. He obtained Jack's telephone number, called him and told him he believed Jack's actions indicated Jack was considering suicide. Jack unhesitatingly told Bob this was true. In the conversation that followed Jack agreed to come to Bob's office in the morning, which he did. Jack told Bob he would prefer to talk with Barbara, who had just transferred to another food service. Barbara was informed of the situation and talked with me about what she should do. Another quick course in intervention was held. Using this information, Barbara was able to convince Jack he should seek professional assistance and accompanied him to the college health service. The gatekeepers in this intervention were not trained mental health professionals. They were, however, university employees who had Jack's trust and respect. Bob and Barbara's personal experience resulted in a presentation on suicide in the workplace being presented at a food service conference [19]. This illustrates the value of educating any person within the university or college community.

Another effort that emphasizes the link between prevention and postvention is a preventive outreach program [20]. This particular program is aimed at staff training to prepare a college or university staff to implement outreach programs following an attempted or completed suicide. This is a combination of an education/training program that is done on a regular basis with the recognition that there is both a short term reaction and a long term aftermath following a suicide. Prevention efforts are discussed in this chapter and the concept of a team intervention is presented in Chapter 8 on postvention. While these are convenient divisions for the sake of discussion it needs to be understood that there are no clear delineations between prevention, intervention, and postvention in the real world of the campus.

"Shneidman advocates mass-media campaigns like that which helped 30 million Americans give up smoking in the past decade. 'It's like V.D. and cancer,' he says. 'Education is more important than crisis intervention. I don't like putting out fires; I think it's more important to build a hotel where fires don't occur'" [21, pp. 51-52]. Within an educational institution there are a number of approaches for these educational endeavors. The University of Florida's approach incorporated a variety of activities including out-reach programs and media campaigns combined with printed materials [22]. Their theme "This Campus Cares" must have had a positive accent as "many faculty, staff, and students have reported that the materials, programs, and information provided have helped them feel less helpless and less overwhelmed in the face of student problems" [22, p. 278-279].

Some of the possibilities for awareness and prevention activities are presented here. There are obvious "variations on a theme" that can be developed to strengthen these activities on the campus.

PROGRAMMING

A major thrust of most residential life units is programming to provide students with stimulating programs to meet their perceived needs. This effort is also made through student unions, various student organizations who wish to promote their own points of view and organizations and individuals who are invited to the campus to present information on a broad range of topics. These programming efforts are important for they not only provide immediate information and discussion opportunities but it is possible they will also stimulate further discussions on an informal basis among students. Chickering has noted these latter sessions are very important for it is "in bull sessions and individual debates, intellectual skills are sharpened and new information is acquired, values are clarified, stereotypes are questioned and destroyed" [23, p. 223]. These programs offer opportunities to present information and strategies for coping with depression and suicide, recognition of clues and intervention tactics. Students are often seeking ways to cope and it is possible to present programs that provide suggestions on personal coping strategies. In their study of students with mild depression, Franzini and Johnson found students preferred behavioral to cognitive strategies for coping with their depression by a ratio of five to one [24]. While this has obvious implications for counseling staff working with depressed students, it has great applicability for programming. Programming can provide information on the behavioral strategies for students to employ.

Programming efforts can also teach students how to intervene in a crisis situation. Range and Pryor found fraternity and sorority members are apparently more helpful to someone who has a physical rather than a psychological problem [25]. This probably occurs because there is a lack of knowledge about intervention tactics. What is more important, there may be a distinct lack of knowledge about how to manage their own emotions. College mental health and other trained staff can provide programming to these groups. This programming could incorporate role plays and other interactive exercises that would permit students to try intervening with a peer, providing the students with a greater sense of comfort. This would enable them to respond more effectively to individuals in crisis and obtain professional assistance. Programming results are often calculated in terms of how many people attended the program. The results of programming in this area should be calculated on the effectiveness of the program as an awareness, prevention and intervention effort for the individual and the group.

COLLEGE COURSES

At both the undergraduate and the graduate level, courses could be developed which either incorporate materials relating to suicide or as courses specifically on suicide. There are now some specific courses in psychology, sociology, anthropology, counseling, public health, mortuary science, medical school curriculum, and perhaps others that include coursework on dying and death. Most of these courses devote one or two lecture periods to the topic of suicide. However, we need to go beyond this minor inclusion in coursework. For example, coursework on suicide could be expanded to courses in history (discussing the effect of suicides in history, e.g., Masada), literature (the effect of suicide within a work, e.g., *Romeo and Juliet,* or of a body of work, e.g., the works of Sylvia Plath), journalism (the effects of various types of reporting of suicide as demonstrated through research relating to vulnerability and contagion) and communication (the need for accurate, unambiguous verbal and written interactions).

Beyond incorporating work on suicide into these courses, it would be useful to have courses that are devoted specifically to the multi-dimensional aspects of suicide. While a few courses exist in some educational institutions, they are the exception. Even within departments that are devoted to the training and development of teachers and professional counselors the existence of coursework in suicide is rare. An understanding of the dynamics of the process of suicide would enable counselors to undertake proactive rather than reactive approaches to suicidal individuals.

However, beyond the instruction of teachers and counseling professionals this specific coursework would have another impact. Coursework on suicide would assist in the removal of the stigma from suicide. It would become acceptable to discuss suicide. This educational effort would make an open and meaningful interchange possible not just within the classroom but also would provide a tacit permission to students to discuss the topic anywhere on campus and not just in quiet whispers as is the current habit.

WORKSHOPS AND CONFERENCES

Currently two professional organizations, the Association for Death Education and Counseling and the American Association of Suicidology hold annual conferences where suicide is a major or specific issue dominating the conference. Other associations have annual conferences where papers and workshops on suicide are presented as part of a wide ranging group of topics. It is necessary, however, to go beyond these organizational settings. Workshops of varying lengths and one-day conferences need to be organized at very local levels and publicized in such a manner that anyone wanting to learn about the issues of suicide, death, and grief would feel welcome. Eckstein has developed one format for such workshops [26]. He presents an approach that can be used in any setting. This is important for these workshops must meet students where they live and work, within residence halls, student unions, or fraternities as part of regular programming efforts. Workshops may be organized for a very specific group of people to address very specific concerns. An example would be the development of a workshop for clergy who wanted to learn how to work effectively with and to preach a compassionate sermon for the survivors. These events should be organized to present information in a sequential order. Beginning with the basic information allows individuals the opportunity to work through the material and not become overwhelmed. It is important to scale the material to the level of the audience so that those who are involved will learn new information as well as reviewing previous information. This type of workshop could be developed with staff from the counseling service and mental health units on the campus.

CAMPUS RADIO AND TELEVISION STATIONS

Both of these media offer excellent opportunities to reach the entire campus community. Informational programming during suicide awareness week is one way to focus efforts. It is important that information be consistently presented so it becomes part of the campus climate. Made for television productions as well as commercial movies can be used with discussion groups. In this way, learning becomes part of the everyday experience. Students will learn to observe movies and television productions more critically. Both media can use individuals or panels who are knowledgeable about the issues of suicide. Questions from an audience or a call-in show can provide members of the community with an opportunity to ask the questions that are most pertinent to them.

PUBLICATIONS

As part of an awareness effort, small, inexpensive publications such as pamphlets and brochures can provide a significant amount of information in an informal and effective manner. At the University of Minnesota we use a ten page booklet entitled, *The Issue Is Suicide* as part of the educational program [27]. It is available throughout the campus. The booklet provides some information on suicide, indicators of potential suicide, a number of agencies that are available for counseling and hot line and crisis agency telephone numbers. There is information on the aftermath of a suicide. A bibliography provides a listing of twenty-one books for further reference. Several times a year my phone will ring and the person will begin by saying "I've read your book and . . . ." My response is "Are you thinking about committing suicide?" Our dialogue begins and another intervention takes place. The booklet has been copied or adapted for use at many colleges and universities. It is a very cost effective and easy way to provide the campus with informational material that becomes part of the awareness, prevention, and intervention activities on the campus.

TRAINING

A complete training program encompasses prevention, intervention, and postvention. However, it begins by developing an awareness of how an individual personally reacts to suicide. This is very important for each individual has a personal history that has some disposition toward suicide. Whether it is a developed value judgment or a personal emotional experience as a result of an attempted or completed suicide, everyone has their own private reaction. However, it is possible that this has never been explored and understood in the context of being a person who will be involved with a suicidal person and expected to provide some relief for him or her.

Within the educational institution it is expected that all matters will be rationally considered and the response will be a product of this consideration. That's utopia and it generally does not exist when we hear someone respond to the question, "Are you thinking about committing suicide?" Rather, if we are honest, there is more likely a tightening of muscles, a change in breathing pattern and heart rate that indicates that we are now involved in a matter where someone is considering whether to live or die. While it is necessary to remember and use all the skills that we have learned, it is also necessary to understand and listen to our "gut feelings." It is completely possible that our own value systems or our experiences may prevent us from effectively interacting with a suicidal person. That's OK! We must recognize this and refer the suicidal individual to someone who can effectively engage them.

How do we recognize our limitations and our potentials? In training, I use a simple sentence stem exercise to engage participants in a discussion of their values and experiences. I ask them to complete the sentence stems with the first word(s) that come to them as that is most likely what will occur if they encounter a suicidal person. The sentence stems are:

> I believe that suicide is . . . .
> I believe that anyone who attempts or commits suicide is . . .
> I am/am not comfortable discussing suicide because . . . .
> If a close friend or family member told me that s/he was considering suicide, I would (emotional reaction) . . . .
> If a close friend or family member told me that s/he was considering suicide, I would (action taken) . . . .

Once the statements are completed, participants are asked to move into groups of three or four and discuss their reactions. Participants find their reactions may be very similar as well as quite different depending upon their own personal experiences. Then all participants are invited to share their thoughts and reactions as well as what they learned from the group interaction.

Participants realize almost immediately that their reactions to the sentence stems become more personal as they proceed through them. Their reactions become more personally intense and sometimes they find it difficult to share these in the large group. However, since this sharing is optional there is no pressure to do so. Sometimes participants are surprised at their level of self-disclosure.

This is not a complicated exercise but it provides participants with the opportunity to understand their own strengths and limitations. From this exercise educational information on the mythology of suicide, the warning signs and assessment techniques, referral techniques, and lastly how to cope with an attempted or completed suicide is presented.

Who should be trained? Persons who are interested and emotionally capable of working with suicidal people. A different format of training may be developed for those who may not be as interested but whose work setting places them in contact with members of the academic community and the need to be aware of potential suicidal behaviors is essential. Individuals in this category include residence assistants, residence hall directors and housing staff, staff members who have contact with students, instructors, secretarial and administrative staff, counselors, physicians and nurses, security staff, chaplains/clergy, ROTC staff, supervisory persons in fraternities and sororities, and others.

Out of this listing, there is one group that should receive a significant amount of training in understanding depression and suicide. Resident assistants have often been referred to as the "front line" in working with individuals who are most likely to be identified as depressed and suicidal as well as having to work in the aftermath of attempted and completed suicides. Maierle, Groccia, Korn, Geer, Jorgenson and Slimak conducted a survey and found that after counseling center staff, resident assistants are the group that is most involved in working with potential or actual suicidal behavior among students [28].

Training formats can provide solid educational material that extends beyond prevention efforts into intervention and postvention activities. The more all of the human resources of the campus are involved in awareness efforts, the greater the resource nucleus. The greater the nucleus is the more individuals there will be who have accurate information and the ability (and hopefully willingness) to engage in the identification and intervention of depressed and suicidal persons. Having a significant number of people on a campus who are aware of the signs of an impending problem can be a significant part of crisis management efforts on a campus.

Does training work? Will non-counseling or student personnel staff react? Remember the joke, "How many psychiatrists does it take to change a light bulb?" Answer: "One, but the light bulb has to want to change." The same answer applies here, the person has to want to change and engage himself or herself with a depressed or suicidal student. An experience that I had following a training session illustrates not only the change, but the significant worth of involving all members of the academic community.

Following a training session at a college, I received a call from a professor who was, as he put it, the reluctant dragon who attended only because his friend had "dragged him along, huffing all the way." He told me that he remembered comments I had made about students giving hints about their mental state in their assigned work. He had asked that students in his writing class to write an essay that would convey a specific mood. He then read me the opening lines of one essay. "It was a dark and stormy day but that merely gave everyone the excuse they wanted to stay away. After all who wanted to go to a funeral anyway. So, there they were, a few relatives and even fewer friends, and of course, his mom and dad. And an old minister who didn't know what to say. What could anyone say that made any difference? They all talked about how young he was, how good looking he was, how much he had going for him. But no one really knew why he had put the gun to his head. He knew, but he could no longer tell them. He had wanted to tell them that he couldn't take it any more, the pressure was too much." The essay continued to its full required length in the same mode. It was hand written and toward the end there were a number of instances where the word "I" was crossed out and replaced with "he." The professor said, "This seems to be what you were talking about, am I correct?" He was. He contacted the student and talked with him about what was happening in the student's life. He later called and told me the student had agreed to counseling to resolve the difficult issues in his life. What he had learned reluctantly, he acted upon energetically.

PEER COUNSELING

Part of the training program effort, particularly on small college campuses, may be the development of peer counseling efforts. Salovey and D'Andrea conducted a survey of colleges and universities to determine funding resources and the interaction between professional staff and the peer groups [29]. For peer groups, the most common concerns for the clients were of academic difficulties and relationships between friends and lovers. Suicide and crisis intervention was the eighth most common problem.

A valuable peer counseling group is resident assistants who serve this function consistently throughout their employment. A number of models of education for identification, intervention and referral have been developed for this group [30-33]. A sense of trust usually is developed between residents and resident assistants that is enhanced by an ongoing relationship. The interaction between two students also relieves much of the pressure of "having to see the shrink" and alleviates some of the concerns about potential stigma by the resident in this initial involvement. This facilitates the resident in his or her willingness to reveal problems and concerns and advances the helping process.

HOT LINES

Hot lines require well-trained personnel to staff them and this has been done with both professionals and para-professional staff consisting of students and other interested individuals. These are particularly effective if they are staffed during hours when other campus agencies are not open (most often between 4:30 p.m. and 8:00 a.m.). It is often during these hours that the crises occur and students who may wish to remain anonymous in their initial contact will use these services. The efficacy of hot lines in suicide prevention efforts was reported by Stewart and Glenwick [34]. In their study, one service reported "the six most frequent categories of calls were: information and referral (36%), loneliness and depression (19%), pregnancy problems (12%) dating and social skills (10%), prank and obscene (5%), and drug abuse and emergency (4%)" [34, p. 547]. Another service's frequency of calls was 1) relationship problems, 2) suicidal ideation and 3) alcohol and drug concerns. The incidence of calls relating to depression and ideation indicates that this can be an effective prevention (and intervention) program.

ADVOCATES

A sense of advocacy is involved in the programs that are listed above. There may be, however, the need to develop a group of students who are trained and have the emotional stability to become advocates for suicidal students. These advocates would be available to accompany students to a crisis center, a hospital emergency unit or to a police station for observation until transportation can be arranged to a mental health unit. The advocate would accompany the student together with other officials. As this is a particularly emotional and frightening experience, having a peer to advocate for and accompany the student could have a very calming effect.

PEER GROUPS

There are a number of different peer groups that have been formed to meet the needs of students. Many of these are related to specific health issues such as chemical use and abuse, survivors of sexual assault, incest survivors, adult children of alcoholics, and others. Awareness and prevention efforts in these groups are very important. Many of these groups consist of students who have had significant, traumatic events in their lives. In Chapter 2 the discussion of high risk students related risk factors and their impact upon students. While these students may be in a specific group to resolve what they perceive to be a primary problem, there may be secondary problems that also have considerable impact on their lives. For example, women and men who have been sexually assaulted and are in a group to attempt to resolve issues relating to the assault, are also high risk persons for suicidal behaviors. One sexual assault center decided to ask about possible suicidal thoughts or behaviors during their intake procedures. They found that 100 percent of the victims experienced some level of suicidal ideation or behavior following their assault. The development of preventive responses in the center's repertoire has enabled them to meet the needs of their clients more completely.

SUPPORT SYSTEMS

After a student has arrived on campus and gone through new student orientation, what happens? Students are generally "on their own" unless they either seek out some new group or are sought out by a group. While in high school, more than likely they were surrounded by a group of friends with whom they interacted mentally, socially, and physically. They may have been involved in a group centering on certain functions (e.g., sports teams, clubs, religious groups). And, they usually had a family that they returned to each evening. If they are now commuting to college, they will find fractures in these support groups. Their friends, including significant others, may be attending another college. Other friends who are working and not attending college are developing new interests or their work schedules conflict so they don't get together as often. The family may seem different as they enter this new period of their life. The student may not want any family interference in his or her activities since they "aren't in high school anymore." If they are attending a college away from home, probably few of their high school friends are also at the same school. The family contact is now by long distance telephone calls. The transition adjustment has arrived! Schmid and Trickett evaluated social networks prior to and after high school graduation [35]. They found while there was only a slight decrease in the size of a student's network, there was a substantial amount of specific person change (52%). The family network was the largest and was rated not only as the most helpful but also as the most stressful network.

If this transition does not meet the student's expectations, he or she may begin to isolate himself or herself from other students in the residence hall or elsewhere. For those students who are living alone off campus, isolation has the potential for the development of substantial feelings of loneliness.

It will not be possible to reach all students, but efforts that can be made through residence halls, fraternities and sororities, various interest groups and clubs can produce new social networks for these students.

COUNSELING SERVICES

While counseling services would be one of the most natural prevention units on the campus, an article in *The Chronicle of Higher Education* raises some important questions about the availability of this service [36]. Cage states, "college students are under pressure as never before as their institutions raise tuition, slash services, and reduce course offerings to balance their budgets. But even as those pressures mount, the number of psychological counselors available to help them handle the stress is dwindling" [36, p. A26]. The article points out that there has been an increase in students seeking counseling at 84 percent of the counseling centers. In addition, on some campuses the counseling centers are now involved in providing services and in-service training to college employees who are also feeling the stress of cutbacks. What services must be available to this relatively high risk population that is recruited for the college or university? What importance is attached to the out-of-classroom experience? What support does the institution wish to offer to these young men and women who are in a major transitional phase of their lives? Administration, faculty and staff need to work together to answer these questions for their particular campus. These questions must be positively addressed if awareness and prevention are to be the hallmarks of the campus.

REFERENCES

1. G. Domino, L. Gibson, S. Poling, and L. Westlake, Students' Attitudes toward Suicide, *Social Psychiatry, 15*:3, pp. 127-130, 1980.
2. J. D. Minear and L. R. Brush, The Correlations of Attitudes Toward Suicide with Death Anxiety, Religiosity, and Personal Closeness to Suicide, *Omega, 11*:4, pp. 317-324, 1981.

3. M. Limbacher and G. Domino, Attitudes toward Suicide Among Attempters, Contemplators, and Nonattempters, *Omega, 16*:4, pp. 325-334, 1986.
4. R. S. Gordon, L. M. Range, and R. P. Edwards, Generational Differences in Reactions to Adolescent Suicide, *Journal of Community Psychology, 15*:2, pp. 268-274, 1987.
5. L. M. Range and W. C. Goggin, Reactions to Suicide: Does Age of the Victim Make a Difference?, *Death Studies, 14*:3, pp. 269-275, 1990.
6. A. Droogas, R. Siiter, and A. N. O'Connell, Effects of Person and Situational Factors on Attitudes Toward Suicide, *Omega, 13*:2, pp. 127-144, 1982.
7. R. M. DeLuty, Physical Illness, Psychiatric Illness, and the Acceptability of Suicide, *Omega, 19*:1, pp. 79-91, 1988.
8. J. B. Ellis, G. Meade, and K. Bjornstad, *Social Attitudes of Traditional and Non-traditional College Students Toward Suicidal Behavior,* paper read at the Southeastern Psychological Association, Knoxville, Tennessee, March 1992.
9. D. Lester and J. Bean, Attitudes toward Preventing versus Assisting Suicide, *The Journal of Social Psychology, 132*:1, pp. 125-127, 1992.
10. G. Domino, Attitudes toward Suicide among Mexican American and Anglo Youth, *Hispanic Journal of Behavioral Sciences, 3*:4, pp. 385-395, 1981.
11. Latino Task Force on Community Mental Health Training, *Latino Community Mental Health,* Spanish Speaking Health Research and Development Program, UCLA, Los Angeles, 1974.
12. Group for the Advancement of Psychiatry (Report No. 130) *Psychotherapy with College Students,* Brunner/Mazel, New York, 1990.
13. D. L. Peck, The Last Moments of Life: Learning to Cope, *Deviant Behavior, 4*:3-4, pp. 313-332, 1983.
14. H. L. Pruett and V. B. Brown (eds.), *New Directions for Student Services on Campus: Crisis Intervention and Prevention* (No. 49). Jossey-Bass, San Francisco, 1990.
15. A. W. Astin, K. C. Green, W. S. Korn, M. Schalit, and E. R. Berz, *The American Freshman: National Norms for Fall 1988,* University of California Higher Education Research Institute, Los Angeles, 1988.
16. W. Morris (ed.), *American Heritage Dictionary of the English Language,* American Heritage Publishing Company, Inc., Boston, 1969.
17. E. S. Shneidman (ed.), *Death and the College Student,* Behavioral Publications, New York, 1972.
18. E. A. Grollman, *Prevention, Intervention, Postvention,* Beacon Press, Boston, 1971.
19. R. L. V. Rickgarn, Suicide and the Workplace, *NACUFS Journal, 14,* pp. 39-40, 1989.
20. N. B. Webb, Before and After Suicide: A Preventive Outreach Program for Colleges, *Suicide and Life Threatening Behavior, 16*:4, pp. 469-480, 1986.
21. G. H. Colt, The Enigma of Suicide, *Harvard Magazine, 86*:1, pp. 47-66, 1983.

22. J. R. Funderbunk and J., Jr. Archer, This Campus Cares: A Suicide Prevention Project, *Journal of College Student Development, 30*:3, pp. 277-279, 1989.
23. A. W. Chickering, *Education and Identity,* Jossey-Bass, San Francisco, 1969.
24. L. R. Franzini and B. R. Johnson, Students' Preferred Strategies for Coping with Depressive Affect, *Journal of College Student Development, 32*:6, pp. 553-559, 1991.
25. L. M. Range and R. P. Pryor, Fraternity and Sorority Members' Response when Fellow "Greeks" are Suicidal, Physically Ill, or Dangerous, *College Student Journal, 24*:2, pp. 184-188, 1990.
26. D. Eckstein, Reflections Relative to Death, Dying and Grieving Workshops, *The Personnel and Guidance Journal, 61*:3, pp. 138-142, 1982.
27. R. L. V. Rickgarn, *The Issue is Suicide (4th printing),* University of Minnesota, Minneapolis, Minnesota, 1983.
28. P. Maierle, J. Groccia, H. Korn, C. Geer, J. Jorgenson, and R. Slimak, *Counseling Center Involvement in Campus Crisis Management,* Campus Crisis Task Force State University College, Fredonia, New York, 1983.
29. P. Salovey and V. J. D'Andrea, A Survey of Campus Peer Counseling Activities, *Journal of College Health, 32*:6, pp. 262-265, 1984.
30. G. S. Blimling and L. J. Miltenberger, *The Resident Assistant: Working with College Students in Residence Halls,* Kendall/Hunt, Dubuque, Iowa, 1981.
31. R. D. Grosz, Suicide: Training the Resident Assistant as an Interventionist, in *College Student Suicide,* L. C. Whitaker and R. E. Slimak (eds.), Haworth Press, New York, pp. 179-194, 1990.
32. J. B. Hersh, Interviewing College Students in Crisis, *Journal of Counseling and Development, 63*:5, pp. 286-289, 1985.
33. W. C. Phillips, Suicide Education for Residence Staff: Identification, Intervention and Referral, *Journal of College Student Personnel, 24*:4, pp. 376-378, 1983.
34. A. M. Stewart and D. S. Glenwick, Patterns of Usage of a University Based, Peer-operated Hotline, *Journal of College Student Development, 33*:6, pp. 547-553, 1992.
35. K. Schmid and E. J. Trickett, *Social Network Functions during the Transition to Post-high School Living,* paper presented at the American Psychological Association annual conference, Washington, DC, August 1992.
36. M. C. Cage, Students Face Pressures as Never Before, but Counseling Help has Withered, *The Chronicle of Higher Education, 39*:13, p. A26, 1992.

CHAPTER 7

Intervention

The Clown—Part I

The word—alone—holds no company
Feeling alone,
I hold no one.

A clown in the circus of life
is a fixture, only needed when to perform.

He takes care, when painting his face,
to show no signs of what lies beneath.

A painted smile goes a long way,
but, there is no way to disguise a broken heart,
it shows in the eyes.
And tears from the eyes,
of one who holds a broken heart,
are much too sour to kiss from the painted cheek.

As a clown, I have always walked the high wire.
I am
just to fill the spaces between the main attractions.

I want to drop from this thin line,
on which, I walk.

The fall would be long,
the impact hard,
but, this world would never feel the difference.

This poem appeared on a student's room door in a residence hall. The residents of the floor all knew that he was an aspiring writer. There had been other occasions when he would place a piece of his writing on the door for others to read. He enjoyed their comments, criticism and praise for his writing. They were always a free flowing pieces that seemed in character for David, himself a sort of free spirit. Some fellow residents remarked that this poem seemed more "morbid" than others he had written. The following week, the original poem was posted a bit higher on the door and another poem appeared beneath it.

Part II

Did you hear of the clown.
falling to his end?
They thought it was only part of his act,
until there was no one
to make the children laugh.

As a child they say,
he was not as different
from what you and I are today
trying to get a grasp on his dreams,
a perspective on the whole.

And when the paint came off,
his face was wrenched with despair,
and his heart broken,
but, they said it was not a result of the fall,
oh no,
it had started long before then.

They could tell,
by the eyes.

Residents began to talk among themselves about the morbid poetry on David's door. They didn't really want to talk with him about the poems. His other material had been "more fun" and "provocative" in a far less depressing way. Two of David's women friends stopped by and told him they didn't like what he was writing, that it was quite disturbing to them. They told him clowns were supposed to make people laugh, especially children, as he had written. David told them clowns didn't always make people laugh and asked them if they had ever heard of Leoncavallo's *Pagliacci*. They told him that they had not and he suggested they should go to the Metropolitan Opera when it came on tour. They could learn a lot about life and love from this opera. They felt they were being put down and David seemed to have a very "snotty" tone in his voice. They left. On their way past the resident assistant's room, they remarked to Jim that David was "getting to be just plain weird." They told Jim of their conversation and Jim told them he would talk with David. Jim did check, but David was not in his room for the rest of the evening. The next morning, the poems were moved to form a line across David's door and there was a third poem.

Part III

The Sun never rose,
and the clown was buried today.
The air was a glaucous haze,
and no one was there.

The grass hung their heads in silence
or, was it from the rain
which had fallen the previous night.

The gray clouds gazed down
upon the trees, slowly dancing in the wind—
swaying to and fro,
to and fro.

As if to say,
"To this world he came—
from this world he departed."

And alone
always alone.

Jim was awakened by a resident knocking on his door. The resident blurted out, "There's another one, and this one is just awful. I don't know, but I think something's wrong." Jim quickly dressed and went to David's room and read the poem. He knocked a couple of times and not hearing any response he announced he would have to use his pass key if the door were not opened. There was a bit of noise and David opened the door. Jim asked if he could come in and was told he could. Jim noted David's eyes were very red, as if he had been crying. "David, this clown that you have been writing about, it's really you isn't it?" "Yes, I thought no one would ever figure it out. I was so afraid of what I might have to do. I was afraid I really was all alone. I don't know what to do. Help me please!"

Interventions often begin like this. Someone like David begins to tell us their life has become very difficult and they feel alone. They put on the clown's painted face to hide their pain and they walk the high wire of life, hoping that someone will either stop them from taking those first steps on the thin line or will have a net to catch them when they fall. Someone like the two women may tell another person of their perceptions of the changes taking place within the life of this person. And, someone like Jim needs to care about what is happening in other people's lives, to be willing to take a risk and to ask that person what there is in their life that apparently makes it so difficult for them to continue to live.

Interventions hopefully may begin at an earlier stage. Students who are involved in a number of extra-curricular activities and employed in addition to their academic work manifest their stress in several ways, one of which is writing.

When over-committed becomes the norm,
When stress and pressures take over,
Then fun dies.
Time management seminars are for the young
and organized.
This is not me.
I can work 23 1/2 hours a day
Just wind me up just a little more
and watch me go!
Ooops! Another toy is wound up too tight.
Another spring is snapped.
That will never happen to me.
It's amazing how many toys have been thrown away.
I guess they didn't want to be played with anymore, or
they broke down.
I have to be the favorite toy.
I need a new energizer battery.
I'm slowing down.
Help!
Some other toy might replace me.
My spring has been sprung.
The trash can is so cold.

—Arthur (senior)

Fortunately, Arthur had a strong support system and he was able and willing to talk about his stress. If these were not the case, the emotions expressed in this piece of writing could easily have been turned toward more depressed thoughts and actions.

To intervene is to care! To intervene is to make a commitment! Can you do that? In fact, anyone can "intervene" but there is more to the process than that. In many ways, intervention can be compared to swimming in a lake. Some people arrive at the lake and gingerly touch their toe to the water to see if it is too cold. Others rush into the water and immediately dash for the shore again having experienced the direct effect of the water upon their bodies. Others rather methodically wade out and deliberately plunge into the water and swim for the raft and having reached it, pull themselves onto the raft and enjoy the sunlight. While it is possible that anyone can intervene with a suicidal person, there may be reasons why they should not do so. And, this does not make that person any less caring or concerned. It is just that she or he has some issues in their own life that makes it more appropriate for them to limit their intervention to helping the suicidal person reach another helper. Some examples of this might be:

- the person simply does not feel comfortable talking about suicide because of his or her own beliefs and values.
- the person has a significant number of problems in their own life and does not have the energy to engage in this activity.
- the person may have recently experienced a loss of a significant person in their life and they are not emotionally prepared to cope with the emotional demands of the suicidal person.

O'Neal and Range wanted to determine if specific circumstances would encourage or discourage helpful responses to suicidal threats [1]. They provided 141 undergraduates with short vignettes about various persons with an HIV+ test, depression, drug abuse, anxiety, or adjustment problems. Students written responses were relatively unhelpful regardless of the circumstance. However, the responses to the suicidal person who recently tested HIV+ were very unhelpful, probably because of the stigma of AIDS. While they found students relatively unhelpful when presented with hypothetical cases, they wondered if this would change if actual people who they knew were involved. This seemed to be the case in other studies [2, 3]. They suggested that strategies for intervention be developed and tested to determine any changes in helpfulness.

Intervention with a suicidal person is both very time consuming and very energy consuming. Therefore it is important to understand that there are different levels of intervention and to acknowledge which level is appropriate for our own action is crucial. Initially, anyone who wants to can begin an intervention when they detect that someone appears to be (or is) expressing suicidal ideas. I would call this the *every person* intervention level. The intervention at this level is to give permission to the person to talk about whatever there is in his or her life causing them to consider suicide. This is the development of a rapport and trust which communicates to the suicidal person that there is an empathic relationship and the intervener wants to facilitate the person's access to a more professional level of assistance.

At this level we need to be certain that we include students. Often it is the suicidal student's peers who become aware of his or her suicidal thoughts or impending actions. Lawrence and Ureda surveyed 1,131 university freshman and found they were able to recognize suicidal behavior in their peers [4]. The problem was they were either unsure or did not know how to make a helpful response. As noted in the previous chapter, programs can be developed to enable students to achieve a reasonable comfort level with their suicidal peers. This can be done through accurate information, skill training, modeling, and role playing. These activities can be offered on a volunteer level and will increase emotional comfort in situations that are stressful and emotional. The combination of knowledge and the belief that a person can take appropriate action are needed for effective intervention.

The second level I would call the *skilled helper* level. The previous intervener may accompany the suicidal person to an individual who has had training in para-professional counseling skills (e.g., a teacher, a resident assistant, a student affairs staff member) or who occupies a position where some formal training in counseling has taken place (e.g., a clergy person, a crisis line worker, a physician, a dentist, or a nurse). The intervention may begin at this level as the suicidal person seeks some assistance. For persons involved in the medical profession it is important to note that at least 50 percent of individuals who have committed suicide have sought medical attention within the previous six months. This has profound implications for the staff of college health services. Intervention at this level may provide some persons with the interaction they need to resolve their life situation, or they may be referred to persons at a third level.

The third level I would call the *professional* level. The interveners at this level are those persons who are professionally trained and include school counselors, social workers, psychologists, psychiatrists, and others who have had advanced training in counseling. Intervention at this level may involve out patient counseling, medication, and hospitalization. Again, intervention at this level may begin through referrals or by initial contact with a suicidal person seeking resolution of a life problem.

Active outreach by professional staff can have an impact on the campus' intervention efforts. Dashef reported on the efforts by one campus mental health service [5]. The service emphasized ties to such groups as residence life, freshman orientation, undergraduate advisement offices, teaching assistants. Staff from the mental health service met with these groups and organized workshops on suicide intervention. They emphasized the importance of mental health and encouraged referrals as a primary prevention effort. Their secondary prevention effort was with students who were either referred or were self-referrals. While the staff did not wish to claim any testable cause and effect relationship, during the two year intervention period studied, there was a decline in the rate of suicide on the campus.

This type of intervention program could be developed by any professional group although sometimes there may be a need for training at the professional level as well. As previously noted, suicidal persons often consult with medical staff about problems before their suicidal action. Michel and Valach have offered some suggestions for training of general practitioners [6].

Intervention begins at any level with a recognition of a person's suicidal inclination. While this may be as obvious as someone coming directly to a person and asking for help, it is more likely that the intervener will have to be cognizant of the clues related to suicidal behavior. It is usually not mental health or other professionals who become aware of the potential risk of suicide. Rather, it is usually the suicidal person's peers, colleagues, friends, and family that become aware of the suicidal clues. This is precisely why it is very important to have programs for the general public on the recognition of the clues to suicidal behavior. These programs can assist in the elimination of attitudes of denial, teach people the clues to suicidal behavior and to recognize that all suicidal clues and threats should be taken seriously. Otherwise there is a genuine possibility that a significant clue may be avoided or missed and a suicide attempt or completed suicide may take place. "Intervention in and the prevention of adolescent suicide often fundamentally depends on the awareness and sensitivity of key people in the young person's life who seriously respond to obvious and veiled suicide clues and make referrals to those who can help" [7, p. 123].

There are a number of clues to suicidal ideation and action. These may be behavioral, emotional or statements which are made, indicating that the individual has some level of suicidal risk.

BEHAVIORAL CLUES

Noticeable changes in the everyday patterns of an individual's life that are relatively sudden and otherwise unexplained are significant indicators that the individual, if not suicidal, has had something happen in his or her life that needs to be explored. These changes in patterns cover the entire spectrum of that person's behavior. The following are some examples:

- There is a noticeable change in the person's appetite. He formerly ate heartily but now claims not to be hungry or picks at his food.

She never ate a lot and now she seems to consume everything in sight. Both are changes in eating patterns and illustrate that not all suicidal persons do "less" of everything.

- There is a change in the person's sleeping habits or a disturbed sleeping pattern. She might be one of those students who seemed to be awake and actively studying until one or two in the morning. Now she is sleeping at ten in the evening and still can't seem to get enough sleep. He might have been up early in the morning and enjoying eight o'clock classes. Now he sleeps until noon and misses classes regularly.
- There is a definite increase in the person's consumption of alcoholic beverages. While he previously drank a beer or two "with the guys," he is now drinking alone in his room and seems to be intoxicated at least twice a week.
- There is a change in the person's smoking habits. She never smoked before and now she is smoking heavily but doesn't seem to derive any pleasure from it.
- There is a change in the person's physical appearance. He previously looked as if he had stepped out of the pages of *GQ*. Now, he looks as if he slept in his clothes the last three nights.
- There is a change in the person's social activities. She was the social chairperson for the group and always arranged activities and made certain that everyone knew about the events and encouraged their participation. Now she spends most of the time in her room and doesn't want anyone to bother her.

All of these are indications that something significant has caused a change in the person's life. This is only a partial listing and it can be extended to religious activities, sexual behaviors, loss or gain of weight, use of chemicals and any other pattern of behavior that was normal for the individual but now there is an unexplained and noticeable change.

Another clue is a different level of energy. Usually for a suicidal person this involves a diminishment of energy, a lethargy or fatigue. The person may exhibit a decrease in their ability to concentrate as well as a lack of interest. However, there are times when there is an increase in the level of energy to a point of restlessness, agitation, and annoyance with anyone who doesn't immediately respond to a request. As there is a generalized impression that all suicidal people are depressed, this hyperactivity often is deceiving and missed as a suicidal clue.

Diminished levels of energy are often accompanied by a loss of pleasure in usual activities and a lack of interest in everyday events.

Often the suicidal person will describe themselves as no longer deriving pleasure from anything. This is a psychological state known as anhedonia and it is very common in suicidal persons.

Somatic complaints are often a clue to potential suicidal behavior. These clues are most often discovered by medical personnel who can find no cause for the frequent severe headaches, the pain in the stomach, or the problems with breathing, for instance.

Impulsiveness, recklessness, and aggressiveness which have not been part of the person's previous behavior may be clues to suicidal behavior. Sometimes a self-destructive behavior, not immediately recognized as a covert suicidal action, appears. This may take the form of extremely reckless driving, impulsively running across a street against the traffic light, consuming a large quantity of an alcoholic beverage, or deciding that walking on a bridge railing would be exciting. There may be deliberate aggressive efforts such as attempting to engage others in physical contests or searching for dangerous situations.

Students who are making their "final arrangements" and are not ill, are distinctly saying that they have suicidal thoughts. These activities take the form of buying insurance, writing wills, and planning their funerals. These are not normal activities for college students. However, this may take a more subtle form known as the "living will." Students begin to give away their favorite possessions. This is a very common phenomenon among high school and college students. They want to make certain that their special friends receive something that will provide a remembrance of them to that person. For example, a young man who had a complete set of weights and lifted regularly by himself and with friends, suddenly gave away all of his equipment. His friends thought that this was strange and asked him why he was doing this. His response was, "I don't plan to be around and I want you guys to have them." Sometimes when a student has very little that she or he considers to be of value, they may choose to leave advice as was the case in the following written by a young man.

> In the movies, everyone gets a dying speech so I figure I get one too. First I'll tell the people I know what I have observed about them and I hope it will help them to make it in this rat race. John—you worry about hurting others too much. Tell them what you think and if you're right enforce it. Don't let people push you around so much. Bruce—You'll have it made wherever you do if you cut down on being so proud of everything you do. Joe—be open, it seems to agree with you but watch those sarcastic comments. Tweety—it's time to stop playing games with people. They deserve a little more respect.
> —Eldon (sophomore)

EMOTIONAL CLUES

There are a number of emotional clues to potential suicidal behavior. Expressions of low self-esteem and unreal expectations of self combined with feelings of despondency and depression are observed. Feelings of guilt, remorse, and self-reproachment for real or imagined transgressions against someone or some group are often the first steps towards the development of feelings of isolation, loneliness, and alienation. It does not mean that another person or group has avoided or rejected the individual. It is that individual's perception of what is happening and it may or may not have any basis in reality.

Pronounced mood swings may take place without any apparent stimulus. One of the most pronounced is that of sudden crying spells, tearfulness, and sadness for which there is no immediate explanation. While this is a phenomenon seen reasonably often in young women, it is not a common phenomenon with young men. Having been taught that "men don't cry" the appearance of this phenomenon in young men clearly indicates a serious situation. Changes from withdrawal and sulkiness to hyperactivity indicates something is out of control. Often there is a high level of anxiety that is not substantiated by any external force. This is referred to as the person who always seems to be "walking on the edge."

Lastly and most importantly are the feelings of being powerless, helpless, and hopeless. In his book, *Definition of Suicide*, Shneidman presents ten common characteristics of suicide and lists the two common affective characteristics of suicide: hopelessness and helplessness [8]. As was noted in the chapter on etiology, hopelessness has been extensively researched through the use of the Beck Depression Inventory and the Beck Hopelessness Scale. In a prospective study of 1,958 outpatients, Beck, Brown, Berchick, Stewart and Steer found that hopelessness was significantly related to eventual suicide [9]. They were able to identify sixteen to seventeen patients who eventually committed suicide by using the Beck Hopelessness Scale. Hopelessness is closely related to the seriousness of suicidal intent. Beck et al. provides an answer to the question of how hopelessness becomes a predictor of eventual suicide.

People who respond with marked hopelessness in one personal crisis will be likely to respond in the same way at the next crisis. . . . hopelessness may constitute a stable belief, incorporating negative expectancies that are very resistant to change in suicide prone patients [9, p. 194].

Individuals give clues to their hopelessness through such statements as "There's just no hope." "There's no use, nothing can be done," "I feel so absolutely helpless," or "There's nothing anybody can do." The statements are usually given in the most absolute of negative terms, featuring the words never, nothing, and no one. Expressions of hopelessness are regarded as cardinal clues to impending suicidal action.

STATEMENTS OF SUICIDE

Individuals also tell us that they intend to engage in some suicidal action through indirect statements like:

> "I won't be around much longer."
> "They would be better off without me."
> "Who'd care?"
> "Nobody would miss me if I wasn't here."
> "It won't be long before this pain is gone."
> "Did you ever wonder what it would feel like to be dead?"
> "I just want to lie down and sleep forever."

Then they also present very direct statements.

> "I want to die."
> "I just can't take it anymore, I want to end it all."
> "I'm going to commit suicide."

It is at the moment that these statements are made that the denial systems of those who hear them are most readily apparent. This is true of people of all ages, but with college students the whole idea that someone in their peer group would want to commit suicide just seems very unreal. Often statements of suicidal intent are met with such comments as "You've got to be kidding." "You'd never do anything like that!" "Stop fooling around, I don't like to hear talk like that!" or "Why would you do something like that?" (and it isn't intended as a question). These responses are viewed as rejections by the suicidal person. So, they go on looking for someone who will respond to them.

> I didn't know what else to do! No one took me seriously! I told them that I was going to kill myself and I even told some of them how I was going to do it. The usual response was 'You'd never do a crazy thing like that!' But, I would and I did. . . . You want to know how many people I told? I told fourteen people who I thought were my friends. I thought they would do something and they didn't. So, it seemed like it was true that nobody cared and when I figured it out,

> you know, how many I'd talked to, I knew it was inevitable because
> nobody would stop me. So, last Friday I was alone. I took my knife
> and slammed it into my wrist. God, it hurt and then Mike walked
> in. I don't think I'll ever forget the look on his face. He grabbed a
> towel and wrapped it around my wrist and drove me to the hospital.
> —Lauren (junior)

Had Lauren really told fourteen people about his impending suicidal action and had fourteen people really taken no action? He did give me the names of the people and I was able to contact most of them. They were shocked at his attempt. They readily admitted that he had told them he was thinking about suicide. They all had thought Lauren was too bright and had too many good things going for him. They had responded to him with variations on the theme—"You wouldn't do *that*!" While a single instance, it is illustrative of what can happen when suicidal people communicate their intentions.

The oblique method of communication used by most suicidal persons has its roots in the psychological pain that they feel and the resulting constriction and perturbation. The suicidal person advances through a series of distressing events that results in an increasing level of psychological pain, often referred to as the unendurable psychological pain. Recently Shneidman has referred to this as psychache, "the hurt, anguish, soreness, aching, psychological pain in the psyche, the mind" [10, p. 145]. Concurrent with the development of this pain, the individual becomes more constricted in his or her thought patterns. The range of options and alternatives that would appear available to someone who was not suicidal, gradually disappear or appear to be unobtainable. As the suicide person becomes increasingly vulnerable and dichotomous in his or her thinking patterns, the options eventually narrow to two—do I live or do I die? While there is still an ambivalence about dying, the options are reduced. However, even in this highly charged atmosphere, ambivalence still plays an important role. For example, Louis was a very dramatic person in his dress and personage. He liked to be known as the person with a flair for the dramatic. This also affected how he dealt with his suicidal feelings.

> It seemed that nothing was going right. My lover had moved out a
> couple of weeks ago and we had a nasty fight on the phone. Well, as
> I hung up I realized this fantastic thunder storm was moving
> nearer. I was really fascinated by the power of the lightning and the
> thunder. And, I thought to myself, 'What a way to go, right in the
> middle of this storm.' I left my apartment and walked to the bridge.
> It was just pouring rain and I loved every minute of it. Thunder,
> lightning rain—I was going out in style. Imagine jumping to your

death while all of nature is raging around you. I thought we felt as one. Just as I came to the bridgehead, there was this instantaneous flash of lightning and simultaneous crash of thunder. It was so near I could feel all of it. And, I said, 'That could have killed me!'

—Louis (senior)

Louis said that he suddenly realized what he had said and started to roar with laughter. He realized that on his way to die, he didn't want to die and ended up seeking emergency help that evening. Louis' ambivalence won that evening. He sought assistance to find another option. However, these types of incidents do not always have happy endings. The duality of living and dying can take more critical turns.

Now, when this becomes combined with various levels of anxiety or perturbation the situation becomes increasingly lethal. As the level of perturbation increases the possibility of an action taken in what might be described as a type of anxiety attack increases. Consequently, combining a high level of constriction with a high level of perturbation equals a high level of lethality.

It is in this process that the suicidal person engages in the "cry for help." She or he is still ambivalent about choosing to die but needs to know that there is someone who cares about her or him. The open communication of depression and suicidal feelings may be stifled by any one of the many factors that were discussed in the chapter on the mythology of suicide. Many suicidal persons communicate their intentions by indirect methods. These indirect methods are used to determine if anyone will take them seriously, if they really care, and if they will take some action.

ARE YOU THINKING ABOUT COMMITTING SUICIDE?

This is the question to ask. To do otherwise is to send someone like Lauren searching for another person who may hear his plea. The question will not put the idea into someone's mind. That is the myth. Rather, it will enable the person to speak of the intolerable situation that has brought him or her to this point. This question is special in two ways.

First of all, it doesn't avoid the issue. Interestingly, one of the most common ways of responding to indications of suicidal thoughts or behaviors is to ask, "You're *not* thinking of committing suicide are you?" There is an emphasis on the negative and the communication given to the suicidal person is that the answer that is desired is, "No, not me." And, that is more than likely the answer that will be given. It is apparent to the suicidal person that the responder is not desirous of entering into an interaction with him or her, for whatever reason. It has become apparent to me that regardless of other constriction(s) in their thinking, suicidal persons appear to be extremely capable of "reading" another person's intent. They are looking for a direct involvement not an indecisive possibility.

Second, this question says the word *suicide*. Some other responses are very ambiguous using euphemisms such as "hurting yourself," "doing harm" or even as ambiguous as "doing something to yourself." These responses communicate to the suicidal person that any involvement is tentative at best. For the suicidal person, the question becomes, "How much can I say before I will frighten you away?" Suicide is what we are talking about, the word "suicide" is what we need to say. It communicates clearly that we are willing to take a risk, that we are willing to engage in an intervention. Perhaps, most frightening of all, we are willing to take the risk of becoming a survivor.

THE CONTRACT

An effective tool with a suicidal person is to ask them to engage in a contract. The contract has the suicidal person make the following promise, "I will not attempt or commit suicide until I have contacted you and we have discussed options and alternatives to my impending actions." Some people prefer to have the suicidal person sign a contract. I personally prefer to maintain this as an oral contract because I believe that an oral contract means that I accept the person at their word. I believe that it gives the suicidal person more power when it is accepted in this manner and since the person usually is feeling very powerless, any appropriate means I can use to return some sense of power is essential.

It is very important to remember this contract does not say the intervener *can stop* a suicide. It says that the intervener and the suicidal person will discuss options and alternatives. It should be very obvious the suicidal person can contact anyone from a location that would be undetectable. Then, if he or she is intent on suicide, fulfill the contract, hang up the phone and commit suicide. However, the contract seems to create a bond that has significant meaning for the suicidal person. They recognize that there is someone who will listen to their pain and who will work with them.

Since it is highly unlikely that the primary person with whom the contract is made is always available, an important part of the mechanics of the contract is to provide the suicidal person with an alternative set of contacts. These usually consist of crisis line phone numbers, emergency room phone numbers or the names and phone numbers of other counselors or therapists who would be available. An effective means of making these alternative contacts readily available is to have them on a small card that can be given to the person to keep in a billfold or purse. This avoids having the information in another place (or losing it) at a critical moment.

Does a contract work? From my own experience and from the experiences of others, the answer is a definite "yes." The commitment to keeping the contract is very strong even when the individual is close to committing suicide. Sandra is an illustration of this commitment. Sandra and I had a contract from our first meeting. I had referred her to a therapist and we both knew that she had a lethal quantity of medication that she had hidden somewhere and would not tell us of the location. Her advisor told Sandra that perhaps she should consider another field of study after receiving an unsatisfactory grade. That evening she wrote letters to the significant people in her life explaining why she was committing suicide that night. When these were complete, she showered, applied makeup, dressed in her best peignoir, arranged herself in bed, and was about to begin taking the medications when she remembered the contract. Sandra said she debated whether she should call me at that hour of the night (3:00 a.m.). She remarked later that her thoughts went "He'll think I'm crazy for calling him at this hour. Well, I'm suicidal, but I'm not crazy." After about an hour of debating, she decided to flush the medications down the toilet and was waiting by my office door when I arrived in the morning. "Guess what I almost did last night." was her greeting. Even when Sandra was close to taking her final action, the commitment to the contract was remembered and honored. This contract is an important part of any intervention.

There are other actions that also need to be taken once the question has been asked and the response has been, "Yes." At this point, people are very concerned that they will do something that will "push the person over the edge" or make the matter much worse. A caring, empathic response and posture by an intervener will rarely produce a negative reaction. To allay these types of fears, let's start with the things not to do, the "don'ts." Once these are avoided, the do's become that much easier.

THE DON'TS OF INTERVENTION

Don't tell someone, "You can't do it!" Indeed they can. In fact, making this statement may sound like a type of dare or a challenge of their capabilities. This statement may sound like "You're not a capable person, you don't even have the capacity to do this." Suicidal people do not need further challenges to their battered self-image and feelings of inadequacy or incompetency.

Don't tell someone "You wouldn't dare!"

> My mother was probably really upset with me since I think she saw
> me as her problem child. When I told her that I felt like killing
> myself she responded, "You wouldn't dare, you don't have the guts
> to do it!" I was furious with her. For the first time I believed that
> she really wanted me to die and get out of her hair. I decided that
> she wasn't going to get rid of me that easily. I would show her! I
> would live! Doesn't that sound weird? But, it's how I managed to
> live through college. I defied her all the way.
>
> —Karen (graduate)

The potential of a dare having a positive ending like this is minuscule and should not be a part of any intervention.

Don't say, "This is only a phase, it'll go away in a day or so!" There are two implications in this statement. The first is there is nothing really wrong with the person that time won't cure. This is not true. The second implication is that the suicidal person's emotional state is perceived as insignificant, thus discrediting and rejecting their statements. This will only add to their current feelings of isolation and rejection.

Don't be drawn into a bargaining or manipulative situation where the suicidal person wants something done, probably inappropriate, in return for their action(s), (e.g., "I won't attempt suicide if you will promise not to tell anyone.") Manipulative suicidal persons are difficult and very often they have found this manipulative behavior has enabled them to achieve their goals. Manipulative behavior is often used to obtain otherwise unobtainable goals, often with parents. "I won't do anything if I can have the car this weekend." is an example of manipulative behavior and inappropriate bargaining combined. If the manipulations don't succeed, the level of suicidal threat will escalate. In this manner, the manipulative person attempts to or actually does maintain control and achieves his or her goals.

Don't promise what you cannot deliver. Most importantly it is inappropriate to promise someone that you will "keep them from committing or attempting suicide." Unless you are capable of remaining with the person twenty-four hours a day, seven days a week, fifty-two weeks a year *ad infinitum* you cannot keep this promise. You certainly can say you will do everything possible to insure their safety, including calling 911 for assistance if there is a dangerous situation. There may be a tendency to make substantial promises in the hope that this will relieve some of the stress of the moment for both the person and the helper. Remember, however, that promises may be called to account and inappropriate promises may become counter-productive efforts.

Attempt not to appear shocked at what the suicidal person may say. There may be attempts to shock the intervener to test his or her ability to stay with the person. Or, the suicidal person may reveal intimate details of his or her life that are distressing or lurid and which are intrinsic to his or her psychological pain. At this point it is important to support the individual and not concur with their negative self-image.

Don't get into a philosophical debate on the merits of suicide. This may be a deflection by the suicidal person to determine if you have a position that may support his or her decision. Philosophical debates may be engaged in at a more appropriate time.

Don't leave the suicidal person alone until you are certain there is no danger she or he will attempt or commit suicide. If you are uncertain, seek assistance from someone who is better qualified to make such judgments.

Don't talk about past suicide attempts in terms of "successful" or "unsuccessful." Talk about suicide in terms of ideation (thinking about suicide), suicide attempts and completed suicides. Several years ago, I found myself being chastised for the use of inappropriate words by a student who had made a sublethal attempt. We were beginning our fourth session when he said he had something to tell me.

> You know, I'm really pissed off at you! I've been wanting to tell you this and since you asked if there was anything I wanted to say, I'll say it. Do you remember our first meeting? (I said I remembered the meeting but perhaps not specifically what he was referring to and so asked him to tell me.) Well, you said that my attempt was unsuccessful. Well, all I could think of was there was my dad sitting in front of me telling me "You damned kid, you can't even do this right!"
>
> —Kelly (junior)

Kelly was right. I had used an inappropriate descriptor and I immediately removed those two adjectives from my suicide vocabulary (And, I learned a great deal about Kelly's relationship with his father as well.)

Don't look for several reasons for the person to live. For some reason we have become accustomed to asking people for lists of ten things, in this case ten reasons to live. Suicidal people, particularly when they are highly perturbed and constricted, are having a difficult time figuring out how to live, let alone looking for ten reasons. A list of reasons may be one more unachievable task, another failure. It is appropriate to look for *a* reason to live, just one reason is enough to start the process. The reason to live may be a person, a belief, a pet. Whatever the reason, start with *one*.

THE DO'S OF INTERVENTION

First and foremost, listen carefully to everything that is being said. Check out what you think you have heard. This not only indicates you *want* to understand what is being said, it also demonstrates you want to *understand* it accurately. It shows you care. If there are smoke screens, diversions or inconsistencies seek to have them clarified or gently challenge them. Listen to the words for context, content and affect, and observe the body language.

In the event you come upon someone who is suicidal and you do not know the person's name it is important to establish a connection by asking her or his name. You only need a first name to establish this very human linkage. This will demonstrate to the individual that you care enough to want to address her or him by name. Also tell the person your name so she or her can call you by name. This introduction is a very normal part of a human interaction and it lends some degree of normalcy to a stressful situation. Whatever the incident, using names is a powerful recognition of the individual as a distinct individual.

The focus of an intervention is upon the suicidal person. You want to find out as much as possible about them. Ask the person about themselves. Learn some basic information about where they live, their marital status, and other parts of their life. What is happening in their life at this time that would precipitate a suicidal behavior? Ask the person direct questions about the details of his or her planned action. Who is involved? What means are they planning to use? When are they planning to attempt/commit suicide? What has brought them to this decision? If possible, avoid questions that begin with the word, "Why?" "Why?" questions tend to have an accusatory sense for adolescents and young adults (probably for anybody) conjuring up a mental image of a parent or an authority figure saying, "Why did you do this?" These questions are important as they provide the basis for an assessment of suicidal risk.

Who is Involved?

Is it just one person or is it a suicide pact between two or more people? Is there any indication that this might be a suicide following a homicide or other illegal act?

What Means are You Planning to Use?

This is often regarded as a very intrusive question, perhaps even suggestive. But, there is a need to know the means to determine the level of lethality. At the low lethality end of the scale would be the use of a small amount of aspirin, a scratching of the arm or perhaps no idea at all as to what might be used. The lethality increases as the use of knives, prescription medications and more potentially harmful devices are considered. At the high end of the lethality scale, would be the use of a gun, hanging, or jumping. The higher the lethality, the greater the risk.

It is most appropriate to ask the person to give you whatever they plan to use to attempt or commit suicide. This removes the object and may defuse the situation making it easier to continue with an intervention. There is a concomitant benefit to this action. It indicates to the individual your concern and your willingness to take appropriate actions to prevent the suicidal behavior. This provides the suicidal individual with another resource person, an affirmation that there are people who value him or her. At times there are unexpected benefits from this action.

In an intervention with a suicidal student I asked for the knife he said he was going to use to commit suicide. He said he had a special knife and gave me a knife that had a puma engraved on its blade. After he had completed his counseling, I met him and asked if he would like to have his knife returned. "No, you keep it." he said. When he was leaving the university I again asked him and again he responded with, "No, you keep it." I told him there was the possibility we would not meet again and I didn't want to keep his valuable knife. "Don't worry about it, I'll always know where it is." was his response. The knife remains in my desk drawer. I have become convinced the knife was the only weapon he would use to commit suicide and as long as I have it, I am a form of "insurance policy." I can keep it in my desk for a long time if that's the case.

When are You Planning to Attempt/Commit Suicide?

This may range from an "I don't have the slightest idea." which is a very low level intentionality. As we move towards situations with greater risk, the more specific and imminent a time reference, the higher the risk level. The higher the level of intentionality, combined with a higher level of lethality, the greater the risk level for the individual.

As stated before, assist the individual in finding *one reason to live*. That's all you need to start the process of hopefulness and enabling the person to regain some control over their life. Ask for a *reason* and avoid specifying something definitive, such as a person. For it may be that the person does not have anyone that they consider important. A *reason* permits the person to find an object of value and love that may be quite beyond anything that may have been discussed.

I remember being thoroughly frustrated during an intervention with a young man, Jim, who was seriously contemplating suicide. Jim said there was no one who cared about him. As we talked, the circumstances of his chaotic family life and other stresses in his life did make it appear that he had no good reason to live. More out of frustration than anything else, I said, "My god, man there has to be someone or something that will miss you when you're gone." Interestingly, there was not the usual immediate response of "Nope." Instead, after a pause, in a very quiet voice Jim said, "Kitty would." Now sometimes we get so caught up in the process we focus only on what was heard and not what was said. That was my problem this time. I couldn't recall anyone named "Kitty." So, I asked, "Who's Kitty?" "My little kitten in my room at home." He proceeded to tell me about a kitten he had rescued and cared for at home. His parents didn't like the kitten, so he had to keep it in his room. The kitten became a reason to live and we progressed from there to acceptance of therapy and eventually a happy student. Reasons to live do not have to be people, they can be anything the person values.

Assist the person in obtaining professional help by working with them to find a counselor. At colleges and universities there are usually mental health units whether they are part of the campus, as a health service, or an arrangement with a local medical or mental health facility. The individual may be very threatened by his or her emotional state and quite frightened at being out of control. Students may view the situation as representing yet another failure in their life, believing that they will be seen as incompetent. Therefore, it is extremely helpful to accompany the person to the counselor or doctor's office. They need support as they work to begin resolution of this life crisis. This action demonstrates a further caring for the individual at a time when they believe few if any people care what happens to them.

ASSESSMENT

A complete psychological assessment should be performed by a mental health professional. The dynamics of suicide and the legal and ethical implications for counselors have been summarized by Fujimara, Weis and Cochran [11]. Their work is an effective synopsis providing a short refresher for anyone working with suicidal clients. There are some initial assessments that can be made to make some determination of the degree of suicidal risk and the immediacy of professional intervention. Hatton and Valente's book on assessment and intervention is an excellent reference book that can be used by persons who have some intervention and assessment training [12]. An assessment can determine the risk level of the individual as one of the following:

Low—the individual has some feelings of isolation, has only vague thoughts of a suicide plan, has significant others who are regarded as supports and generally functions fairly well in daily activities.

Medium—the individual is beginning to feel hopeless, has more frequent thoughts about suicide, may be beginning to formulate some plans, has begun to rely upon alcohol or other chemicals for "relief" from stress, has few significant others to rely upon for support and has a life style that is relatively stable but deteriorating.

High—the individual is in severe psychological pain, feeling hopeless, helpless and highly anxious, denies having any support or anyone who cares about him or her, may be significantly abusing alcohol or other chemicals, has a generally unstable lifestyle and has frequent thoughts of or actually developed a highly specific plan for suicide.

These are generalized levels and it is important to assess individual factors to come to a determination of the level of suicidal risk. Risk factors constitute individual pieces which, like the pieces of a puzzle, need to be put together to develop the complete picture and make a determination of suicidal risk. Some factors, like the pieces in a puzzle, are larger and more important in the final assessment. An important part of this assessment may not, however, be in what is heard, rather in how it is heard. Sometimes we call this a "gut feeling," something we know instinctively. Hatton and Valente call this "intuitive feeling" [12]. In doing this, the caregiver is responding to

> Nonverbal cues or some feeling tone that suggests that the cry for help has been muffled by some interference as yet unidentified, which is actually stifling a piercing scream. Such intuitive feelings warrant further consideration and generally turn out to have accurately appraised the risk [12, p. 76].

The following are some of the risk factors, behaviors or symptoms of potential suicidal behavior. A caution—the suicidal individual may or may not fit the given potential. It is critical to remember that each person should be assessed as an individual for even without the risk factors usually attributed to their "group," they may be suicidal.

Age—In the fifteen to twenty-four years of age group, suicide is the second leading cause of death. However the increase in the nontraditional, older student on campus requires attention be given to the fact that among Caucasians and Asian Americans, the risk increases with age. Native American and African American males have a high risk of suicide between the ages of fifteen and thirty-four, then the risk declines. There can be significant variations between individuals of the same and different races.

Gender—Males commit suicide about four times as often as females. Females attempt suicide about four times as often as males. The highest risk category is for males.

Race—There are significant variations as previously noted. Among college age students, being a Caucasian, African American or Native American male, produces the highest risk. It is important to note recent data on Asian American students and the stress factors they perceive in achieving a higher educational status seems to have propelled this group, males and females, into a higher risk category.

Marital status—Persons who live alone, are divorced or widowed are at highest risk. For the college student group, living alone, whether in a residence hall or in an off-campus unit, creates a higher risk as they may perceive themselves to be isolated, and can isolate themselves more easily. With more non-traditional students on campus, divorced persons as students become more common. Widows or widowers would seem unlikely in this population. However, I would submit that the break-up of an intimate, long standing relationship may be perceived in emotional terms by students as a death or a divorce from the other person. It is not a situation to ignore even if it does not fit generalized frames of reference.

Method—The more lethal and non-interruptable the method, the greater the risk. At greatest risk are those persons who are contemplating suicide by use of firearms, hanging, or jumping from a height. Men generally choose these more lethal methods. Drug ingestion, gas, smothering, and slashing are less risky and are the methods most generally chosen by females. However, there has been a noticeable increase in the number of women who are committing suicide by firearms and hanging. The increase in the number of women using firearms as a means of suicide was reported by Marks and Abernathy in 1974 [13]. Rogers presented a synopsis of the trends towards increased lethality in method of choice among women [14]. In reviewing the data from 1964 to 1984, Rogers found there was a 55.91 percent increase in the use of firearms and explosives, and a decrease of 20.99 percent in poisoning. "In 1984, 39.60% of the female suicides used firearms and explosives, and 36.50% employed poisoning. Furthermore, the category of hanging also increased by 3.15%" [14, p. 37].

By 1989, the use of firearms accounted for 65.1 percent of the male and 40.8 percent of the female suicide deaths in the United States. The trend toward increased lethality, particularly among women, means the method of suicide must be carefully assessed and stereotypes must be discarded.

Sexual orientation—The risk of suicide among gay, lesbian, and bisexual young adults has been estimated to be three times that of their heterosexual agemates. Within a college age population there is a significant risk as these individuals come to terms with their sexual orientation and make difficult decisions about acknowledging their sexual preference. This may be a high risk factor depending upon the identification and integration of the person.

Religion—In general, suicide rates are higher for Protestants than Catholics or Jews. Statistical data on other religious groups are generally not available. An individual's religious beliefs may provide the person with a sense of hope. Beliefs may also be a restricting factor if the person believes that he or she is destined to an eternal damnation, but that is not always the situation.

> I know if I commit suicide I will go to hell. I've heard that from my priest as long as I can remember. And, I believe it. But, you need to understand that hell in hell cannot equal the hell I am experiencing. It can't be worse!
>
> —LuAnn (senior)

It is essential to determine what religion means in the life of the suicidal person. If the individual is like LuAnn, the risk is very high as the inhibiting factors have been removed.

The crisis—The intensity of the crisis is the strongest indication of the level of risk. The individual's perception of the level of crisis is the important factor. If the perception of the crisis is that it is immediate and unresolvable the risk factor is high. If the crisis is less immediate and there are potential intervening variables, the risk becomes less.

The communication of intent—The level of risk is determined by a number of factors. What is the availability of the method? This can range from fantasy or non-availability (low) to can be obtained easily (medium) to has the method available and has a specific plan (high). What is the time reference? This also ranges from having an idea (low) to a generalized time frame (medium) to a specific date and time, perhaps coinciding with another suicidal event or anniversary of a suicide (high). What is the capability (or belief) of the person? A low level of risk would be a statement like, "I don't think I could ever do that." While "I think I might be able to do it." indicates moderate risk. "I know I can and I will." exemplifies a high risk.

Deception and concealment—The more deceptive the person is about their impending suicide and the greater the efforts made to conceal the method, time, date and place, the greater the risk. This is referred to as the risk-rescue ratio. What is the risk and what is the chance of rescue? If the risk is low and chance of rescue high, this would be regarded as a less lethal effort. However, if the level of risk is high and the chance of rescue is low, then the lethality of the action is very high.

Coping strategies—The greater the number of effective coping strategies the person has the lesser the risk. However, as the coping strategies lessen and impulsivity increases, the risk level increases. If the coping strategies have become destructive, such as dependence upon alcohol or other chemicals to resolve the crisis, the risk also becomes high.

Significant others—Who are they? What is the quality (intimacy) and quantity of the relationships? If the individual has a number of significant people in his or her life and they are perceived to be strong supports there is less risk. The fewer people of significance and a low quality of contact and relationship with these individuals indicates a higher risk for the suicidal person. Sometimes these significant others are fantasized and provide no actual support but may be perceived as people who really care. In the following illustration, Andy's fantasized support system did not materialize creating a higher risk level for him.

> All through high school Mary was the only person who was always nice to me. When we came to college we ended up in the same dorm. Sometimes I would sit down and eat with her and her friends. I know they thought I was a geek, just like others did in high school. But, Mary was always smiling and asking me how things were going. When I really felt bad, I decided to ask her to go to a movie with me. I knew that would help. She just smiled at me and said she had a boyfriend and wouldn't go with me. I was so hurt. I thought she was the only one who cared about me.
>
> —Andy (freshman)

Functioning level—How well does the person function in his or her daily life activities? Life activities include such routines as sleeping, eating, getting to classes and work, social activities, study, and other routines of college life. If the individual functions fairly well in most areas, the risk level is low. If there is reasonably good functioning in some areas the risk level is moderate. However, if the person is not functioning in any activities, the risk level is high.

Previous suicide attempts—This is a critical area. The level of risk increases exponentially as the multiplicity and lethality of previous actions increase. Once the level of lethality has increased it will more than likely remain at the higher level in subsequent attempts.

Previous therapy history—The level of risk associated with this factor is dependent upon the person's perception of previous therapy. If the therapeutic sessions were perceived to be helpful the individual may accept further psychological intervention. If the perceptions are negative there is probably little chance the individual will want to return to therapy.

Previous psychiatric history—There are some disorders that present a higher risk ratio. These include schizophrenia and paranoia where there are delusional and hallucinatory factors to confound a state of anxiety. Previous depressive and/or suicidal states contribute to situations where an individual, having been through a previous episode, may attempt at an earlier stage to avoid a recurrence of this emotional state as evidenced by Dick's statement.

> Why did I try to kill myself? Because I know what it feels like to be depressed and moody. It's so awful I can't even describe it to you. I just couldn't let it happen again. I never want to feel that way again. Never! Never!
>
> —Dick (junior)

Dick described himself as "falling into that black hole again." As he began to experience depression again, he decided that he would avoid the pain and attempted suicide. Each attempt seems to bring the "plateau" of non-acceptance of further psychological pain to a higher level increasing the risk of suicide at lesser levels of stress.

The concept of being in a black hole is often reported by college students. Sometimes the hole is perceived as having slimy sides that not only makes it impossible to climb out, but the individual keeps slipping further downward. At other times the perception is that the individual is floating in the middle of the hole and is unable to touch the sides as they move further and further down. These statements are often tied together with feelings of hopelessness and helplessness.

Previous medical history—A history of accidents requiring a medical attention or a poor or chronic health condition may indicate higher levels of risk. A history of accidents may indicate an effort at other self-destructive behaviors and/or attempts at a "cry for help." For college students a poor or chronic health condition that inhibits their activities may result in a lessening of a desire to live for they do not see a productive lifetime ahead. Significant numbers of individuals have consulted with medical personnel within six months of their suicidal behavior. It appears they have tried indirectly to inform the medical staff of their problems. It would also seem wise to be aware that students who ask to be tested for HIV+ antibodies or AIDS may present a high risk factor. Fear of the disease may create a highly stressful life situation and a diagnosis may produce a life threatening crisis.

Stressful (negative) life events—Students who have had a significant number of stressful, negative life events (or they have perceived the events as being negative) are at greater risk for suicidal behaviors. There is a direct correlation between the number of stressful life events and the risk of suicidal behavior.

Chemical use and abuse—The use and abuse of alcohol and other chemicals contributes to a higher level of risk. Alcohol is the most commonly used substance. The risk level increases as the level of use and abuse increases. A depressed person is ingesting a central nervous system depressant that provokes other psychological changes. The disinhibiting effect that alcohol may have on the individual also produces a higher risk factor. Students also recognize that alcohol use or abuse may be used as a "cover up" in the event the behavior does not achieve the desired result. I have had several students state they would never have attempted suicide if they had been sober. My response has been that this wasn't true, they were simply denying what had happened. They have agreed this was the truth.

Anger and hostility—These two factors can play an important role in the level of risk. Anger towards someone may be a precipitant and may result in behavior intended to strike back at the individual—"they'll be sorry!" Hostility plays the same role especially as an individual becomes more alienated and isolated from a general population. The "I don't need them." attitude creates hostility and rejection and an increasing level of risk.

Family history—A number of factors related to a family's history can contribute to a higher level of risk. A family history of suicide can become accepted as a "predestined" or "genetic" factor in the life of a student. The potential instability and chaotic lifestyle of a family may create a mental disposition to a sense of hopelessness and helplessness. The loss of a parent (particularly a father) during a student's early years has also been shown to be a risk factor.

Issues of loss—Loss can be many things to a student. The loss can be through death of a sibling or parent or other significant person. Loss may involve separation or the divorce of parents. Loss may be the break-up of a relationship between two individuals. This latter loss is a significant factor for young adults. A relationship loss is often the final factor precipitating a suicide crisis. Loss essentially means that an individual has become deprived of something that had an essential significance in his or her life. Any loss must be treated as a potential risk factor and the greater the grief, the greater the risk level.

Legal status—Current or impending legal difficulties can create a highly negative environment. While some judicial actions may be seen by students as a badge of "coming of age" (e.g., an arrest for intoxication) other action may be seen as changing that individual's status or level of self esteem. For students this may create an even greater crisis as they may perceive their lives have been ruined and all friends lost because of this violation of the law. The greater the perception that this will have a significant impact on the future life of the individual and feeling out of their control, the greater the risk level.

Future orientation—The student's orientation toward the future is an important factor in risk assessment. A student who has extensive and realistic plans for the future may not be at much risk for suicide. There is movement across a spectrum of convictions, so too does the risk change. For the student who, at the opposite end of the spectrum, sees no future and who has no plans, there is a high level of risk for suicidal behavior.

Assessment essentially involves the examination of multiple factors in the life of an individual and determining whether they constitute inhibitors or precipitators. There are also those behaviors that initially serve as inhibitors until they reach a certain threshold at which time they become precipitators. Some of these have been identified by Himmelhoch such as wrist cutting which may relieve stress and reestablish a contact with reality [15]. "The act and the subsequent bleeding become a way of defining their own reality and of relieving the intense anxiety that usually correlates strongly with depersonalization" [15, p. 48].

It is apparent assessment is a complex task. The use of clinical tests as well as judgment of the factors that have been presented here provides an assemblage of components from which the practitioner must develop a risk assessment. It is part science and part art as there is no perfect assessment instrument. The use of this information will be more developed by the skilled helper than the person intervening at the "every person" level. And, there will be a higher level of development at the professional level. The important part is that some understanding of the complex factors entering into the suicidal situation be understood by everyone. Each person needs to understand their own level of competency and when it is met they then need to refer the suicidal person to someone at a higher level of competency. In this manner intervention can begin with any person and hopefully produce a positive outcome for the suicidal person.

Intervention also takes the form of hospitalization. Sometimes there is the need to convince students that hospitalization is not incarceration. Peers often have this view of hospitalization particularly if a student is placed in a locked ward for their own safety. Rosecan, Goldberg, and Wise did a pilot study on psychiatrically hospitalized students at Georgetown University Hospital over a three year period [16]. Of the forty-eight admissions, thirty-three students were admitted with suicidal ideation. They found freshman and sophomores were more likely to be admitted in the first two months of each term and probably were more vulnerable to psychological aspects of separation. The academic cycle was a major stressor for all classes. They noted that college students in psychiatric wards "typically present in crisis, stabilize in hours or days, and focus very quickly on discharge" [16, p. 14]. Likewise, the students had a capacity for reintegration that was "not surprising, given that students represent a preselected group chosen by an office of undergraduate admissions and that admission is based upon, among other qualities, past accomplishment and personal adaptivity" [16, p. 14]. These positive factors related to hospitalization need to be communicated to students. This will not only reduce the stress among peers, but also provide a sense of assurance to those students who perceive themselves to be in a similar situation.

Intervention is prevention, the anticipating or countering in advance of a suicidal action. Prevention, consequently intervention, begins with education and training for all persons. These efforts could reduce the mythology and the apprehension that is present during an intervention and enable a greater number of persons to begin this process at the "every person" stage.

Interventions will only be as good as the knowledge that we have for understanding the diversity and the complexity of the risk factor matrix and the suicidal process. Interventions will only be as good as the people who are willing to engage their time and their energy in attempting to inhibit the suicidal process.

REFERENCES

1. S. E. O'Neal and L. M. Range, College Students' Hypothetical Responses to Suicidal Individuals who are HIV Positive, Substance Abusing, Depressed, or Anxious, *Death Studies, 17*:2, pp. 143-149, 1993.
2. S. K. Martin and L. M. Range, Extenuating Circumstances in Perceptions of Suicide: Disease Diagnosis (AIDS, Cancer), Pain Level, and Life Expectancy, *Omega, 22*:3, pp. 189-199, 1991.
3. L. M. Range and S. K. Martin, How Knowledge of Extenuating Circumstances Influences Community Reactions toward Suicide Victims and Their Bereaved Families, *Omega, 21*:3, pp. 191-198, 1990.
4. M. T. Lawrence and J. R. Ureda, Student Recognition Of and Response to Suicidal Peers, *Suicide and Life Threatening Behavior, 20*:2, pp. 164-176, 1990.

5. S. S. Dashef, Active Suicide Interventions by a Campus Mental Health Service: Operation and Rationale, *Journal of American College Health, 33*:3, pp. 118-122, 1984.
6. K. Michel and L. Valach, Suicide Prevention: Spreading the Gospel to the General Practitioner, *British Journal of Psychiatry, 160,* pp. 757-760, 1992.
7. A. L. Berman and D. A. Jobes, *Adolescent Suicide: Assessment and Intervention,* American Psychological Association, Washington, DC, 1991.
8. E. S. Shneidman, *Definition of Suicide,* John Wiley & Sons, New York, 1985.
9. A. T. Beck, G. Brown, R. J. Berchick, B. L. Stewart, and R. A. Steer, Relationship between Hopelessness and Ultimate Suicide: A Replication with Psychiatric Outpatients, *American Journal of Psychiatry, 147*:2, pp. 190-195, 1990.
10. E. S. Shneidman, Commentary: Suicide as Psychache, *The Journal of Nervous and Mental Disease, 181*:3, pp. 145-147, 1993.
11. L. E. Fujimara, D. M. Weis, and J. R. Cochran, Suicide: Dynamics and Implications for Counseling, *Journal of Counseling and Development, 63*:10, pp. 612-615, 1985.
12. C. L. Hatton and S. M. Valente, *Suicide Assessment and Intervention* (2nd Edition), Appleton-Century-Crofts, Norwalk, Connecticut, 1984.
13. A. Marks and T. Abernathy, Towards a Sociocultural Perspective on Means of Self Destruction, *Life Threatening Behavior, 4*:1, pp. 3-17, 1974.
14. J. R. Rogers, Female Suicide: The Trend Toward Increased Lethality in Method of Choice and Its Implications, *Journal of Counseling and Development, 69*:1, pp. 37-38, 1990.
15. J. M. Himmelhoch, What Destroys our Restraints Against Suicide? *Journal of Clinical Psychiatry, 49*:9, Suppl., pp. 46-52, 1988.
16. A. S. Rosecan, R. L. Goldberg, and T. N. Wise, Psychiatrically Hospitalized College Students: A Pilot Study. *Journal of American College Health, 41*:1, pp. 11-15, 1992.

CHAPTER 8

Postvention

> I expect that you assume no responsibility. I am assigning no blame. I am dead because I no longer believe in life, not because it has failed me. Reality for me is a trap. I believe that life is ultimately pointless. We don't know why we're here or how we got here, but we usually try anyway.
>
> —Sam (junior)

About a fourth of the people who commit suicide leave a note like this one. It was on the back of an envelope that contained some instructions on the disposition of Sam's personal effects and sealed envelopes which police gave to the people whose names were on them. For the person who committed suicide the intense pain is over. Now the pain begins for the survivors. Once again, there is the difficulty of discussing suicide. However, this time the difficulty is in talking about the suicide and meeting the needs of the survivors, efforts known as postvention.

Postvention is a relatively new term coined by Edwin S. Shneidman, founder-president of the American Association of Suicidology to "describe the help and intervention of others that is needed by *all* survivors of suicide (attempters, families of suicides, friends, associates, etc.) [1, p. 225]. I would suggest postvention goes beyond the Shneidman description of help and intervention to survivors. Rather, the derivations of the fraternal triplets of prevention (to come before, to anticipate), intervention (to come between) and postvention (to come after) suggest a common parentage—to come—which inextricably links them. Earlier I suggested that the more obscure meaning of prevention (to anticipate or counter in advance) provided that concept with two meanings. The first was to anticipate or counter in advance and the second was to preclude. Likewise the concept of intervention also has two meanings. The first is to come between and the second is to intercept and prevent. The concept of postvention, like its siblings, also has different meanings. The first of these is to come after and respond to the suicide. The second is to be part of both effective intervention with families *and* if its educational effect is used, to intervene with potentially suicidal persons and prevent their suicidal activity. All three concepts exist in interdependence with one another. All three concepts when used interactively and effectively can result in a powerful endeavor which could have some positive effects on the suicide rate of college and university students.

Postvention is an intervention with survivors. Who are the survivors of a suicide? The obvious answer is those persons who are part of the family of the person who committed suicide. They are easily identified and are the people usually responsible for the funeral arrangements. But, there are so many more! There are the members of the sports team, the brothers and sisters in the fraternity or sorority house, the residents of a residence hall, the members of a religious institution, the boyfriend or girlfriend, the lover, the spouse, the faculty members, the lab partners, the co-workers, in fact survivors include anyone whose life was touched in some way by the presence, and now the absence, of the person. Given that the death may not be socially recognized or deemed significant to these individuals, the members of these latter groups often are not thought of as survivors. LaGrand referred to these individuals as the forgotten grievers [2] and they have also been referred to as the disenfranchised grievers [3].

Grief is not reserved just for the completed suicide. It exists in the case of the attempted suicide because grief is the total emotional response of an individual to a loss. And there is loss following an attempted suicide. The attempt brings forth the emotions characteristically associated with loss, among them anger, relief, sadness, distress, anxiety, resentment, and confusion. The attempt can change relationships, immobilize families, destroy some friendships, and elicit new ones. Suicide is not a neutral action and the reactions from survivors are not neutral.

The aftermath of an attempted suicide involves two perspectives. First there is the perspective of the attempter who needs assistance to resolve his or her unmet needs. Second, there is the perspective of those individuals who were involved in the life of the attempter and their reactions to the attempt. This latter group may consist of family, friends, neighbors, people who were associated in a number of ways, and possibly counselors. It is usually a broader assemblage of people than expected as people touch each other in many ways and at different times.

What happens following a suicide attempt depends on a number of variables. There are times when the attempt may not even be recognized. An individual may make a very sub-lethal attempt through ingestion or minor cutting. Quite often these are covered up by the attempter and may never be known to anyone. Or they may be discovered by chance.

> I'd never seen Allison wear a jacket in the dining room before. She told me she was just chilly, but that was stupid it was so hot in there. She said she was tired and needed to get some rest so she left before the rest of the house finished dinner. After dinner I went to her room and asked her what was wrong. She said "Nothing." I asked her to take off the jacket and she started to cry. She took it off and showed me a bandage on her arm. Then I knew, but I didn't know what to do. She begged me not to tell the other girls in the house. She told me she had used a razor blade but had thrown it away. We talked for a long time. But, I don't know what to do now. It wasn't that bad, the bandages stopped the bleeding. But she's so afraid people will think she's crazy. I think she needs some help but how do I get her there.
>
> —Becky (junior)

An alert sorority sister discovered this attempt and convinced Allison to seek some help. The attempt remained known only to Becky, Allison, the therapist, and myself. In this instance, professional assistance was obtained. However, many such attempts go unnoticed and nothing happens unless a later attempt attracts attention.

There are also instances where the attempt is known but is felt to be simply an attention getting maneuver since there was little danger and the person making the attempt was very public about the action. Often these actions are not recognized as a "cry for help," but are regarded as manipulations. There is a need to have the action evaluated to determine more precisely what is happening in the life of this person. Manipulations can be dangerous as they tend to escalate when the initial desired effect is not achieved. This escalation could become a near-lethal or lethal accident where there was no intent to die but to produce another effect through a dramatic action. Low level lethality attempts can become part of an escalating pattern if the issues are not dealt with as soon as possible. These attempts can have significant long-range effects. In many instances there is an apprehension by the family and friends of "waiting for the other shoe to drop."

Then, there are those attempts that are observed, have varying levels of lethality and result in professional intervention. While the attempter is receiving counseling to facilitate resolution of his or her problems, quite often the students who have interacted with the person are simply waiting for the person to return to the residence hall, fraternity, or apartment. They are not certain how they should act when the person is released from a hospital, much less how to react while he or she is in therapy. This produces a significant tension for the individual and for his or her friends. It is important for peers to receive information on how to react to the individual to relieve some of their tension and so that they are not counterproductive during the individual's therapy.

An example of this type of occurrence took place when a male resident assistant, Julian, attempted suicide. The action would have been lethal except friends began to search for and found him. Julian was taken to a hospital where he remained in a locked ward for a period of time and then spent some time in an open ward. He had visitors from the residence hall throughout his period of hospitalization. Julian was very open and talked with residents about the experience and why he felt compelled to commit suicide. After this hospitalization, Julian returned to the residence hall and resumed his work on the floor. He noticed changes in the residents. They seemed to be very careful about what they said while he was present. One evening he heard a resident comment, "That's crazy!" Another resident said, "Shh, you know we can't use words like that around Julian." Another resident who had visited Julian in the hospital walked up to him and said, "Hi Julian, where have you been?" Julian called a floor meeting and told the residents they were driving him crazy through their actions. He had kept no secrets from them about his action, his hospitalization or his continuing therapy, so why were they acting this way. What happened was the residents could cope with Julian's attempt as long it was within the confines of the hospital. Once he was back in the residence hall there were no "rules of conduct" or social conventions upon which they could draw.

Attempters are going to reenter the college and university society. There needs to be an understanding that they are valuable members of the community. Students, staff, and faculty need to be able to openly communicate with the students. They need to be able to express their concern over the incident and, if they so choose, to make it known that should the student feel overwhelmed again, they are available. If this is not done, there is a distinct possibility the student will begin to feel alienated and isolated again as she or he is avoided by other students, faculty, and staff. For many there will be the feeling they were right. Their original feelings of alienation and isolation are now being verified by what they see and feel. What may have been a fantasy before has become a reality now.

The adherence to various forms of the mythology and fears about what might happen if we have contact with a suicidal person as well as the threat of becoming a survivor creates many barriers. Education and training can overcome these barriers and make students, faculty and staff more comfortable with their emotional reactions. For the suicidal student, the postvention after an attempt consists of professional intervention, psychotherapy, and sometimes medication to assist them in returning to a productive life. For those who are in contact with the student, the postvention after an attempt consists of education and training that will enable fellow students, faculty, and staff to contribute to the well being of the student.

Postvention in the aftermath of a completed suicide is a more complicated and traumatic experience. Survivors may have to deal with the initial shock without having an established pattern of behavior upon which they can rely. Staff may be involved with police, coroners, and other officials in circumstances where they have not had any experience. Administrators may be called upon by the media to answer questions for which they have no answers. Parents may arrive demanding answers to questions that no one can answer. The question, Why?" will be a dominant theme with many asking and not receiving any answer. A few years ago, in a meeting with Rabbi Harold Kushner, I noted that this question was the hardest one to cope with under these circumstances. His response synthesized many thoughts into a concise, powerful statement. "Remember, 'Why?' is not a question. It is a cry of pain." The "Why?" that we hear across the campus in the aftermath of a completed suicide is indeed the cry of a campus in pain—its students, its staff, and its faculty. Shneidman defined this happening in a different way [4]. He said, "The person who commits suicide puts his psychological skeleton in the survivor's closet" [4, p. 22].

The aftermath of a completed suicide is replete with powerful emotions. While accidents, natural deaths, and homicidal deaths of students are difficult situations, a death by suicide has a definite difference, the person apparently chose to die. I use the word apparently because I am personally aware of a couple of instances where the rescue possibilities that were calculated by the suicidal person almost did not take place. For instance, Lou wanted his roommate, Jim, to know that he was in severe psychological pain but could not figure out how to tell him. So, he planned to take all of his anti-depressant medication just a few minutes before Jim came back to the room after class. He believed that if Jim saw the empty vial and Lou lying on the bed he would get help. So, Lou carried out his part of the plan. Jim, on the other hand not knowing of his part in the plan, met a friend and spent some time in the student union drinking a coke and talking. When he returned some time later he found Lou unconscious and having difficulty breathing. Fortunately, Lou lived to tell of his plan as Jim called 911 for assistance. However, had Jim returned a half hour later Lou would probably have been dead and no one would ever have known that he did not want to die. Lou just wanted to try to tell someone about his pain. Still, the element of choice was there and for many the idea of attempting or choosing to die is a difficult concept.

There are three words that are often used interchangeably but which have different meanings in the language of dying and death. They have special significance to deaths by suicide. The first of these words is bereavement. The etymology of this word is from a root word meaning to be ripped or torn up. For survivors of suicide this is an apt description of how they feel. Their world has had a piece torn from it and it was ripped away by the same person who committed suicide. The second word is grief. Grief is the total emotional response of an individual to a loss. Grief in the aftermath of a suicide not only encompasses all the emotional range of any other death, but does so with an intensity usually not found in other types of deaths. The third word is mourning. Mourning is the process by which we incorporate the loss of the individual into our life histories and move forward eventually investing our energies in another relationship. Each of these—bereavement, grief and mourning—is a phase in the process that each individual in the campus community must move through to complete their adaptation to a loss by suicide.

LaGrand suggested that there are three pivotal issues relating to the resolution of losses in the lives of students [5]. These three issues are "initially confronting and dealing with one's emotions, relating these feelings and emotions to others in the hope of gaining understanding, and adapting to an environment without the person or object of loss" [5, p. 247]. Respectively, these are concise ways of describing how students cope with the processes of bereavement, grief, and mourning. As we assist students through these processes, we may need a cautionary note. We make assumptions about how individuals proceed with the process of coping with loss. Wortman and Silver examined some assumptions and found they do not always hold true [6]. In their review of the myths of coping with loss they stated that 1) depression does not inevitably follow a loss, 2) distress is not a necessary factor in resolving grief, 3) many people continue to exhibit distress far longer than commonly assumed, and 4) for some individuals a resolution of their loss may not be achieved. Their work reminds us that we are working with individuals and that individuals respond in an individual manner. Consequently, as we facilitate students in their movement through the bereavement, grief and mourning process, we need to recognize their vulnerability and their wide range of differences. And, we need to remind students of this as well.

BEREAVEMENT

The shock of a death by suicide seems to surpass the shock of any other death. Indeed, it is as though something had been ripped from the fabric of the campus. Depending upon the circumstances of the suicide and the prominence of the student on the campus there will be variations in the impact. Regardless of how limited or how expansive the impact, it is important that the campus have protocols in place to begin to cope with the trauma to the campus community.

Each campus will differ with regard to the internal staffing available, outside agency availability, and other factors. However, a coordinated and caring response by members of the institution is necessary to provide assistance and support to the survivors. The principal responders will probably be staff from the student affairs offices, public information office, residential life office, student counseling services and/or psychiatric unit, police department, and campus counsel. Students should be involved as they provide an excellent source of information for the development of campus action plans. More than anyone else, they have a sense of the "pulse of the campus" and can provide valuable advice about students' reactions to the proposed strategies. As an incident of attempted suicide will have an impact upon the campus, particularly residential groups, it is important to have a policy developed to cover such incidents. If a written policy is not in place, at least a more formalized understanding should be developed between various administrative staff members for consultation. Moorman, Urbach and Ross presented some guidelines for consultation with university personnel in the event of student psychiatric emergencies [7]. Their work addressed such issues as the student's right to confidentiality, the responsibility of the therapist to the student and the complexities involved in such an emergency. Their information provides a valuable resource for the development of campus guidelines including how to cope with difficult students. They point out that if the student is unwilling or unable to consent to contact with various persons,

> the psychiatrist needs to proceed on the basis of what he feels to be in the best interest of the student. Both long term (e.g., suicidal behavior) and short-term (stigmatization) consequences of consulting or not consulting need to be considered [7, p. 94].

The development of another campus' response was presented by Furr and Simpson [8]. It included a structure for the development of a policy and its use following a student death. They included the delineation of roles of campus groups, the variation in circumstances of a death, follow-up responsibilities, and the implementation and evaluation of the policy. They arrived at a conclusion that is very valid. "Being prepared for a tragedy that may never happen is a far superior strategy to making decisions in the midst of a crisis" [8, p. 21].

However, this is not the usual pattern for campus responses. Wrenn conducted a survey to determine how colleges managed student death and what these institutions found effective during the postvention process [9, 10]. He found there was often a lack of policy, very little training and difficulties relating to the relaying of information to official and other parties. To alleviate many of these problems, the following are questions that need to be addressed in developing a campus protocol before a death by suicide (or any other manner) occurs.

1. What individuals, offices or agencies are to receive immediate notification of a death by suicide? Is there a different protocol for weekends, evenings, weekdays, holidays, or working hours?

2. Who is responsible for making determinations relating to confidentiality issues and how are they to be contacted?

3. Who is responsible for contacting other individuals, offices or agencies that would have an important role in this response process?

4. Who is responsible for contacting the local police department?

5. Who is responsible for contacting the local coroner's office?

6. Who is responsible for contacting the parents of the deceased?

7. Who is responsible for contacting the roommate or other individuals in a small living unit?

8. Is there a campus emergency response team? Who is responsible for contacting team members? Are the members or someone else responsible for assessing the situation on the campus and determining the impact of the suicide on the campus?

9. Who is responsible for handling any unpredictable behavior that may occur as a result of the traumatic experience?

10. Who is responsible for handling media contacts? What are the guidelines for providing information? Are the guidelines consistent with the guidelines of the American Association of Suicidology (presented in Chapter 10)?

11. Who is responsible for rumor control on the campus?

12. Who is responsible for crowd control on or near the site of the suicide?

13. Who is responsible for securing the deceased's personal effects until they are released by the police and claimed by parents or next of kin?

14. Who is responsible for any room reassignment for survivors of the deceased if the suicide took place in a living area? What arrangements are to be made regarding the physical condition and equipment in the room?

15. Who is responsible for immediate intervention with the members of a residence hall, fraternity, sorority or other living group? Who is responsible for follow-up contact with the group?

16. Who notifies other offices on the campus of the death to avoid late fee mailings and overdue notices to the parents or next of kin?

17. Who sends a letter of condolence from the campus to the parents or the next of kin?

18. Who is responsible for any meeting with counsel for the family and/or reviewing any legal implications?

19. Who is responsible for a follow up assessment of the impact on the campus and any need for further intervention?

20. Who is responsible for debriefing the campus emergency team and making any recommendations for change in protocols as a result of the incident?

21. Who is responsible for filing reports, what reports are to be filed and within what period of time following the suicide?

22. Who is responsible for maintaining any records relating to the incident and for what period of time are these records to be maintained? Who has access to them?

23. Who is to be responsible for training that is needed, updating the protocols and convening either the emergency response team or an appropriate group of staff on a regular basis to review training needs as personnel and circumstances change.

There may be special issues relating to a particular campus that also need to be addressed. The protocols should be developed with consultation and cooperation between all departments that would be affected by a suicide on the campus. Protocols that are in place at the time of a suicide provide all segments of the campus with a defined format for action at a time when anxiety, sadness, and confusion dominate the campus.

> Our campus had always seemed so idyllic. No one ever thought any of *our* students would even consider suicide. After all, we were a school that prided itself on our Christian heritage. Then it happened and we somehow managed to work through it. Not without a lot of anxiety and some tense situations as we all had suggestions. We were lucky! There's no other word for it. We weren't prepared and there's no way we ever want to go through that again. It may never happen again, we hope it doesn't. But, we no longer live in delusion. We now are ready to deal with the reality.
>
> —Dean of Students

There is a Chinese proverb, "We cannot stop the birds of sorrow from flying over our heads. But we can prevent them from making nests in our hair." The establishment of working relationships that enhance the synergy of all segments of the campus community begins this process. Once the immediate crisis is past, there is a need to begin to work with the grieving process of the campus community.

GRIEF

Grief is the total emotional response to the event of loss. It begins with the shock of learning of the suicide and is characterized by disbelief, confusion, anxiety, bewilderment, anger, and often by feelings of total numbness. Individuals may experience significant denial as their defense mechanisms protect them from the full impact of the suicide.

When I opened the door and saw a young policeman standing there I could tell from the look on his face that something horrible had happened. Then I saw our priest standing next to him and all I could think of was that George (husband) had been hurt or killed in an accident. Father asked if they could come in and I let them in. I could only say, "What? What's happened to George?" "It's not George it's Greg. He hung himself in the gym. We just got the call from the campus police." I couldn't believe what Father had just said. I just stood there and my whole body was ice cold and I just started to shake. I couldn't believe a priest would lie, but I couldn't believe him. There had to be a mistake. We had just talked with Greg on the weekend and he said everything was fine. Fine! How the hell could everything be fine! Somebody had to be lying. It was like I was in a dream world. Nothing seemed real, for some crazy reason I asked them if they wanted some coffee.

—Greg's mother

When I turned the corner I saw a police car in front of our house and I just had this terrible feeling that something had happened to Peggy. I parked the car in the driveway and as I got to the front door, it opened and there was Father. He had a most peculiar look on his face. Peggy was standing by the sofa and she looked like she had seen a ghost. Father said, "I'm really sorry George, we just found out that Greg hung himself in the gym at school." I know that he said something else, but I didn't hear a thing. I just remember Peggy saying, "It has to be a mistake, Greg would never, never do anything like this." I held her and we just stood there, frozen. Father asked us to please sit down on the sofa and we did. I know he was talking, but I don't remember hearing him. I just remember seeing Greg as he was waving to us before he got in the car to go back to college. A hundred images from the past flashed in my mind. He was alive, this was some cruel hoax.

—Greg's father

After the shock begins to erode, the pain begins to increase and the level of affect changes. Crying may be followed by feeling abandoned. Angry outbursts may take place, directed at anyone or no one in particular. There may be a sense of disorientation and a need to be very exacting in details. The full range of human emotion may occur and emotions may change without regard for any "normalcy" because there is no normalcy. This intense period of grief is like any other grief and yet there is a special intensity of grief following a suicide.

There are a number of factors that make this grief different. Deaths from illness or old age can be anticipated. A death by suicide is usually not anticipated. Deaths from accidents or homicides are also unexpected but they usually are not precipitated by an action of the deceased. Deaths by suicide are committed by the deceased. A death by suicide is also seen as a violent act. The suicide is seen as a self-murder and the means of committing suicide are often very violent given that 65 percent of the men and 40 percent of the women who commit suicide do so by using firearms. Suicide may also evoke emotions that are usually not present in grief following other deaths. The suicide can provoke intense feelings of failure characterized by such questions as "What didn't I do?" or "If only I had . . ." Survivors' feelings of blame are characterized by such statements as "I should have been able to . . ." or "It's all my fault, I should have listened." Blame can become a very destructive force as survivors seek to find scapegoats. Blaming is represented by statements like "If he hadn't broken up with her this never would have happened!" or "I never wanted him to go away to school, but you insisted." Lastly, there are the feelings of guilt. "It's my fault for not . . ." or "If I had . . ." are typical of statements of guilt. Unfortunately, it seems that when the unexpected or the traumatic happens there is an almost uncontrollable desire to find a reason. This demanding urge to find a reason often ends up with an excess of blaming and guilt being assigned. Someone, or something, other than the deceased has to be responsible for this shocking act.

And then there's anger. Anger is a predominant emotion in the aftermath of a suicide. Survivors are angry at the deceased, at themselves, at others around them, and sometimes angry without any discernible object of their anger. Anger is a very powerful emotion and is the most repressed emotion following a suicide. Generally people are taught that anger is not an appropriate emotion—it is bad! Consequently, they are unable to fully express the range of their emotions because a particularly powerful emotion is not permitted. Anger may be appropriate and it may be inappropriate depending upon the circumstances. This needs to be communicated to the survivors so it does not become a destructive, internalized force. Unexpressed anger will be expressed and most likely at a time when it may be inappropriate. It may be a trite analogy, but it is a true one—unexpressed anger becomes like the volcano waiting to erupt. No one knows what will trigger the eruption, but it will be triggered. Like the volcano no one knows when it will happen, but it will happen.

As an example, while guest lecturing to a university class I made statements to the effect that I had not come across a survivor situation where there was no anger. Suddenly, a young man jumped up in the back of the classroom and shouted, "My father shot himself three years ago and I have never been angry with him!" The anger projected in this statement startled everyone in the classroom. I remarked, "You could have fooled me, I hear a very angry person." He continued to protest for a short time and then sat down. After the class he told me I was totally wrong and he was an instance where there was no anger and I had better accept it. He left the room and the regular class instructor agreed she would need to be aware of him. A few weeks later the instructor told me the young man had run across the street to meet her. He asked if she remembered him and she acknowledged she did (he would be hard to forget). He said that while sitting in the living room with his house mates he had suddenly begun sobbing and was unable to explain what was happening to his friends. The next morning a friend accompanied him to the counseling services. He said, "I was taught to honor my father and my mother. To be angry at my father was to dishonor him and I couldn't do it. That guy was right, I was very angry. But I hadn't learned how I could love my father and at the same time hate what he did. But, I'm learning and I thought you'd like to know."

There is the emotional response to the person who committed suicide and an attitude toward those persons who were most intimately connected to the deceased, especially the family. Research has been conducted in both areas and there are some studies that provide important information on these responses. Gordon, Range and Edwards studied the reactions of college students and their parents to fictitious reports of deaths [11]. They found reactions to a suicidal death were more negative than to a non-suicidal death by both groups. Students did not view the deceased as being as psychologically disturbed as did the parents. Students indicated they would be more tense and have greater trouble expressing sympathy to the family than did the parents. Parents indicated they would have a less positive liking towards the parents of a suicide. Gordon et al. believed this information would be useful to persons who interact with students and parents in the aftermath of a suicide. They suggested further study to validate their findings.

Goldney, Spence and Moffit used the Aftermath of Suicide Instrument to determine the experiences of some people who were immediate survivors, psychiatric social workers and a community sample [12]. Both the bereaved and the community sample agreed suicide was caused by mental illness (which is often a common view). Goldney et al. suggested there may be another reason for this interpretation. "It is possible that such a view may grow out of denial of the interpersonal components of suicidal behavior, thus minimizing one's personal responsibility in a given suicide case" [12, p. 146]. The community sample reflected some social stigma in their responses. They stated they would be less likely to invite friends to a suicide's funeral, would probably not mention the suicide's name when talking with the family and would perceive shame as an appropriate emotion for the family. Social workers disagreed "markedly" with the bereaved and with the community sample about the role of mental illness in suicide" [12, p. 146] and were viewed as sympathetic to the family. The role of mental health professionals to the family and other survivors is important. The reaction of college mental health professionals can be extremely helpful to the survivors as they provide both professional support and empathy.

That mental health professionals may be the major support for survivors was illustrated in a study by Thornton, Whittemore and Robertson [13]. "Since the emotional and social support that the griever receives helps modulate the effects of the death, knowledge about various factors that influence these supports is important" [13, p. 122]. They found there were fewer social supports when there was a death by suicide as evidenced by a greater likelihood of the survivor being held responsible for the suicide. This would certainly exacerbate feelings of guilt and blame and further complicate an already complicated grieving and mourning process. These circumstances need to be anticipated and become a part of the caregiver's support for the survivors.

As students will be survivors when there is a suicide on campus, it is important to understand how they perceive the grief process. Vickio, Cavanaugh and Attig studied 123 undergraduate students (48 males, 75 females) and found there was "substantial awareness of the various facets of the grief process, including the emotional, physical, interpersonal and temporal features" [14, p. 239] and sensitivity to grief reactions due to various circumstances. This study did not deal specifically with grief after suicide and there may be differing reactions following a suicide. It is noteworthy, however, that sensitivities to the grief process are present in the student body.

What happens on a campus when a suicide or other death takes place was explored by Thompson and Range in a study involving 112 undergraduates (32 males, 80 females) [15]. This group was selected from about 400 students to match bereaved students with non-bereaved students. They found considerable differences in the perspectives of the two groups. The bereaved recalled more blame and less helpfulness in the support process and were viewed as extremely vulnerable. When there was a suicide, the responses of the non-bereaved were more varied and extreme. This included less helpful statements like, "put it behind you" and "go out and have fun," and helpful statements like "you're not to blame" or "he's at peace." The non-bereaved students believed they knew how to comfort and provide support for the bereaved but were unable to do so.

From the last two studies it is apparent there is a knowledge of the grief process and a belief that students know how to address the grief of their peers. However, knowledge and desire do not necessarily translate into effective action. This may happen because the responders believe that they will "say something wrong" or it may occur because they have no familiar patterns of behavior in their interpersonal skills repertoire to cope with a suicide. Educational institutions can facilitate the development of these skills through various means.

To cope with the pain of the campus and to lessen the effect of the "skeleton in the closet," institutions should take a proactive approach. At the very least this would mean there would be literature readily available to provide information for students. Educational programming to assist in the development of responding skills would be a further step. Indeed, if peers were trained to respond in what their peers perceive to be the most helpful manner, by "expressions of personal willingness to help or listen" [16, p. 30] it would greatly assist the bereaved as well as the general campus climate. A further step would be for institutions to have teams of paraprofessional or professional staff trained and ready to respond to a death or deaths on the campus or affecting the campus community. The availability of support groups is another tactic that can develop a positive campus climate. These support groups can be provided through the counseling or mental health centers and engage in significant therapeutic intervention. There are two different groups that can be organized. The first would be a group for those students who have either seriously considered or attempted suicide in the past. Suicides on a campus can elicit painful memories for those who have had serious suicidal ideation or who have made attempts. There are probably few of these groups in existence. The second would be a group for the survivors of suicide.

There have been a number of survivors' groups developed in the general community, but there appears to be only a modest effort to do this on campuses.

Some useful information that can be adapted for use in these groups has been developed by Berenson [17]. While this support group was designed for college students who had suffered a death in the family, Berenson describes the course of this time-limited model and makes suggestions for the use of similar groups. Freeman offered a structured format specifically related to students bereaved by suicide [18]. He utilized Yalom's curative factors [19], Parkes' stages of grief [20] and Worden's tasks of grief resolution to facilitate movement through the grieving process [21]. Freeman's structure was a closed-ended group that met for two hours a week for eight weeks. The self-evaluation of the group members indicated that it had been helpful. A more open ended model that continued over an eighteen month period was initiated by Balk, Tyson-Rawson and Colletti-Wetzel [22]. They developed a social support group intervention designed to assist any bereaved college student. They found that the commonality of experience among group members enabled an openness and sharing of emotions. The leader of the group had to be able to tolerate intense emotional situations as well as integrate didactic materials that would assist group members. The group functioned most productively when it followed its own natural progression as opposed to a set agenda. This material is useful in developing support groups for students.

USE OF LITERATURE

The least involved method is to make literature available where students congregate on the campus—student union, residence hall, health service, or any other place appropriate to an individual campus. The information is available and accessible. This gives students permission to pick up the material. The literature may relate to suicide in general such as the booklet, *The Issue is Suicide* which was developed at the University of Minnesota [23]. In twelve pages there is a brief introduction, some facts and myths about suicide, indicators of suicide, intervention tactics, a list of referral agencies, comments on grief in the aftermath of a suicide and a bibliography of selected books. The booklet is available in college offices, student union, health service, counseling service, residence halls and police department. Chee's reaction sums up its usefulness.

Can I talk to you about this booklet I picked up on campus? You see, I saw it in my dorm and I was really surprised since we wouldn't have thought about anything like this on my old campus. It was, like, taboo! Anyway, I read it and realized that my friend is doing a lot of things that are mentioned in the book and I'm really concerned. I like what it says to do, but I need to know more because I'm not sure exactly what to do.

—Chee (junior)

Another booklet that is more specific to the grief process is *Grief After Suicide* [24]. This eight page booklet discusses the emotions following a suicide and looks to the future. Having this booklet in an open, well-traveled area allows students to pick up the material and read it without having to discuss their reasons for doing so with anyone. Many students need to begin their explorations in this non-threatening manner.

Another tactic is to develop educational programming and training. Educational programs conducted on the campus provide students with accurate information, lessen the effect of mythology, give permission to students to express their emotions when they are bereaved and encourage other students to engage in helpful, supportive behaviors.

Training programs can provide para-professional staff (i.e., resident assistants, health advocates, peer counselors) with the background that will enable them to engage in prevention, intervention, and postvention activities. These same training programs can be developed in greater detail for student affairs personnel, campus security/police departments and other campus staff. Some suggestions for training programs for student affairs staff have been made by Butler and Statz [25], and for training residence hall staff by Jacobs and Towns [26] and Charles and Eddy [27].

Minimally, a training program needs to address the following:

- the incidence of suicide nationally, on campuses, and, if possible, on the specific campus.
- attitudes towards suicide in general and by those who are involved in the training program in particular.
- understanding of the process of bereavement, grief and mourning in general, and as they relate to a death by suicide in particular.
- knowledge of the clues to impending suicidal action.
- knowledge of intervention tactics.
- knowledge of postvention tactics.
- knowledge of the campus policies and procedures relating to deaths on campus.

INTERVENTION TEAMS

The suicidal death of a friend, classmate, neighbor on a residence hall floor, fraternity brother or sister or sports team member creates a significant trauma in the lives of students. They are not only confronted with their feelings of loss, but they are reminded of their own mortality at a time when they feel invulnerable. The conflicts that take place create anxiety and uncertainty. For students, under these circumstances, "when a death occurs, particularly of an unexpected nature, there is no pattern of behavior to draw upon, and confusion results" [28, p. 105]. It is at this point that an educational institution can move beyond its routine, its impersonal role and procedures and engage in a significant and meaningful relationship with the survivors. This can be achieved through the development of a team of professional, para-professional, or a combination of both, persons who will engage in an intervention with the group that has been affected. The description of the development of a team to provide information and support to students will be that of the University of Minnesota's Death Response Team [29].

At the University of Minnesota there were a number of services available for students. However, simply having the information and offices available did not meet the needs of students. There was a need for staff to move from a passive to an activist stance by reaching out to students and meeting them where they lived, in the fraternity and sorority houses and in residence halls.

Initially, the concept was to develop a team which would respond to suicide deaths only. Staff from housing services, counseling services, mental health clinic, police department, office of the vice president for student affairs, campus clergy and public health faculty met and discussed the necessity for an organized effort to meet the needs of students following any death of a student. Numerous questions were raised during the discussions including the objectives, who would be involved as team members, the establishment of contact points, departmental auspices and legal liabilities.

The group determined that the objective of the newly named Death Response Team would be to provide a professionally trained volunteer group who would respond to requests from residence hall groups, fraternity and sorority house groups, sports clubs and other organized student groups when the death of a member occurred. Initially, the intent was to provide services to only student groups. However, as the reputation of the Team spread throughout campus, the Team has responded to faculty and departmental groups requesting interventions.

The Team provides the following types of service to these groups:

1. To serve as a resource to facilitate individual and/or group reactions to the death of a member of that group. This would include telephone and on-site consultation, counseling and group meeting(s).
2. To serve as a resource for follow-up consultation and/or counseling services for the group and its members.
3. To serve as a referral resource for individual(s) or group(s) which required either short or long term counseling contact to resolve the issues brought about by the death.

At the University, the Team consists of professionally trained counselors, psychologists, social workers, and chaplains. For the University this resolved the issue of legal liability as all staff would be acting within the scope of their professional responsibilities. Campuses that do not have enough professionally trained staff may have to either recruit members from the community and/or train para-professionals to assist in the effort and make determinations about how to manage potential liability.

While the University Police Department is the twenty-four hour contact point for the Team, contact may also be made through any residence hall director or the counseling service. Each contact point maintains a list of Team members who have agreed to be contacted and will respond to these requests. The Team functions under the departmental auspices of University Counseling and Consulting Services.

When a Team member is contacted, he or she initiates an assessment of the situation with the contact person. Decisions are made whether an immediate intervention is needed because of severe distress within the group or if there should be a short delay (a day or two) to permit the reduction of the effect of shock and to notify all members of the date, and place of the meeting. The Team attempts to engage in rumor control through specific members of the group to avoid distortions and misinformation that can create greater difficulties. The Team member then contacts another member so there will usually be two Team members present at the intervention. This permits one Team member to be engaged with the survivors while the other observes the reactions of the group or individual members.

Before the meeting, Team members meet with the leaders of the group, residence hall director or resident assistant to learn of any new consequences that might affect the group. The Team is alerted to the possibility of any group members who may be having particularly difficult reactions.

The Team is introduced by a member of the host group. Team members discuss the purposes of their visit, the dynamics of loss and grief and ask members of the group to share their own reactions. Group members are advised they should not expect their reactions to mirror that of others as they are all individuals who are reacting as individuals. This is particularly reassuring to members of the group as they do not want to appear different from their peers and may feel isolated by their reactions if they are not synchronous with other members of the group. The session lasts between two and three hours during which time members of the group share their reminiscences of the deceased, the reaction that they have had to the death and the effect the death has had upon the community. The Team members encourage interaction and ask members for clarification of their statements. Special efforts are made to support members who have apparently taken some risk to reveal their relationship with the deceased and to discuss openly their emotions. At the end of the session, the Team members summarize what they have perceived happening during the session and ask for summaries from members of the group. The Team members also provide information on the various counseling and crisis facilities that are available and encourage group members to use these facilities if they have some unresolved issues they would like to discuss in a more private setting. The Team members also announce that they will remain for a while after the meeting to talk with any individuals who have specific issues.

After the session, the Team members again meet with the leaders or staff and assess the intervention and make some initial determination about possible follow-up meetings. Concerns about reactions of specific individuals are expressed to the leaders or staff together with suggestions about interventions with these individuals. Staff members or leaders are encouraged to express any concerns they have and Team members address these concerns.

The following morning, Team members alert the counseling services about the intervention (if this has not been done previously) and briefly discuss the situation. This allows the counseling service to be prepared for walk-ins, which happen frequently.

At least once a quarter the Team members meet and report on the interventions that have taken place. Experiences are shared, feedback is given to the members and future intervention tactics are discussed. Team members are also brought up to date on the incidence of deaths on the campus since not all deaths have Team intervention. This is particularly important in a large commuter school such as the University of Minnesota where many deaths take place off campus. Some of these deaths are reported directly to the campus but others are discovered by campus people reading newspapers or being told of a death. When deaths are reported, the accuracy of the report is determined. If the report is correct, notifications are mailed to a number of offices to delete the person's name from mailing and other lists, for example.

While the Death Response Team was initially formed to work with student groups, the positive nature of the Team's efforts has become widely known on the campus. This has resulted in interventions with faculty, staff and office groups as well as mixed groups of staff and students.

A similar team can be formed on any campus. Donahue [30], Hipple, Cimbolic and Peterson [31], Moats [32], Crafts [33], Zinner [34], Halberg [35] and Scott, Fukuyana, Dunkel and Griffin [36] all provide information and variations on the Team concept that can be used in the development of a model for any particular institution.

In the brochure that is used to advertise the services of the Team at the University of Minnesota, the following statement is made. "Death intrudes itself into campus life suddenly and significantly. The time of the quarter, the press of midterms, the interruptions of routines—none of this matters when someone within the University community dies as a result of an accident, a homicide, natural causes, or suicide. A group of individuals at the University of Minnesota, from such diverse areas as the University Counseling Service, Boynton Health Service, Public Health faculty, Housing Services staff, campus clergy and the University Police Department, met and discussed how to best meet the needs of groups when a member of that group dies. Out of these discussions the concept of the Death Response Team was developed. The Team is now available to serve your organization or group." In this manner the Team had taken the University beyond its routines, its rather impersonal roles and procedures and its large size. Team members become truly involved with the men and women of the University at the moment when their lives have been diminished by the death of a friend, a colleague, a teammate, another human being who has a special relationship with them.

SUPPORT GROUPS

The Death Response Team is an example of a singular event support group. However, in the event of a suicide the survivors may need an ongoing support group to assist them in their grief and mourning process. There has been a significant proliferation of suicide survivor groups in communities through the nation. But this does not appear to be the practice on campuses. The general impression seems to be that students have the services of counseling offices where they can work one on one on the resolution of their concerns with a counselor. However, on many campuses either due to limited staff, budgetary constraints or both, there is not enough time to engage in individual counseling without significant waiting periods between sessions.

There is a second group that can use the services of a group therapy situation. This group consists of those students who have either seriously considered or actually attempted suicide and who have unresolved issues related to these events. These students also can benefit from a suicide support group situation. While individual therapy has been the primary mode of therapy for suicidal students, Hipple has noted that there were twelve articles written on the use of group treatment of suicidal persons [37]. Hipple's article provides an overview of some essential aspects of a counseling group for suicidal individuals. He points out that the therapists' style (3 therapists are recommended for a group) must be active, directive and confrontive while at the same time supportive and accepting. Clients should be moderate to high suicidal risk and that there be very specific group limits relating to behavioral acting out and other matters. There is a necessity for the immediate crisis to be discussed so that alternatives can be developed. Mechanisms for emergency hospitalization and crisis management need to be in place. Hipple noted that while these groups have been underutilized in the past, the increasing numbers of suicidal students on campuses may require this therapeutic format be used to best utilize human resources.

The use of a group therapy model for these two student groups may seem unusual, particularly for the students who have experienced significant ideation or made attempts. Often these students feel this part of their life history is shameful or no one will understand their experience. For these and other reasons the student's suicidal experience may inhibit them from expressing their emotion should they again begin to become depressed or again experience suicidal ideation. In my conversations with students who had undergone these experiences, it appeared that resolution of the suicidal experience was incomplete. For this reason, a suicide support group was formed at the University of Minnesota. A staff member from University Counseling Services and I acted as facilitators for the group. Posters on the campus solicited participation by students who had seriously considered or attempted suicide and who believed they still had issues to resolve. Intake evaluations were performed and a couple of students were referred for individual therapy because of their high suicidal risk. Unlike Hipple's group format, the students in this group were low to moderate risk. For the members of this group, this was the first time they had been with a group of students who shared similar experiences. The therapeutic value of the group may be illustrated by a quotation from a student involved in the suicide support group as he was being interviewed on a campus television program.

> It was a normal thing, but I reacted in an abnormal way. After the attempt you go on, you just move forward I guess. I move a lot sideways, but I make strides I guess. I find the easiest thing to do is to talk to a group of people who know what you're feeling and that's the main reason I'm in the group I'm in now. Our support group meets once a week on campus. We sit and talk, you know, we can talk about anything. We can bring up anything, it's non-judgmental. There's two counselors and they do a really good job. They know what questions to ask and can bring things out of you in a non-threatening type of way. It's really nice to know you can go there and say anything and know that you're not going to be judged and you can go there and find out that a lot of things that you're feeling and a lot of thoughts you have are normal.
>
> —Dean (junior)

Group therapy for these students is like group therapy for any other group that needs assistance in the resolution of specific needs. Group therapy provides an opportunity for members of the group to come to the realization they are not unique in their needs or interests, that there are others who also experience similar types of pain or discomfort and who want to make changes in their lives, to eliminate these adverse situations. The group members are supportive of each other because they can draw upon each other's strengths and challenge each other's perceptions of inadequacy.

A group therapy model developed by Yalom provides a solid framework for both the suicide survivors and suicide support group [19]. Yalom suggests that "therapeutic change is an enormously complex process and occurs through an intricate interplay of various guided human experiences, which I shall refer to as 'therapeutic factors'" [19, p. 3]. Yalom's factors are:

1. Instillation of hope.
2. Universality.
3. Imparting of information.
4. Altruism.
5. The corrective recapitulation of the primary group family.
6. Development of socializing techniques.
7. Imitative behavior.
8. Interpersonal learning.

9. Group cohesiveness.
10. Catharsis.
11. Existential factors.

From my viewpoint, these factors provide a solid basis for the development of the two groups. Each of these factors will be reviewed with a commentary on their impact upon each group. The suicide survivors group will be identified as "survivors" and the suicide support group identified as "support."

Instillation of Hope

Survivors

In the aftermath of a suicide there is an overwhelming feeling of helplessness together with all the other emotional impact. The intensity will vary with the degree of intimacy that the survivor had with the deceased as well as the previous life experience of the survivor. Within these groups there is a need for the instillation of hope. From my experience, the survivor who is seeking a support group does so because he or she already accepts the group process and hopes that the group will make a difference in their chaotic life. As groups develop and continue there will be individuals who have already begun the process of resolution. They provide hope for the newcomer as they relate their positive experiences to the group. The survivor can begin to understand that his or her personal pain, while different in some respects from others in the group, also has a common basis, hence the possibility of a common healing.

Support

The person who has experienced serious suicidal ideation or has attempted suicide, may believe that they are "outcasts," that there is no one else who has experienced what they have endured. They have found that very few people want to listen to this traumatic part of their life experience. In the group they encounter other students who have had similar experiences and share similar emotional baggage. There is a sensation of "if they have made it, so can I."

Universality

Survivors

As student survivors share with each other their experiences it becomes apparent that they are no longer "alone." The stresses that they have endured as a result of the suicide are recognized by others. Their grief is recognized and their psychological and physical pains are understood by both the members of the group and the counselors. Survivors are often socially isolated by their peers and others who cannot cope with the trauma of a suicide,

> I knew I had to talk about Mike's suicide. I wanted people to know about him and what a really neat person he was. I wanted them to know that he meant a lot to me, that we were good friends. And, I also knew that I needed to talk about the awful feelings I had because of his suicide. I thought I knew who my friends were. I really thought I knew who would listen and care about how I felt. Instead, I found that every time I would even mention Mike's suicide people would find an excuse to do something else, to get away. I confronted one of our best friends and asked him if he didn't have any feelings because he wouldn't talk about it. He just said, "I can't." and walked away. I began to think I was really weird and wondered if I was going crazy too.
>
> —Lisa (sophomore)

Particularly with college students, the group can provide a universality, a similarity that is important for a person struggling to be an individual who still walks, talks and acts like those around him or her.

Support

Even with the significant numbers of students who have and are experiencing suicidal ideation and/or attempting suicide there is a feeling of uniqueness. Indeed, no one else may have experienced their psychological pain for precisely the same reasons. However, within the group they can find others who shared similar experiences. Yalom noted that secrecy may often be an isolating factor. For individuals who enter a support group this is often very true as they have not previously confided their ideation and they may have concealed an attempt.

> My parents never knew what made me so ill. They were gone so they never heard the vomiting and I had cleaned it all up. But, I was still shaking and crying when they came home. I told them I thought I had the flu. Dad wanted to take me to the doctor, but I didn't want to go. I was afraid they would find out what I did so my Mom stayed with me the rest of the night. I just couldn't tell them and hurt them and I felt so guilty about it and I still do.
>
> —Shirley (senior)

In addition to this type of secrecy, there is the secrecy that may be imposed through a family reaction of "we don't want anyone to know what happened. We'll just keep it within the family." The result is a feeling that this is a very shameful act. Further emotional distress may be inflicted if the individual feels she or he will be blamed if the community discovered the family secret. Self-disclosure about the ideation and/or attempt by members of the group provides a commonality, a sharing of this life experience with others.

Imparting Information

Survivors

Within this group, those who have been in the group for some time can provide personal testimony about their experiences and what has resulted from their interaction with other group members and the counselors. The counselors can provide information on the recovery process. This can probably be done more successfully by weaving the information into the discussions thus avoiding a more formalized or teaching style of information giving. The providing of information serves the purposes of legitimizing the survivor's emotional reactions and acknowledging their individuality as well as their commonality with the remainder of the group and integrates this factor with others such as universality. These factors do not operate in isolation.

Support

For members of the support group there seems to be a unique need for each individual to recount his or her suicidal experience. Later the factor of catharsis will be discussed, but it appears that it is extremely relevant and therapeutic for the attempter to be able to present the details to a group which he or she believes understands the dynamics more clearly because of their similar experiences. Once this catharsis takes place, the individual appears to be ready to move toward a resolution of the issues surrounding the attempt. This is a unique form of imparting information for the attempter. In an interactional format both members and counselors can provide information on the psychodynamics of suicide. Often there is a need for the counselors to provide information so that members will not feel they are abnormal. An example would be reassuring a group member that his or her feelings of anxiety about revealing suicidal ideation to a family member are not unusual. The counselors' most productive method for providing information is by interweaving the information into the discussions of the group.

Altruism

Survivors

The concern for the welfare of others may seem an odd part of a survivors' group. Members seem to have their own "burden" and often perceive themselves as incapable of adequately coping with their own loss let alone provide solace and comfort to another in similar circumstances. For students, in particular, this may seem an insurmountable task. And, yet in the interactions within the group a sense of wanting to help the other person develops. Members discover that sharing their experiences creates a sense of belonging (universality)— "we're all in this together"—and a sense of hope begets a further development of self esteem. As levels of self disclosure deepen, each member discovers she or he has something of value to contribute. Counselors play an important role in this process by acknowledging the contributions of the members and seeking feedback from other members about the impact this is having upon them. The ultimate culmination is the group where people can feel needed.

Support

Because of the stigma of suicide, ideators and attempters may find it difficult to believe they could have anything to offer that would assist another person in understanding their own situation. They've all heard the comment, "You'd have to be crazy to do anything like that!" If they are "crazy" or mentally ill what could they possibly offer anyone. Within this group, the role of the counselor is to provide appropriate, positive feedback to members who make contributions to the group and to solicit contributions from those who are reluctant to share their experiences. In this manner members of the group begin to share their experiences and realize this is helpful to others. The desire to be able to offer something that assists another member develops throughout the group process.

Corrective Recapitulation of the Primary Family Group

Yalom stated that "without exception, patients enter group therapy with the history of a highly unsatisfactory experience in their first and most important group—the primary family" [19, p. 15]. The group resembles a family and the interactions within the group may resemble reactions with parents, siblings or significant others. The task is to challenge and correct such issues as fixed roles, relationships that inhibit growth and unfinished business while at the same time encouraging productive, new behaviors. I would suggest that within a college or university setting, students often develop new "families" which may resemble their family of origin. Authority figures such as professors, deans, residence hall directors, and residence assistants may become surrogate parents. Members of a fraternity, sorority, sports club, or residence hall floor may become surrogate siblings. The interactions between the student and these individuals becomes a secondary family experience. Consequently, the disruption of a suicide will have similar effects upon their reaction and interaction with members of this surrogate family (and very likely with their own family as well) which may manifest itself in behavior on the campus.

Survivors

Survivors are often trapped in specific family roles that are now intensified as the result of a suicide. For example, a male student has become the leader or a "big brother" in a group. He has said that this is very natural for him because he has always been the "man in the family" since his father died while he was in high school. He is now confronted with the suicide of one of his close friends in the group. He may not want to be the leader or big brother at this time when he is attempting to cope with his own grief. However, members of the group will want the stability of his leadership and may even demand that he fulfill this role. So he searches for a group to help him cope with this unwanted responsibility.

> I can't take this any more. When my dad died it was bad enough that I had to be the "man of the family" since I was the oldest. I didn't do anything after that. I mean I didn't have any fun or go out with the guys. I always had to be taking care of family business. We could have hired someone to do it but mom thought that was a waste of money and she was so worried about money even though there was plenty. Someone even said I looked like I was "seventeen going on forty" because I was replacing my dad and that was how old he was. I didn't feel good and I was afraid I would have a heart attack and die like he did. Obviously I didn't even though at times it seemed easier. Now, here I am again. Everybody wanting me to take over again. I just can't do it.
>
> —Sean (sophomore)

For Sean, a survivors' group would enable him to cope with his grieving of two deaths and an opportunity to seek out new ways of relating to people without becoming the exclusive leader. For many other survivors, the suicide may elicit emotions connected to past family struggles and unresolved issues. While survivors enter the group with a primary purpose of learning how to cope effectively with the immediate trauma of a suicide death, the suicide may open a very large and complicated Pandora's box of unresolved business from within either the primary or the secondary family.

Support

Suicidal individuals bring with them many issues relating to their families. "Family" does not necessarily mean only parents and siblings, but it can include a very extended family including grandparents, aunts, uncles and cousins. While many of these issues will relate to the functioning of the primary family in terms of conflicts, and rigid roles and rules, there often are very specific issues such as alcohol use and abuse, and physical and sexual abuse that have created a very dysfunctional family unit. A further complication may be that the family does not wish to recognize suicidal ideation or an attempt because it would reflect adversely upon the family. The attempt becomes an "accident" leaving the original contributing factors unresolved and even further complicated by the denial of the attempt.

There are several other scenarios that could be discussed. However, the point is the family can be a major component of suicidal behavior and this needs resolution within the group.

Development of Socializing Techniques

Survivors

A major issue with survivors is how they will react and interact with people in various settings. Students are generally anxious not to appear significantly different from their peers. Their past experience has usually not included the development of social skills related to coping with the suicidal death of a peer. Such questions as "How do I talk to people about this? I don't want to say anything wrong." or "I don't know what to wear. Will people think I don't care if I wear the dress I wore on our date?" or "We had a party scheduled for three weeks from now. Should we do it?" or "I can't even look her boyfriend in the face because I don't know what to say. What can I do?" Survivor groups permit students to talk about their emotional reactions and the behaviors they see happening as well as their own. The group provides an opportunity for testing skills through the use of role plays where members receive feedback from the group and counselors. In this "laboratory" setting they can develop the new skills needed to cope with the process of bereavement, grief and mourning.

Support

For these individuals the group provides them with the opportunity to learn how to discuss their suicidal behavior appropriately with other students as well as their primary family. It provides an opportunity for them to vent their frustrations when they find other people either ignoring or denying their suicidal behavior. This is also a time when they can learn new skills for reintegrating themselves into their previous social groups. Their previous social groups may not know how to react to them after they return from a hospitalization fearing that something they say may trigger another suicidal response. While unfortunate, it may become the person's responsibility to teach the members of the group how to effectively interact with him or her. The group provides the members with two different yet integrated forms of developing socializing techniques. The first of these is to develop social skills to reintegrate themselves into social groups. The second is to encourage the development of new socializing techniques for members of these social groups to facilitate the reintegration of the student back into the group. There may be instances where the student may have to develop new social support groups as previous groups may be unwilling to adapt to the new circumstances and realities.

Imitative Behavior

Survivors

The observation of new behaviors being modeled by both group members and counselors can have a significant impact upon survivors. Survivors are often "stuck" with the idea that they are expected to behave in certain prescribed ways after any death, but particularly after a suicide. One of the most pronounced destructive behaviors following a suicide is the "we don't talk about it" syndrome. Within the group, survivors can talk about the suicide and the fact that their fellow group members are doing so in an open and honest fashion encourages similar behavior. The group becomes the place where they can develop new behaviors as well as a safe place to express their emotions. In the group, survivors can discover new ways to cope with their loss and to function effectively within their peer group. As their behavioral repertoire increases and they perceive positive feedback they become models for the newest members of the group. At this point they are not only modeling new behaviors for the instruction of new members, but they are gaining positive feedback on their new behaviors and further developing their own self esteem.

Support

When the idea of a suicide support group was first proposed at the University of Minnesota, I received many comments to the effect, "suicide support group, what are you going to do, teach them how to do it?" There was concern the group would develop imitative behaviors that would be negative. There was some risk students might seek out the group to justify their suicidal behavior or gain support for their actions. As co-counselors, we made it very clear at the beginning of the group that we were all in the group to enable members to work through the issues that had brought them to this group. We also asked members to support each other in a positive manner. One of the groundrules was that no member would attempt or commit suicide while they were in the group. All members agreed to this groundrule and agreed that they would either contact one of the counselors or another group member should they have suicidal thoughts. During the course of the group, one member made a suicidal gesture by ingesting a small amount of aspirin. When this was revealed, it was the group members who immediately confronted the behavior and unanimously stated this was unacceptable and a violation of their pact. The individual apologized to the group and stated she was now convinced that the group members did care about her and it would not happen again. There were no further incidents during the group process. As group members disclosed their concerns it became apparent that sexual assault was a commonality and the resolution of this issue provided several opportunities for members to develop imitative behavior as they adapted what worked for other individuals to their own life situation. Imitative behavior is a powerful tool for individuals who have come from situations where hopelessness and helplessness were predominate factors in their psychological lives.

Interpersonal Learning

Survivors

Survivors often have significant interpersonal distortions because of the relative rarity of death by suicide. These distortions occur because the survivors are not certain how they are being perceived by their peers, their friends or their colleagues. It seems that the closer the relationship the greater the distortions.

> God, I don't know what people are thinking about me. They probably think I'm some kind of an uncaring monster. Barb and I dated from high school days and things weren't going so well for us now

and most people knew we weren't getting along too well this past couple of weeks. We had some, well, shouting matches because I didn't think we were ready to get married and she did. Then this happened. I know people are saying I'm the reason she killed herself. Her friends won't even speak to me, they look at me like . . . I can't even tell you how it feels.

—Doug (sophomore)

The importance of interpersonal relationships is illustrated by Doug's belief the community was blaming him for his girlfriend's death. The rejection he was experiencing could have a basis both in reality and in his imagination. The apparent rejection by Barb's friends was being translated into the distortion of total rejection. Participation in a survivor's group can facilitate the development of interpersonal learning so that the individual can begin to discern what is reality and what is fantasy. In addition, the group provides an outlet for the pain that he or she is feeling. It is not uncommon for people to begin to move away from a dying individual and to begin to speak as though the person was already dead, a concept called "social death." In the same way, people avoid survivors. They may avoid the survivor by simply making certain that they have little or no physical contact. Where this is not possible, as in a living situation, the avoidance becomes manifested in verbal avoidance. No mention is made of the deceased or the relationship between the deceased and the survivor. For the survivor this is tantamount to becoming an outcast or as one student said, a social leper. For the survivors the group becomes a place where the acceptance of other members and their involvement with him or her is an essential part of the reconstructive process. The group becomes a place where the survivor can move through their tasks of mourning. Indeed, it is particularly in a survivor's group that students can work through Worden's four tasks of mourning [38]. They can accept the reality of the loss. They can effectively experience the pain of their grief. They can learn how to adjust to an environment in which the deceased is missing. And, lastly, they can learn how to emotionally relocate the deceased and move on with their lives. The group provides a social microcosm where students can learn how to function effectively during and after their recovery from loss.

Support

Interpersonal distortions are a common factor for students who have experienced ideation and/or attempts. They experience interpersonal distortions as a part of the process that brought them to serious ideation and/or attempting suicide. While they are attempting to recognize these distortions and relieve them, in the aftermath of an attempt they are also prone to further distortions much like those of the survivor. They may believe people have extremely negative thoughts about them and their behavior. They may experience real or imagined rejection at a time when there is a serious need for acceptance and involvement with other people. If interventions are not made, these distortions may become significant contributing factors that will propel the individual into their previous suicidal state of mind. Both members and counselors can challenge these distortions and engage the individual (and the entire group) in interpersonal learning. In this setting, members of the group can engage in appropriate risk taking behaviors to develop new ways of interacting with each other and with the community outside the group. An important part of this experience is the sharing of individual experiences as they engage in new behaviors within the community. Through feedback, members of the group can learn which behaviors seem to have the most successful impact and how to modify behaviors that seem to have a negative impact. As each individual's self esteem increases, the greater the risk taking becomes and the greater the degree of positive change. As with all therapy groups, eventually the group becomes unnecessary and the individual can say their thankful good-byes.

Group Cohesiveness

Survivors

Cohesiveness refers to the attraction that members have for the group as well as for each other. For survivors, this seems to be a natural happening as a "we-ness" develops. Students who are involved in survivors' groups have noted that there was an immediate acceptance as everyone in the group recognized the similarity of the members' experiences. There was acceptance and a sense of support combined with a genuine sense of approval for the student who had sought out the group to begin to resolve their survivor issues. It is not necessary that the survivors' group even have a commonality of age or experience for this to occur.

> I went to the group last night. I had a little difficulty finding it but I was determined to see if the things you talked about would really take place. When I walked in I was really scared since everyone seemed older. But, right away this man came up to me and introduced himself and just made me feel like I was OK there. Two of us were new I found out as we went around and introduced ourselves

and told why we were there. I really liked the guy who was one of the leaders. He let me know I could say as much as I wanted to. I said a lot more than I thought I would. I cried. I never thought I would do that in a group but it was OK. I'm going back next week and I want Mike to come with me if he will. I had my doubts, but it does work and they're neat people. Thanks.

—Chet (senior)

The cohesiveness of the group is expressed in terms of the effective introduction of new members to the group, the members' willingness to attend on a regular basis and the support of other members of the group in the complete expression of their emotions including risk taking behavior and self-disclosure. Self-disclosure may provide some of the most tension filled parts of the group's interaction especially when it appears to be against the accepted aim of the group. For example, the self-disclosure of Ann who said "I was just so tired of his manipulation of me and everyone else. It seemed like everything I did was done just to please him and to make sure he wouldn't get hurt and kill himself. Well, I'm free of that now that he's dead and it feels good." While there was an immediate conflict in the group about whether this was an appropriate thing to say or feel, many group members shortly acknowledged that they had experienced similar emotions. However, they had felt ashamed of having such emotions relating to someone who was in such psychological pain that they had committed suicide. So, they had never expressed these emotions. The ability of group members to make known their deepest emotions and thoughts indicates a strong, cohesive group that facilitates successful interactions and resolutions.

Support

Members of this group share similar attributes. For these students, being together with other students whom they believe understand them and acknowledge the kind of psychological pain they felt either during their ideation or attempt is a powerful catalyst for understanding and change. The students are accepting of each other, they have an immediate understanding of the type of pain expressed by the members and they form meaningful relationships within the group. The University of Minnesota group formed some strong friendship bonds. They socialized together outside the group and they remained in contact with each other after the group's conclusion. The group also promotes self-disclosure that facilitates a full recounting of what had taken place in the student's life leading to the suicidal behavior. What had previously been a most unacceptable part of their being, their suicidal self, was now a focus for change and growth and integrated as part of their life history. The cohesiveness of the group creates a strong bond enabling awareness of the many facets of their lives and an understanding of how they can use new-found self-esteem and different ways of coping with stresses and negative life events.

Catharsis

Catharsis is defined as: "1. Medicine. Purgation, especially for the digestive system. 2. A purifying or figurative cleansing of the emotions. 3. Psychoanalysis. a. A technique used to relieve tension and anxiety by bringing repressed material to consciousness. b. The result of this process; abreaction" [39, p. 212]. All of these definitions are applicable to the therapeutic factor, catharsis, in either the survivor or support group.

Catharsis is a purging for the student. Both groups give members permission to literally "throw up" everything that is of concern to them. These moments are high tension events as the group's energy, focused on the individual who is engaging in catharsis, is as significant as the energy being expended by the member who is beginning the process of eliminating negative forces from their life.

Catharsis is also a figurative cleansing. Groups provide the forums where the members can "come clean." They can confess their innermost thoughts, negative and positive, about themselves and about others. For many this is the first time in their lives this has been permitted and they may need to learn how to label and express their emotions. It is a time when the "unacceptable" is acceptable. For example, students can express anger and find their anger is appropriate and normal. In other settings they might be told it is inappropriate to be angry at someone who committed suicide because they were in such pain.

> Damn him! Damn him! Damn him! How could he hurt us so much! We all told him he could talk to any one of us at any time. All he had to do was walk down the hall. Was that asking too much? This just isn't fucking fair! We did our part, we sat up a lot of nights talking him through his problems. He cheated and we're paying for it. He can't feel anything now but I hurt, I hurt a lot.
>
> —Melanie (freshman)

Catharsis can be used to relieve tension and anxiety by bringing repressed material to consciousness. This is usually the work of the counselors as they gather information and search for underlying causes in the behavior of the members of the group. This cathartic intervention is most useful in cases where there is repression of some shameful event such as incest, sexual abuse, battering, or alcohol abuse within a family. There are instances where the group members will also begin to sense a hidden part of the person's life that is affecting his or her behavior and inhibiting the individual's growth within the group. These incidents and the memory of them may be so painful they have been successfully repressed for a long time. When these painful recollections are shared and the person is supported by the group members, the individual begins an exploration into some of repressed factors that were involved in their suicidal process.

Catharsis is a powerful factor in the recovery of individuals who are survivors or ideators/attempters. It is a necessary factor in the process and it will cause the most discomfort for group members. However, the potential for successful imitative behavior by other members who have repressed incidents in their lives is very high once they have witnessed the therapeutic effect on just one member.

Existential Factors

> It's just not fair! Nobody deserves this! This is such a waste of . . . of everything he ever worked for! He had everything going for him, scholarships, an internship. He never studied that much and he still got the best grades. I worked with him because I could learn more from him than from some of my profs. We were best friends and he never said a word.
>
> —Eli (graduate student)

Survivors

Eli's recognition that at times, life is neither fair nor just is a major part of the existential factors involved in the resolution of survivors' issues. Not only is life unfair but there will be the imposition of pain that is caused externally but which can easily be internalized. The Chinese proverb, "We cannot prevent the birds of sorrow from flying over our heads, but we can prevent them from building nests in our hair." is repeated here because it is part of the existential. One of the major functions of survivors' groups is to prevent the building of nests of grief in our hair. These groups also function as "combs" to remove from our hair those nests that have already been built. For survivors the recognition that there is no escape from the basic issues of life and death and that we must each take individual and ultimate responsibility for our own lives is an important, positive factor. Groups can provide support, challenge, empathize and provide a "safety net" while the survivor must take responsibility for making changes in his or her life and developing mechanisms to cope with the loss and adjust to a new environment.

Support

The recognition that life is not always fair or just is also an integral part of the therapeutic endeavors addressed in this group. Group members develop the realization that, at times, there is pain in living and this is normal. The group can facilitate the recognition that there needs to be a focus on the totality of life events and not just upon those life events that are negative. An invaluable part of the group's focus is addressing issues honestly and with the understanding the individual must take responsibility for their own life. Other group members and the counselors may offer advice and provide support during moments of crisis, but they cannot take responsibility for the other person's life. That is an important issue within this group. For anyone to assume they can totally preclude suicidal behavior is to create an illusion that will have profoundly disastrous results if there is a suicide. The recognition that no one in the group is either omniscient or omnipotent is an important and powerful component for a successful group endeavor. Recognizing and effectively coping with the basic issues of life and death are the ultimate existential factors in these groups.

Each of these eleven therapeutic factors contributes to the success of the group therapy endeavor. They are not separate entities, but are inextricable elements of the total process. The utilization of these factors in either group enables group members to begin resolution of their life issues. The most important factor is the actual establishment of groups to meet the needs of the students who are survivors and the students who are or have been involved in suicidal behaviors. For, in this way, the institution can demonstrate its willingness to become involved with students during a crucial part of their life—their ideation and/or suicidal action or the mourning of a friend, a lover, a roommate, a teammate, a person who affected their life.

In this discussion of grief in the aftermath of a suicide, the role of religion or spirituality needs to be considered. For most individuals, there is a religious or spiritual crisis and they seek comfort from their clergy or spiritual advisor. This is a critical moment for clergy and I have often been asked by clergy, "What can I say when something like this happens. I have to deliver the homily or sermon at the funeral?" There are two references that I use which relate directly to suicide and religion. The first of these is a writing by Fr. Arnaldo Pangrazzi [40]. While this piece was written for a Catholic publication it contains significant reflections that can readily be adapted for use in any religious situation. Pangrazzi discussed the historical and religious views toward suicide and how to live with painful memories, heal and then move forward to discovering peace. "No matter the tragic mistakes, no one has the right to condemn these individuals. . . . As our faith teaches us, one of God's attributes is mercy. . . . He knows the deepest recesses of each of us, and his love and mercy are greater than anyone can ever know or understand" [40, p. 2]. I have found this article to be very useful reading for survivors. The second work is a collection of sermons on suicide edited by Clemmons [41]. These sermons were delivered at the funerals of suicides and are basically a Christian work. However, the range of views represented provides materials that can be adapted for use in funeral services or as a consolation for a survivor.

Postvention also needs to occur with the counselor or therapist who has been working with the suicidal person. An entire issue of the *Journal of Counseling and Development* was devoted to the concept of critical incidents as catalysts for counselor development [42]. Fifty-eight highly personal experiences express a common ingredient of the "notion of 'stretching' oneself, revising one's understanding of human nature and human possibility, and channeling these insights into positive development. A suicide is a critical incident in the lives of everyone who has been involved including the counselor or therapist. Millen and Roll used a case study of a suicide to point out that everything can be done right and a suicide still occurs [43]. While they provide some guidelines on working with suicidal clients, their most important contribution to postvention was their presentation of helpful and nonhelpful reactions to the suicide of a client. Reactions that were less helpful included the following: "What if" statements that encourage self-blame rather than inquiry. Intense anger that may preclude positive expression of other emotions (although it is important to remember that anger is a normal reaction, it is only destructive as it moves to abnormal anger). Denial that anything might have been done or that the death was, a suicide. A helpful reaction was to consult with colleagues to work through the emotional reactions and gain new insights. To me, this is a critical part of working through a death by suicide and recognizing limitations. "Don't try to understand everything. Some things will just never make any sense. Just don't be afraid to let your feelings show" [44, p. 97]. Another strategy suggested by Millen and Roll is that we pardon our teachers who "colluded with us in the fantasy that if we did everything right 'it wouldn't happen'" [43, p. 491]. And then we can proceed with a new humility and become involved with new clients, new students and new situations.

MOURNING

Mourning is the process through which we incorporate the loss experience into our life history. The acknowledgment of mourning has been exhibited by displaying a flag at half mast, by wearing black armbands or dark, somber clothing for a period of time (usually a year), wailing and bemoaning the loss or providing ritual foods and other items at a family or other religious altar. The intensity and length of the period of mourning depends on a number of variables including the relationship with the deceased, the manner of death of the deceased, the psychological state of the bereaved, cultural norms and other factors.

For students, the need to move forward with their lives while at the same time attempting to cope with a loss creates conflicting stresses. When the death is a suicide, the mourning process can become more complicated as they view their own mortality. The following are excerpts from a journal written by a former serviceman who experienced the death by suicide of a cousin. It reflects many of the issues which students face.

> A rather profound bit of irony can be found in the fact that the only class I've missed this quarter was the one where (the instructor) started his discussion on suicide, death and loss. In a routine "How are things going?" call to my grandparents I found out that my 18 year old cousin who just recently completed Marine boot camp and had been home on leave, committed suicide early that morning . . . I've never known anyone who committed suicide . . . This is the first time I have had to deal with death as an adult. Tonight was the wake, or visitation, or whatever you want to call it. Mark was in his dress blues, and he looked so peaceful. It amazes me how they can take a person who died a violent death, in this case blowing out the back of the head with a 9mm, and make them look so peaceful as they prepare for their final rest. I really didn't know what to think. What can one think about something like this? My uncle summed it up when he said, "Kids aren't supposed to do this." It was a fairly difficult evening, particularly the final viewing. I was one of the last people, other than his immediate family to go by. I did the only thing I could think of. I touched him gently on the chest and said "God speed" and saluted. We, wait a minute, I am confused now. The final viewing was the day of the funeral. Here it is actually Saturday, the day after the funeral and I am trying to reconstruct the events. The final viewing was Friday morning. I realize this now because, as one of the pallbearers, I had to wait around inside as they closed up the coffin. One of the other interesting aspects of dealing with death as an adult is that hopefully you are much more in touch with your feelings and hopefully less likely to repress

them. This was the first time I'd actually cried at the occasion of another's death. Twice that day at the funeral home (the final viewing and when they sealed the coffin) . . . The priest really said a lot of good things. He told friends and family that they couldn't blame themselves, that Mark had made a decision. The priest kept saying that Mark was in heaven, that he was no longer hurting. I didn't hear anything that seemed to reflect the traditional Catholic stand on suicide. The graveside was the most difficult point. I stood across the grave from my uncle. I have never seen him really sad or upset before. But at the gravesite, I saw his face so distorted with pain, grief and sorrow, it was like nothing I had ever seen before, I really hurt to see him like that . . . This class (following the funeral) was not only not fun, but downright frustrating. I have heard before and heard again all about the warning signs, signals and formulas for determining all the possibilities of an individual being suicidal. There are levels low, moderate, extreme risk. There are ways of talking to a person who you think may be suicidal so you can find out if they really are, what and how they are going to do, why, and so on. There are referrals you can give. There is this and that and this and that. But what the hell do you do with an individual who shows none of the signs that precede a suicide? What about a person who is smart, happy, gifted, well-loved and liked, is responsible, who has taken care of a younger brother who adores him, and a whole slew of other things that describe Mark. That's all I could think about tonight. I just wish to God that Mark would've talked to me if he was *that* bad. He knew I had been in the Navy and he knew he could talk to me about it anytime . . . He's gone *forever*. That's a damn long time and quite a crappy trade if you ask me. I wish I could have seen him more while he was home. It really reinforces the whole notion of how unpredictable our lives and the lives of others are. It also goes to show that, no matter how much you try not do, we always take things for granted. . . . One last note on death before I wrap this up. You don't like to tell people about it, at least I didn't. The only people I told in the first two days were my two closest friends. It came to a point on Thursday that I had to tell people about it to explain my mood . . . how I managed to get so much damn food in my room . . . Most of the people who found out about his death found out from people other than me. I guess I didn't know how to tell people or if I should since this was all a new experience for me . . .

—Carlos (senior)

The effect that this suicide had on Carlos is apparent. The fact that he was an experienced resident assistant who had received substantial training did not lessen the impact. It is important to remember that even the most well trained or educated person still is not fully prepared to cope with the trauma of a suicidal death. Understanding and counseling survivors, whether they are students, siblings, parents, therapists, police officers, clergy persons or others, is an immediate need. Dunne, McIntosh and Dunne-Maxim provide exceptional material in their book, *Suicide and Its Aftermath: Understanding and Counseling the Survivors* [45]. They begin by discussing the social context of survivorship and then discuss the ramifications of suicide in families, professional relationships, first responders and conclude with some therapeutic approaches. Their material relating to medical, law enforcement, clergy and mental health professionals provides a healing approach for these individuals when suicide intrudes into their professional lives.

Postvention activities are hard work. Whether we are working with students in the initial aftermath of a suicide, facilitating a group or meeting with individuals it is a time when emotions are shrill, anxiety is intense and everyone is looking for an answer to the ceaseless "Why?" The campus that has been prepared by having protocols in place and support staff ready to respond will find it easier to respond to the needs of students, faculty and staff. The campus that is not prepared will struggle to determine what should be done administratively and probably will have little time or energy left to attempt to meet the needs of its human community.

The activities involved in prevention, intervention and postvention efforts are not only linked but support one another. If a campus is to fulfill its responsibilities to its constituents it is essential that these efforts be carefully designed and ready for implementation. To do otherwise is to fail students at the very moment they need support and encouragement.

REFERENCES

1. G. Evans and N. L. Farberow, *The Encyclopedia of Suicide*, Facts on File, New York, 1988.
2. L. E. LaGrand, College Student Loss and Response, in *New Directions for Student Services: Coping with Death on Campus*, E. Zinner (ed.), Jossey-Bass, San Francisco, pp. 15-28, 1985.
3. G. Thornton, D. U. Robertson, and M. L. Mlecko, Disenfranchised Grief and Evaluation of Social Support by College Students, *Death Suicides*, 15:4, pp. 355-362, 1991.
4. E. S. Shneidman, (ed.), *On the Nature of Suicide*, Jossey-Bass, San Francisco, 1969.
5. L. E. LaGrand, Loss Reactions of College Students: A Descriptive Analysis, *Death Education*, 5:3, pp. 235-248, 1981.
6. C. B. Wortman and R. C. Silver, The Myths of Coping with Loss, *Journal of Consulting and Clinical Psychology*, 57:3, pp. 349-357, 1989.

7. J. C. Moorman, J. R. Urbach, and D. R. Ross, Guidelines for Consultation with University Personnel in Student Psychiatric Emergencies, *Journal of American College Health, 33*:2, pp. 91-94, 1984.

8. S. Furr and J. Simpson, Responding to the Death of a College Student, *Journal of College and University Student Housing, 19*:1, pp. 17-21, 1989.

9. R. L. Wrenn, College Management of Student Death: A Survey, *Death Studies, 15*:4, pp. 395-402, 1991.

10. R. L. Wrenn, College Student Death: Postvention Issues for Educators and Counselors, in *Children and Death*, D. Papadatou and C. Papadatos (eds.), Hemisphere, New York, 1991.

11. R. S. Gordon, L. M. Range, and R. P. Edwards, Generational Differences in Reactions to Adolescent Suicide, *Journal of Community Psychology, 15*:2, pp. 268-274, 1987.

12. R. D. Goldney, N. D. Spence, and P. F. Moffitt, The Aftermath of Suicide: Attitudes of Those Bereaved by Suicide, of Social Workers, and of a Community Sample, *Journal of Community Psychology, 15*:2, pp. 141-148, 1987.

13. G. Thornton, K. D. Whittemore, and D. U. Robertson, Evaluation of People Bereaved by Suicide, *Death Studies, 13*:6, pp. 119-126, 1989.

14. C. J. Vickio, J. C. Cavanaugh, and T. W. Attig, Perceptions of Grief among University Students, *Death Studies, 14*:3, pp. 231-240, 1990.

15. K. E. Thompson and L. M. Range, Bereavement Following Suicide and Other Deaths: Why support Attempts Fail, *Omega, 26*:1, pp. 61-70, 1992.

16. L. M. Range, A. S. Walston, and P. M. Pollard, Helpful and Unhelpful Comments after Suicide, Homicide, Accident, or Natural Death, *Omega, 25*:1, pp. 25-31, 1992.

17. R. J. Berenson, A Bereavement Group for College Students, *Journal of American College Health, 37*:3, pp. 101-108, 1988.

18. S. J. Freeman, Group Facilitation of the Grieving Process with those Bereaved by Suicide, *Journal of Counseling and Development, 69*:4, pp. 328-331, 1991.

19. I. D. Yalom, *The Theory and Practice of Group Psychotherapy* (3rd edition), Basic Books Inc., New York, 1985.

20. M. C. Parkes, "Seeking and Finding" A Lost Object, *Social Science and Medicine, 4*:2, pp. 187-201, 1972.

21. J. W. Worden, *Grief Counseling and Grief Therapy: A Handbook for the Mental Health Practitioner*, Springer, New York, 1982.

22. D. E. Balk, K. Tyson-Rawson, and J. Colletti-Wetzel, *Social Support as an Intervention with Bereaved College Students*, paper presented at the American Psychological Association, Washington, DC, August, 1992.

23. R. L. V. Rickgarn, *The Issue is Suicide*, University of Minnesota, Minneapolis, Minnesota, 1983.

24. Mental Health Association in Waukesha County, Inc., *Grief After Suicide*, Waukesha, Wisconsin, 1981.

25. R. R. Butler and M. A. Statz, Preparation for when Prevention Doesn't Work: Responding to a Suicide, *NASPA Journal, 23*:3, pp. 15-21, 1986.

26. B. Jacobs and J. E. Towns, What Residence Hall Staff Need to Know About Dealing with Death, *NASPA Journal, 22*:2, pp. 32-36, 1984.

27. K. E. Charles and J. M. Eddy, In-service Training on Dying and Death for Residence Hall Staff, *NASPA Journal, 25*:2, pp. 126-129, 1987.

28. E. S. Shneidman, *Death and the College Student*, Behavioral Publications, New York, 1972.

29. R. L. V. Rickgarn, The Death Response Team: Responding to the Forgotten Grievers, *Journal of Counseling and Development, 66*:4, pp. 197-199, 1987.

30. W. B. Donahue, Student Death: What Do We Do? *NASPA Journal, 14*:4, pp. 29-32, 1977.

31. J. L. Hipple, P. Cimbolic, and J. Peterson, Student Services Response to a Suicide, *Journal of Counseling and Student Personnel, 21*:5, pp. 457-458, 1980.

32. B. Moats, *Crisis Outreach Following a Suicide or Death*, unpublished manuscript, Counseling-Psychological Service Center, University of Texas, 1982.

33. R. Crafts, Student Affairs Response to Student Death, in *New Directions for Student Services: Coping with Death on Campus*, No. 31, E. Zinner (ed.), Jossey-Bass, San Francisco, pp. 29-38, 1985.

34. E. Zinner, (ed.), *New Directions for Student Services: Coping with Death on Campus*, (No. 31), Jossey Bass, San Francisco, 1985.

35. L. J. Halberg, Death of a College Student: Response by Student Service Professionals on One Campus, *Journal of Counseling and Development, 64*:6, pp. 411-412, 1986.

36. J. E. Scott, M. A. Fukuyama, N. W. Dunkel, and W. D. Griffin, The Trauma Response Team: Preparing Staff to Respond to Student Death, *NASPA Journal, 29*:3, pp. 230-237, 1992.

37. J. Hipple, Group Treatment of Suicidal Clients, *Journal of Specialists in Group Work, 7*:4, pp. 245-250, 1982.

38. J. W. Worden, *Grief Counseling and Grief Therapy: A Handbook for the Mental Health Practitioner*, (2nd edition), Springer, New York, 1991.

39. W. Morris (ed.), *The American Heritage Dictionary of the English Language*, American Heritage Publishing Company, Inc., Boston, 1969.

40. A. Pangrazzi, Suicide: How Christians can Respond Today, *Catholic Update*, July 1984.

41. J. T. Clemmons, (ed.), *Sermons on Suicide*, Westminster/John Knox Press, Louisville, Kentucky, 1989.

42. T. M. Skovholt and P. R. McCarthy (eds.), Special Issue: Critical Incidents in Counselor Development, *Journal of Counseling and Development, 67*:2, 1988.

43. L. Millen and S. Roll, A Case Study in Failure: On Doing Everything Right in Suicide Prevention, *Death Studies, 9*:5-6, pp. 483-492, 1985.

44. R. L. V. Rickgarn, Suicidal Encounters—Suicidal Experience, *Journal of Counseling and Development, 67*:2, p. 97, 1988.

45. E. J. Dunne, J. L. McIntosh, and K. Dunne-Maxim, (eds.), *Suicide and its Aftermath: Understanding and Counseling the Survivors*, W. W. Norton, New York, 1987.

CHAPTER 9

Becoming the Campus That Cares

What is a student's perception of the campus response to suicide? How is a student's perception of this response formed? Does the campus response enable, restrain or even prevent a student from seeking assistance while feeling depressed and/or suicidal? These are important questions. The answers are even more important for they define the institution's response and create the milieu that may inhibit or enhance the possibility of a student suicide on the campus.

Bernard and Bernard studied institutional responses to student suicide and from these responses it is possible to begin to understand students' perceptions and their reactions to college and university activities related to suicidal behavior [1]. Bernard and Bernard sent surveys to 109 accredited university and college counseling services listed in the *Directory of Counseling Services*. They received responses from eighty-eight institutions (81%). They found there was a broad range of actions that might be taken against students who engaged in suicidal behavior at these institutions. The actions ranged from completely ignoring the behavior to dismissing the student from the institution. They also found there was a wide diversity of persons who made decisions relating to a student's suicidal behavior.

A review of the responses to the questions asked by Bernard and Bernard demonstrates that an institution's concern about students' suicidal behavior begins before admission and continues through their academic career. The first question was "Does your institution routinely request information from entering or transferring students concerning a history of mental illness, psychiatric hospitalization, previous therapy or counseling, etc?" [1, p. 110]. While 40 percent of the institutions ($n = 35$) did not request such information, 60 percent ($n = 53$) did make this request. Of these fifty-three institutions, seven filed the data, eleven denied admission until the student could demonstrate that the problem had abated, and seventeen would react after there was an evaluation on campus. The twenty-eight institutions that would deny admission or require an evaluation were asked what "actions would be taken, specifically on the determination that the student was, or was not, a current suicide risk" [1, p. 110]. If the student was perceived to be a suicide risk, eleven institutions suggested further counseling, four would require counseling as a prerequisite for admission and twelve would deny admission until the student submitted proof the suicidal risk had been alleviated.

The survey asked how institutions would respond to suicide threats. Fifteen (17%) of the institutions indicated that they would take no official action. A "suggestion" would be made by forty-one (47%) of the institutions. This "suggestion" would recommend the student seek professional help, live off campus or withdraw from the institution. A "demand" would be made by the remaining thirty-one institutions (36%). This "demand" would include seeking professional help (19 institutions), moving off campus (1) or withdrawing (11).

In response to suicide attempts, six of the institutions indicated they would take no action (7%). Thirty-six institutions (41%) stated they would make the same type of "suggestions" to the attempters as were made to those who made threats. Forty-five institutions (53%) would impose a "demand" which would consist of professional counseling (22), living off campus (3) or withdrawal from the institution (20).

What would occur should a student refuse to comply with the institution's requirements? The responses included offering a hearing (4), providing a hearing if the student demanded one (19), withdrawal without a hearing (10), calling parents (22), calling police (6) and initiating commitment to a mental institution (9). Bernard and Bernard noted that even though there was specific mention of a hearing in the survey, sixty-five institutions did not mention a hearing. Sixty-seven (76%) of the institutions were satisfied with their policies for managing a suicidal student, thirteen (15%) were dissatisfied and eight (10%) made no comment.

Another study on institutional responses to students with mental and life threatening physical disorders in residence halls was done by the Research and Information Committee of the Upper Midwest Region— Association of College and University Housing Officers (UMR-ACUHO) [2]. The Committee received fifty-three responses from a mailing of 225 surveys (a response rate of 23.5%) which included forty-six four year, four two year, and twenty-nine private institutions. A common theme in almost all the survey responses was that each situation would be viewed individually and the response would be contextual to the specific situation. While the responding institutions reported an increase in students with mental problems, only twenty-eight had a policy for responding. The responding institutions reported a 62 percent increase in suicide ideation and attempts and a 25 percent increase in depression among students. A judicial process was used in twenty-five of the institutions to respond to mental and life threatening disorders and thirty-two of the institutions reported they had judicial policies to address these behaviors. Forty-six of the responding institutions noted that their institutional response to a life threatening disorder was an on-site crisis intervention by either mental health or counseling center staff. In their residence halls, thirty-nine institutions negotiated behavioral contracts and twenty-one made therapy mandatory if the problem negatively affected other residents or was life threatening. If the student refused counseling or treatment, removal from the residence halls, suspension and dismissal were the primary responses by the institution. Ten institutions would dismiss or expel a student for refusing to seek or attend counseling sessions and twenty-five would take the same action if the student were threatening to themselves or others (including disruption of the larger community).

Some factions of the educational institution would argue that the only responsibility of the institution is to provide students with an education and engaging in "remedial" efforts is inappropriate to the mission of the institution. Other factions would argue that "remedial" efforts are necessary only as they relate to the educational (i.e., the classroom) mission of the institution. Any psychological "remediation" is regarded as acceptable as long as the student is neither disturbing to the academic nor is disturbed in the psychological sense. Otherwise, the student who cannot function effectively should be removed from the institution. From the studies noted above, it is apparent institutions often elect to remove the student from the campus through eviction from college residences or expulsion from the institution.

There are three important and different ramifications of these actions—psychological, ethical, and legal. The psychological ramifications are: 1) How is the psychological state of the student affected by these actions? and 2) How do other students view the institution as a result of these actions? The ethical and legal ramifications have considerable effect on the student body as they present an institution's understanding of the ethical and legal requirements of such actions and their adherence to them. The psychological, ethical, and legal ramifications are intermingled and have significant consequences for students and institutions.

In their discussion of institutional policies, Bernard and Bernard draw attention to a number of ethical and legal issues that affect the management of the psychological problems of suicidal students on the campus [1]. The ethical issues relate to the fact that counselors have obligations to their counselee including respecting their integrity and promoting their welfare as required by the American Counseling

Association's ethical standards which state "When the client's condition indicates that there is clear and imminent danger to the client or others, the member must take reasonable personal action or inform responsible authorities. Consultation with other professionals must be used where possible. The assumption of responsibility for the client(s) behavior must be taken only after careful deliberation. The client must be involved in the resumption of responsibility as quickly as possible" [3, p. 107]. Hopkins and Anderson's book provides an extensive review of legal implications for the counselor. There is also a compilation of ethical principles and standards that has been developed by The Council for the Advancement of Standards for Student Services/ Development Programs, the Association of College and University Housing Officers—International, the American College Personnel Association and the National Association of Student Personnel Administrators in Winston, Anchors and Associates book on student housing and residential life [4]. These resources provide significant information on the relationship and the rights and responsibilities of both student and institution. It is very important for these ethical and legal issues to be handled in an astute manner.

Bernard and Bernard noted that Section 504 of the Rehabilitation Act of 1973 (amended 1974) has been defined in such a manner as to include emotional or mental illness under the definition of handicapped [1]. There is a requirement for due process including a notice of the consequences of certain acts and an opportunity for a hearing. Their detailed treatment of this material concludes with a suggestion that institutions may not always be acting in the best interests of students and need to exercise care not to violate federal law.

There is always a fine line between the best interests of the institution and the best interests of the student. The Bernard and Bernard study does not specify the level of suicidal risk of the student either in the information given to an institution before admission or in the threats or attempts that would take place on the campus [1]. There is a range of risk ranging from a very low to extremely high suicide potential that involves an assessment of demographic data, clinical characteristics, and risk factors. Since this information is not included and no differentiation is offered, hopefully it can be assumed that these institutions respond to these various degrees with incremental actions. That is to say that a student with a low level ideation/action would be referred for psychological counseling and one with a high level ideation/ action would be asked to withdraw from the institution.

However, there are some troubling issues here. A clear text reading would tend to indicate that the institutions that require a student to move off campus or withdraw appear to be more concerned about the institution's image, what might be called a "protectionist stance." There appears to be little concern about the welfare of the student. Students who are threatening or attempting suicide have moved significantly into the continuum of suicide. These students are already experiencing significant alienation, isolation, hopelessness, and helplessness. Now they are discovering that these feelings are being validated by the institution. If the student is required to move off campus, this communicates to the student that he or she is no longer an integral part of that community. This action creates a significant sense of isolation and alienation from the community that may be all that remains of a student's support system. Being an "outcast" in any society is a traumatic experience. For the suicidal student this action has momentous impact on their psychological state.

> Maggie brought me here because she said somebody would talk to me. Yeah, right! I'm here because she's my friend and she's sitting right here and I told her I would do it, but it wouldn't do any good. (Question: What makes you believe that talking to me won't do any good?") Because I remember what happened at (college). I told my RA that I had taken a bunch of aspirin the night before because I wanted to die. Well, I was in the Dean's office next and was told that my behavior was inappropriate and so my dorm contract was being canceled and I would have to find a place off campus immediately. I couldn't believe it. But, if I wanted to stay I had to and so my friend and I found this room in a house near campus. My friends helped me move and they thought it was terrible. I remember sitting in my room looking toward the campus and feeling so alone. I cried most of the time. I couldn't tell my mom why I moved. I just said it was cheaper. I couldn't study and I couldn't visit my friends because I wasn't allowed in the dorm. Finally, all I did was cry and so I asked my mom to take me home because I didn't like (college) and I needed a break.
>
> —Andrea (freshman)

Perhaps the ultimate action of being "outcast" would be dismissal from the institution that was the action reportedly taken by 36 percent of the institutions for a threat and 44 percent if there is an attempt. It would be appropriate for an institution to seek hospitalization if the attempt indicated there was an immediate danger to the life of the student. If the attempt were sub-lethal, providing counseling services would seem more appropriate than dismissal. If the student rejects such assistance and is a disruption to the campus, the behavior can be documented and the disruption dealt with through the student conduct code. In this process, however, the student has been provided with a notification of the consequences of his or her actions and provided with due process in the form of a hearing before the campus judicial body.

Forcing a student to withdraw does have important psychological, ethical and legal consequences. From a student's psychological perspective the dismissal has ramifications relating to the feelings of isolation and alienation as noted previously. The phenomenon of isolation as a major indicator of potential suicide is well known [5]. Bernard and Bernard found over one quarter of the students in their study reported feelings of isolation associated with their suicidal behavior [6]. They stated that "forcing a suicidal student to withdraw when that student is already feeling isolated may do little to reduce the sense of isolation or decrease the possibility of actual suicide" [6, p. 412]. I would suggest that this will increase the sense of isolation and alienation and confirm what the student already has been considering, "I really don't matter, no one cares what happens to me. They just want me out of the way." I would also suggest there is a high probability the actions may serve to exacerbate the suicidal state and propel the student more rapidly toward serious suicidal actions. This is certainly not in the best interests of the student nor that of the institution.

A campus response that appears to be more punitive than helpful will have a negative influence on the perceptions of students. Those who are depressed, have some suicidal ideation or have made minor attempts, are going to be deterred from seeking assistance for their emotional crises. If they believe they may be required to move off campus or will be dismissed, there may be attempts to cope with their emotional turmoil independently. Since this is usually not a successful endeavor, we can anticipate a deterioration of their psychological state resulting in a more serious attempt or an actual suicide. Under these circumstances, it would appear an institution's reputation would be better served by providing professional assistance to students rather than exacerbating or precipitating suicidal crises through dismissal. A student's perceptions of a campus are developed through the observation of what happens to a fellow student and "there but for the grace of God go I," creates an indelible impression.

However, if we are not convinced that there is an ethical obligation to students, there certainly is a legal obligation to respond appropriately to suicidal students. A definitive discourse on the legal issues involved in mandatory withdrawals has been written by Pavela [7]. Pavela provided a series of judicial decisions but most specifically reminded institutions of the provisions of Section 504 of the Rehabilitation Act of 1973/1974. This act provides that no otherwise qualified handicapped individual shall, solely by reason of handicap, be excluded from participation in, be denied the benefits of, or be subjected to discrimination under any program that receives Federal financial assistance. There are probably few, if any, colleges or universities that do not receive Federal funding in some form thus making them subject to the provisions of Section 504. In the regulations, a handicapped person is defined as any person who has physical or mental impairment that substantially limits one or more of such a person's major life activities, has a record of such impairment or has such an impairment. Major life activities have been defined as meaning caring for one's self, performing manual tasks, walking, seeing, hearing, speaking, breathing, learning and working. Mental impairment has been defined to include mental or psychological disorders, emotional or mental illness. One of Pavela's conclusions relates to suicidal individuals.

> Furthermore, in cases of threatened or attempted suicide, an initial effort should be made to allow the affected student to remain on campus. If the student is to be withdrawn, school officials should refer the student to an appropriate facility for psychiatric observation and evaluation [7, p. 147].

An action like this would create a positive impression among students. The action would indicate they are part of a campus that will take appropriate and caring measures to insure their well-being.

Pavela's 1985 book contains a succinct two and a half pages that should be required reading before any policy regarding the dismissal of suicidal students is considered or any action taken [8]. Some pertinent points made in this section, "Responding to Suicidal Students" [8, pp. 56-58], relate to the causes for a student's suicidal state of mind including stress, loneliness, academic competition, financial problems, social isolation and sense of loss. He argued that academic institutions should do more to create community, enforce standards and make available counseling services and other forms of support. If a student must be withdrawn for psychiatric reasons, Pavela stated that reasonable efforts must be made for an appropriate referral. He pointed out that to withdraw a student to preempt liability without this effort could create greater legal risks "if they simply 'dump' suicidal students in the larger community. Such a practice is embarrassingly similar to the 'obligatory departures' of insane people from medieval European towns . . . and is ethically indefensible" [8, p. 58].

Other articles on legal issues were written by Gehring [9, 10]. In his 1983 work, Gehring discussed legal issues from the singular point of view, is the student a threat to themselves, property, or others. He posed some questions for administrators to consider: Does the student constitute a threat? Is there a foreseeable danger? What actions can be taken? What are the administrator's duties? and when should students be readmitted? Each of these provide answers, drawn from legal cases, to assist administrators. However, the important focus in this article and his 1982 article is that of the "duty to warn." The "duty to warn" was imposed by the 1976 *Tarasoff v. Regents of the University of California* case (551 P. 2d. 334, Cal., 1976). This case held that where "a person stands in a special relationship to another whose conduct needs to be controlled or to the foreseeable victim of that conduct then there is a special duty to control the conduct or to warn the potential victim" [10, p. 10].

Confidentially becomes moot when a student is of danger to themselves and/or others. At this point the major emphasis is on securing professional assistance for the individual and insuring that he or she does not engage in any activities that would be harmful to him, her or others. This needed action was reinforced on 29 October 1991, when the Maryland Supreme Court ruled in the Eisel case that if a counselor foresees a danger of suicide, the counselor has a duty to try to prevent the suicide. Pate [11] noted this was foreseen by Hopkins and Anderson [3] when they examined the Tarasoff case and argued that the case could be extended to knowing when the client was a danger to him or herself, therefore giving rise to the duty to take actions to preclude the suicidal action.

The Eisel case concerned a high school student who committed suicide. She had told her friends that she was going to do so and they had, in turn, told the school counselor. Nicole Eisel denied any problems when confronted by the counselor and so neither school administration or parents were notified. Nicole died in a suicide murder pact with another thirteen year old girl. The Maryland Supreme Court held that the counselor had a duty to use reasonable attempts to prevent suicide when he knew of the suicidal intent. While this is a case involving a minor who was not a college student, it seems apparent it is only a matter of time until this is applied to the collegiate area as well. It is not unreasonable to assume that, like the Eisel case, cases of student suicide will "be evaluated to determine whether the duty of reasonable professional care owed to the student was satisfied" [11, p. 19]. If this is extended to colleges and universities, the level of reasonable professional care will be defined and any failure to provide this care could result in liabilities for both the counselor and the institution.

Some approaches to managing suicidal students on campuses have been developed. Hoffman and Mastrianni reviewed models for creating both work and study environments to meet ethical and educational goals for, as they note "no college is immune from the question of how to approach, in policy and practice, the mentally ill, suicidal, or chemically addicted student" [12, p. 15]. They proposed that with adequate resources and support, an environment that is responsive to and supportive of the student in distress can not only be beneficial to the student but also to the institution itself. They noted that our culture has not encouraged a sense of social responsibility and

> in this cultural context, higher education has an important role to play, demonstrating to students and, through them, to the broader society that concern for human frailties is as great a responsibility of all our institutions as is encouragement of human achievement [12, p. 19].

Another model was offered by Amada who emphasized the need for well defined codes of student conduct and clear procedure while working with disruptive students [13]. Like Delworth he calls particular attention to the differentiation between disruptive and dangerous behaviors [14]. Amada noted that often administrators are reluctant to administer discipline and have often used referrals to mental health professionals to ameliorate or alleviate the crisis. This is regarded as a coercive measure that instills resentment toward the therapist and therapy that may nullify any possible positive efforts. Amada takes the position in this model that administrative staff should avoid using psychiatric withdrawals to remove disruptive students from the campus.

Delworth edited an excellent volume entitled, *New Directions for Student Services: Dealing With The Behavioral and Psychological Problems of Students* [14]. The model that is developed in this work is the AISP Model (Assessment-Intervention of Student Problems). This model incorporates the judicial process into working with the disturbing student, the mental health system working with the disturbed student, and a campus intervention team working with the disturbed/disturbing student to determine appropriate referral. This model does not eliminate the possibility of psychiatric removal or other interventions that would remove the student from the campus. "The combination of problematical student behaviors, intense campus pressures, and the potential for serious personal as well as institutional consequences causes decisions regarding disturbed/disturbing students to be highly complex and unpredictable" [15, p. 43]. The AISP Model involves the responsible campus officials in making the appropriate determinations. Since this has been a policy review and consultation process the chances of an inappropriate or illegal action are greatly reduced.

A campus-as-community mental health model is developed in Pruett and Brown's edited volume, *New Directions for Student Services: Crisis Intervention and Prevention* [16]. This volume defines crisis and crisis interventions, summarizes important findings on college student stress and provides intervention models for a number of crisis situations including suicide. They present information on staff training and supervision and emphasize the importance of updating campus staff on the hazards and stress present among college students.

Dannells and Stuber reviewed the mandatory psychiatric withdrawal policies at all Kansas colleges and universities [17]. They found that there was a decline in psychiatric withdrawals and policies probably as a result of Pavela's work [8]. They recommended that colleges and universities need to carefully consider these policies and if they are to be developed, they should be developed outside of a crisis or in reaction to a crisis. They recommended the institution as a community develop the policies to consider the myriad of issues relevant to such policy formulation. Lastly, they recommended Delworth's source book be used as a focal point in the development of any policies. "A carefully developed psychiatric withdrawal policy can meet the needs of both the institution and the student and 'provides an alternative when behavioral or developmental methods are not sufficient'" [14, p. 167].

A more difficult issue is the question of involving parents when a student is involved in a psychiatric emergency. In most instances, a student is regarded as an adult at age eighteen and issues of confidentiality imposed under various Federal and State laws precludes informing parents. Solky, McKeever, Perlmutter and Gift presented a strong case for involving parents particularly in instances where hospitalization is required and the parents are a considerable distance from the institution [18]. If this can be done, they demonstrated that an early working alliance with parents is beneficial and avoids possible later confrontations over the manner of treatment and perhaps even litigation. There may be instances where the parents are a negative factor (i.e., instances of alcohol abuse or physical and sexual abuse) and it would be advisable to engage colleagues in the decision making process to avoid further trauma to the student.

What happens to students who take medical withdrawals has not been studied to any great extent. Meilman, Manley, Gaylor and Turco studied students who took medical leave from Dartmouth College over a three year period [19]. They found that depression was a major factor in approximately one half of the withdrawals with 24 percent of these being related to suicide. In proportion to the numbers enrolled, both women and minorities were over represented in this group of withdrawals. Students who withdrew because of depression did not do as well after their return as did those who were not depressed. The authors speculated that there may be too much pressure to move students back into the collegiate setting. This premature entry requires an intensive intervention to avoid another medical withdrawal. They urged that institutions not retrench their counseling services even during a period of fiscal constraint. "This study indicates that for students who are temporarily disabled by psychological factors, a university counseling service can directly support the academic mission of the institution" [19, p. 222].

Having reviewed this material that reflects some of the actions and attitudes of institutions toward various forms of life threatening behavior, particularly suicidal ideation and attempts, I would now like to return to the questions that I posed at the beginning of this chapter.

What is a student's perception of the campus response to suicide and how is this response formed? The how is more easily answered than the what. From the information given above and from reviews of our own campuses we can determine how a response would be formed. Students are perceptive and particularly in residential settings they can observe the policies of the institution in action. They quickly become aware of students who are having problems. What they see is the institution's response. Does it appear that the only concern is for the reputation of the institution? Or, does it appear students matter and efforts are made to assist students in the alleviation of their problems and concerns? Ultimately, the institution's reputation may rely upon its response to its constituents. It is very possible that students give little thought to their perceptions of the campus response to suicide until it affects them or their friends directly. Then they become acutely aware of the institution's stance.

Before last night my experience with cops was pretty bad. I thought they were just out to bust heads or dump people in jail. When Jim called the cops to come and help after we found Ellen I was really mad. Jim said they would help but I didn't believe it. Well, I was wrong. They really seemed to care about Ellen even though she was so groggy she could hardly talk. They were so careful and patient while we waited for the ambulance to arrive. They just helped keep things calm. I'd never thought a cop could calm Katie down after she found Ellen (roommate) almost dead. My friends couldn't believe it when I told them what had happened. Cops had always just hassled us because of the way we dress. I always accused them of stereotyping us and I guess I did the same thing with all of them.

—Emily (freshman)

Amazing, Dr. Thorn is just about the strictest teacher on this campus. I really never thought he'd buy a letter from my hall director telling him that I missed my final because I was up most of the night taking care of things after Nick slashed himself in the bathroom. He even asked how I was doing. After we talked about the makeup exam, I thanked him and told him I wasn't sure he'd understand how tired I was and that I had really slept through the exam. All he said was, "I know." It just made me think he had been through it too.

—Steve, (resident assistant)

For these two students there was a very positive perception of some members of the institution that created an overall positive impression. It is not just the actions that are taken with the suicidal student that creates the perceptions. It is all the actions that are taken with other students, staff, faculty, and persons from outside the institution. Perceptions are formed from what people see and hear taking place within the institution. These perceptions reflect the degree of caring and concern experienced.

Does the campus response enable, restrain or even prevent a student from seeking assistance while feeling depressed and/or suicidal? To answer this question it is necessary to determine if the campus response meets the needs of students in these situations. The needs of suicidal students can be understood by examining some of the commonalities of suicide and students' psychological needs. Shneidman stated that there were ten commonalities of suicide that "tell us what suicide is like on the inside, and what is sensible about it to the person who does it at the moment of its doing" [20, p. 121]. He presented two primarily situational characteristics of suicide. The first characteristic of suicide is intolerable psychological pain, the common stimulus in suicide. He later defined this as "psychache" [21]. The second is frustrated psychological needs which are the stressors in a suicidal situation. An effective campus response to the stress of intolerable psychological pain would be to preempt this situation and assist the depressed or suicidal student in his or her search for assistance. The first enabling tactic is to provide information in open and accessible places on campus that indicates that there is a concern about student mental health. This material should discuss depression and suicide in a clear and understandable manner, including illustrations of various symptoms and how to recognize the symptoms both by the student, by peers, and others on the campus. Appropriate intervention tactics should be presented together with referral agencies both on and off campus that may be used by students. This may seem to be a naive approach to this intense stimulus. However, I would suggest these efforts create the "teachable moment" communicating to students that depression, suicidal ideation, and actions are not taboo topics on the campus. This type of action creates a climate of concern and caring. It must, however, be reinforced with human resources that correspond to the material. This can be done through training of staff, faculty, and students in intervention tactics and having a viable professional counseling resource on the campus for referrals. The entire climate of the campus must be in consonance. If this is not the case, students will quickly realize the charade and a distinct cynicism detrimental to all parties will be developed. If this climate of concern and action is created, most students will not reach the point of unendurable psychological pain because they will have been intercepted at a much earlier stage in their suicidal process. If they do reach the point of unendurable psychological pain, they may also be intercepted through the same mechanisms. If the institution chooses to either ignore depressed and suicidal students or attends to their needs in a peripheral or perfunctory manner, their actions will restrain and prevent students from seeking assistance to the detriment of both institution and students.

There will be some students who are not reached and they will attempt suicide. If the institution's response is categorical in terms of demanding withdrawal or dismissing the student there would seem to be little question that the actions will seriously inhibit students from seeking assistance. If the institution provides offers of psychological counseling, hospitalization, or other assistance to students, these actions will be seen as facilitating students' growth and development.

How a campus responds to the second of Shneidman's characteristics of suicide, frustration of the psychological needs of students, the stressors that create suicidal situations, also defines whether it enables, restrains or prevents a student from seeking assistance. Psychological needs are developed from a condition where something that is necessary or desirable is either required or wanted to satisfy the need. Murray defined a need as:

> a construct (a convenient fiction or hypothetical concept) which stands for a force (the physio-chemical nature of which is unknown) in the brain region, a force which organizes perception, apperception, intellection, conation and action in such a way as to transform in a certain direction an existing, unsatisfying situation [22, pp. 123-124].

The suicidal student wishes to move from this "existing, unsatisfying situation." However, this can only be accomplished when these frustrated needs that create the core pieces of this intolerable psychological pain are satisfied. These needs can be met in different ways, through counseling services, remedial courses and tutoring, proper academic advising, the use of judicial actions, and other human resources. In reviewing Murray's needs ("n" is his shorthand for "need"), I have chosen to provide a short definition of the need and a quotation from a suicidal student illustrating his or her frustrated need. I believe it will be apparent that an institution that desires to facilitate suicidal (or any other) students in meeting these needs can find a positive way to respond to their statements and create a "campus that cares."

• *n Achievement*—a desire to excel, to accomplish and master life's circumstances through physical; social; and intellectual achievements.

> When I came here I was determined to succeed. I wanted everything I did to be perfect. I wanted to be involved in a lot of activities so my resume would look very good when I graduated. After a while I had to drop out of some activities because I couldn't get my work done. Then I had to drop a couple of classes to avoid failing them. Perfection is just a dream. I doesn't exist. So, how can I want something so badly when it doesn't exist? Could I do anything perfectly? I remember reading Sylvia Plath's poetry and I copied her 'Lady Lazarus.' That's where she says something like dying is an art, I do it exceptionally well. Perhaps I need to settle for that.
> —Rachel (sophomore)

• *n Dominance*—the ability to control his or her environment and to attempt to influence others.

> This place is run by control freaks. You don't get to do anything on your own. The school tells you what you have to study, the teacher tells you what you have to do and how you have to do it. I had more freedom in my high school than I have here. I'm a number and a seat assignment. There are no choices, just controls and I can't handle it.
> —Eileen (freshman)

• *n Deference*—a need to admire or support another individual.

> I really admired my brother. Joe's five years older than I am and it seemed like there was nothing he couldn't do. Other people expected me to be like him and I guess I copied a lot of his style. Why not, he was the up-and-coming young executive. Last night I got a call from mom. She was crying and told me she didn't want me to read it in the papers first. Joe's been arrested for embezzlement.

She said, "He's just like your dad, please don't be like Joe." Turns out dad did the same thing only he was allowed to quit and pay back the company. My god, how can this happen? We had everything and now nothing. Can you see me getting a business job with this kind of family? I can hear it now, "Like father, like son." I feel betrayed and destroyed all at once.

—Dan (senior)

• *n Autonomy*—to be free to act and be independent.

I didn't want to live in a dorm in the first place. That was my folks idea so I could get acquainted on campus. I wanted to live where I could do what I wanted to do, play my stereo as loud as I wanted and have a few beers when I wanted to have friends over. So, you know what happened, I got in trouble and I got put on probation in the dorm. So, I started hanging around with some guys who lived in a house. This weekend I went to a big party over there and really got hammered. I guess I left and started to drive back, I don't remember. I woke up in detox and then the cops came and took me to jail. I hit somebody going through an intersection. My dad got a lawyer who got me out, but my dad's mad as hell. He's coming here and I don't think I can face him. After he got done yelling at me over the phone I felt awful. I just sat in my room and looked out my window at the bridge and cried.

—Michael (freshman)

• *n Aggression*—to oppose forcefully, to fight, to revenge an injury.

Damn right I'm mad. Every time they (parents) show up they have to do something to remind me that I'm their "little boy." Well, this little scene in the lobby was just the last straw. I've never felt so humiliated. I asked Jill to go out tonight and just as we were talking about where we'd go, they arrived. I introduced her and mom said something like she didn't know if I was old enough to go out with an "experienced senior." Jill didn't say anything, she just turned and left. Mom wanted to know what was the matter with her. They're always doing this and I hate them for it. I'm not a little boy and they're never going to have a chance to say that again. They'll be sorry.

—Tad (sophomore)

• *n Abasement*—to be resigned to fate, accept criticism, admit wrongdoing.

It is my fault. I should have stayed at the library with Mickey. I could have been a little late at work. I should have walked home with her. It seems like everything I do ends up being the wrong thing to do. Lately I just can't do anything right and Mickey got hurt because of me. This is another one of those days where I think the world would be better off without me.

—Sally (junior)

• *n Sex & n Sentience*—to form an erotic relationship and to enjoy sensuous feelings.

It happened again last night. I wanted to go to bed with Jerry and we were, no he was really aroused. Just like always when I thought it would be OK I just froze. I told him I couldn't and he didn't understand. I told him I had been raped and it just wasn't going to work, all I could feel was that other guy. At least he was kind, he said he understood but he got dressed and left quickly. I feel like a slut for even trying it and what's worse I feel like there isn't anyone who would want to have anything to do with me once they find out. I'm ashamed and I'm afraid. I'm so disgusted with myself that I don't even want to live sometimes.

—Lucy (sophomore)

• *n Exhibition*—to be noticed, seen and heard.

When I was with my friends we all dressed in black and everyone noticed us. Then I started wearing black all the time and no one seemed to care anymore. Well, everybody's wearing earrings now so that's no big deal. So, then I started carrying this knife in my boot and that got boring. So, now I know what works cause it got me called in here to see you. I never cut too deep, just enough to get a little blood. It scares people when I tell them I'm suicidal and someday I might cut a little too deep.

—Neal (junior)

• *n Play*—to enjoy free time and have a playful attitude.

You're right, I think everything's a game. The guys I date, the dances, even a few drinks, sex, whatever makes a good time. People like you when you're fun and I like having fun. That's why I always get invited to parties. I can get any party going. I'm always in it for a good time. Life's a game and if you don't play for laughs you'll get hurt and then you'll cry. I just can't do that anymore so I'll just keep on laughing.

—Beverly (sophomore)

- *n Affiliation*—to be friendly, social, trusting and loyal.

> I don't understand why nobody ever comes by my room. I know most of us have single rooms, but I hear them talking with each other out in the hallway. And they knock on other people's doors and ask them to go to dinner or get a pizza, whatever. But, nobody ever comes to my door and I know other girls keep their doors closed like I do. My next door neighbor is Vietnamese or something like that, but I hear them laughing and talking. Nobody ever knocks or talks to me. But, who'd want to. I've heard them say, "She's so depressing."
>
> —Dell (freshman)

- *n Rejection*—to exclude, remain indifferent or separate oneself.

> I like being alone. I like it when nobody bothers me. I grew up alone, I don't need friends. They're usually fakes anyway. I'm damned good at my music and I'm getting a scholarship to go out east and study at a better place than this. So, I don't need anybody. The fewer people around the more music I can write. I compose much better when I'm lonely, I mean alone. Strange you'd say I sounded depressed because that's what my prof said about my music.
>
> —Nicholas (sophomore)

- *n Succorance*—the desire to have needs of love, protection, aid and nourishment met.

> I just can't be around Mark any more! I can't do anything without him wanting to go along. He wants to eat together, walk to class together, study together, He feels like a damned Siamese twin and I just can't handle it. It wasn't too bad in high school, but now he seems to feel that I'm his only friend here. Well, he's driving my other friends away. But, I also know he's really alone and afraid and I don't want to do anything that would hurt him. I feel so . . . trapped, that's right. I worry about what he'd do if it seemed like I was rejecting him. I know what happened before and I sure don't want to be the cause of anything like that. But, I need out!
>
> —Leo (freshman)

- *n Nurturance*—the desire to be sympathetic and meet the need of others.

> I just can't give anymore, I'm wrung out. My roommate always has problems and we spend hours talking about them. Now I just

flunked a test because I didn't study last night because I was taking care of her again. I thought I was good at this, everybody comes to talk to me and says I should be a counselor since I am such a good listener and helper. What do you do when you haven't anything left for anybody including yourself. I just can't take it anymore. I'm a fraud, I can't help anyone, including myself.

—Margaret (senior)

• n *Infavoidance*—a desire to avoid situations where a person may incur failure, where rejection may occur or which would be embarrassing, and n *Defendance*—the ability to defend the self verbally and/or physically against various injuries and criticisms.

I told them I couldn't play sports. I'm just not coordinated. I tried to play football in high school and just ended up making a fool of myself so I quit the team after two years. Well, they harassed me until I did and wouldn't you know it, I did it again. My stupidity cost us the intramural championship and they're not about to let me forget it. The fraternity lost because of me. I don't even want to live there anymore. I'm tired of being ridiculed. It's just high school all over again and I hate it.

—Bob (freshman)

• n *Counteraction*—an effort to engage in positive efforts to overcome obstacles and maintain self-respect and pride.

If there was just one thing I could do that would prove to anybody that I didn't just get here because of who my dad is it would be wonderful. But it seems everything I do is because I have money, or my folks are so-and-so. What the hell do I have to do to let people know I can do something on my own—kill myself!

—Terry (sophomore)

• n *Harmavoidance*—the desire to avoid physical and psychological pain.

I don't like pain. I mean physical pain. And, I don't like this other pain either, the stuff you talked about at the program in the student union. When you ran down your list I kept checking myself off and so I did what you suggested. I'm here to talk and see what you can do. You must know that there are times when I hurt so bad inside that the pain of anything on the outside would feel good by comparison. I don't like any pain but sometimes it seems that a little of one could eliminate the other.

—Nikki (junior)

- *n Order*—the desire to achieve organization and balance in life.

> My roommate bitched because I keep my side of the room a mess? God, you'd think she was St. Clean. I used to be like her and I don't know what happened I just don't seem to give a damn anymore. I can't keep my clothes clean, I can't find my stuff, I can't remember when I have classes. I'm a mess. Is it OK now that I've said it. I don't know what's wrong it seems like nothing is worthwhile anymore.
>
> —Delia (freshman)

In *Motivation and Personality,* Maslow stated an individual desires a state of homeostasis [23]. The individual strives to maintain a constant, normal state. When needs are not met, there is a drive to meet and satisfy these needs. Maslow organized them in a hierarchy of needs from physiological to safety to belongingness to esteem and self-actualization. When lower needs are not met, the individual cannot progress to the satisfaction of higher needs as "the organism is dominated and its behavior organized only by unsatisfied needs" [23, p. 84]. As has been seen from students' quotations, unsatisfied needs can become a very negative dominating force for the suicidal student.

How the campus responds to students who are attempting to resolve issues—personal, academic, psychological or any other matter that is pertinent—establishes the tone of the campus. That tone is communicated particularly to those students who are attempting to resolve major psychological crises in their lives. Students who have already experienced a diminishment in their own options and alternatives as their thinking pattern becomes more constricted will experience heightened anxiety that will contribute to a more perturbed psychological state. As perturbation and constriction of thinking are two key elements of heightened suicidal risk, unnecessary campus "red tape" may contribute to greater suicidal risk.

What is more important, can the student seek a solution to his or her depressed or suicidal state by confiding in residence hall, student personnel, counseling center or other staff of the campus? From some of the material presented at the beginning of this chapter it would appear that on a number of campuses there would be a significant risk for the student. On these campuses, the student would have to decide if a revelation in hopes of a resolution of the psychological pain outweighed the possibility of or outright dismissal from the institution because of their suicidal ideations or actions. It is highly likely that the student will attempt to "wait and it will get better." As this is also unlikely the student may move further along the suicide continuum and eventually make a serious attempt or commit suicide as his or her needs are not met. If this occurs, then the institution's posture restrains or even prevents seeking assistance. This would thwart the third of Shneidman's common characteristic of suicide, the seeking of a solution.

The student does not want to die, but to cease consciousness, the fourth of Shneidman's characteristics. He or she has not managed to alleviate the unendurable psychological pain most often expressed as "I don't want to die, I just can't figure out how to live." Students often use alcohol and other chemicals to "numb" the consciousness, a complicating negative factor. The number and incidence of negative life events are often key factors in the movement toward suicidal actions. The campus can provide resources that will assist in the alleviation of these stresses. Many of these negative life events involve such issues as alcohol use and abuse, sexual assault, incest, physical abuse and battering relationships that are not only viewed as negative events, but also as shameful issues. The development of support groups based on specific issues communicates to students that the campus is concerned about the ramifications of these events and there is a willingness to provide services that will facilitate student growth. A key by-product of this service is that as the student becomes less perturbed and less constricted in his or her thinking patterns, he or she may also develop new interpersonal living and academic skills. Providing these resources on campus can facilitate the relief of the intolerable psychological pain and eliminate another common characteristic of suicide, the cessation of consciousness.

Students' hopelessness and helplessness are the affective aspects of Shneidman's fifth common characteristic of suicide. These young women and men have accumulated a stockpile of negative events and circumstances. These may include feelings of academic inadequacy (real or imagined), serious concerns about financial problems, difficulty in balancing time required for academic work with time required for employment, interpersonal relationship difficulties, conflicts with parents, issues of sexuality and other issues. Quite often these feelings of hopelessness and helplessness are generated within the student because he or she simply does not recognize that there are many other students who are also experiencing these events and that they are a normal part of the college scene. Student support groups could be developed to enable students to become acquainted and develop friendships. Residential units provide the greatest possibilities in this effort. There also needs to be an effort directed towards the commuting student. This might be developed around special interest groups. These groups could counter one of the most significant emotions—loneliness.

The larger the campus the greater the possibility for "getting lost" in the masses. If groups are developed, beginning with activities welcoming students to the campus, and providing students with opportunities to participate, this feeling could be countered. Tutoring and peer groups developed around academic work would enable students to discuss their concerns and to develop support systems. A hopeful by-product would be a reduction in the amount of competitive pressure as well as imparting of information. If students only see the campus as a competitive enterprise fostering a "do-or-die" attitude towards academic achievement, those students who are having difficulty will consider exiting the campus in one way or another.

The most powerful tool in suicide prevention is that of the suicidal person's ambivalence, which is the sixth of Shneidman's common affective characteristics. Even as the student views his or her options and alternatives being reduced to two options—living or dying, he or she still remains ambivalent. Consequently, we may have a woman who slashes her wrist and calls the police for assistance. If the campus can assist her in this moment of crisis and provide psychological referral her ambivalence toward living will be enhanced. Not only will this strengthen her willingness to live, but the action will also communicate to other students that there are resources on the campus that will respond to their needs at a moment when they believe there is no hope.

Following these affective characteristics, there is a cognitive aspect, the seventh characteristic of suicide defined by Shneidman, constriction. The ultimate constriction is when the student moves to a point of considering only two alternatives—living or dying. But, this very dichotomous pattern of thought is not present in the suicidal student alone, it is present in society. Much of our thought pattern is developed around dichotomies: black-white; right-wrong; gay-straight; pro-life-pro-abortion; life-death; hero-coward; us-them; good-bad; passive-aggressive; love-hate. The view of either—or is not the real world. The real world is not black and white, but rather an innumerable range of shades of gray. The real value of an educational institution may be seen in the effort toward developing alternatives or new ways of seeing things. The effort that any campus can make toward the development of alternatives reduces the possibilities of students becoming frozen in worlds of dichotomies and enables students to make other choices.

The relations that students have with each other and with the institution is an important aspect of their academic career. Shneidman's eighth and ninth characteristics are both concerned with relational aspects of suicide. The first relational aspect is that suicidal persons engage in an interpersonal act. They communicate their intentions. The fact that students give clues to their impending suicidal actions is well known and has been estimated to occur in 75 to 80 percent of the instances of completed suicide. The ultimate test of a campus is does the campus permit and encourage this type of communication? Campuses that are open to students make this clear by providing information on depression and suicide. The campus provides emergency contact numbers and referral agencies for students to use. The campus encourages individuals to talk about their depressed and suicidal feelings with professional staff. Has all of this been said before? Yes, definitely, but this is the critical test. A campus that creates a hostile environment by forcing students to move off campus or automatically dismissing students without other interventions cannot be perceived as friendly to students and their interests. Actions taken without consideration of the level of risk or a determination of the student's danger to him or herself or others create an intimidating environment. Such unilateral or precipitous action is not in the best interests of the student or the institution and quite probably is illegal.

The second relational aspect is what Shneidman labels eggression. "Eggression is a person's departure or escape, often from distress" [21, p. 144]. When a student dies from suicide, he or she has completed the escape. However, the members of the campus community are involved in the bereavement, grief, and mourning processes, their distress has only begun or been exacerbated. The test of the humanity of the campus is how the campus responds—students, staff and faculty. The manner in which the incident is handled communicates volumes to all members of the campus community and particularly to the students. It is unwise to create memorials to the suicide as this may be quite seductive to someone who has serious suicidal thoughts. However, the presentation of programs relating to depression and suicide as suicide awareness programs are an appropriate gesture. The campus is saying to those who want to listen that there is sorrow at the loss of one of its members. However, some good can come from tragedy if a well-developed suicide awareness program can produce interventions and give permission to other students to disclose their depressed or suicidal thoughts. A campus that can react with empathy towards survivors, opportunity for those who are somewhere on the suicide continuum, and a sense of caring for all of its students will be held in high regard.

When students come to the campus, the mental states of some of them are healthy, some of them doubtful and some of them quite damaged by their previous life history. In Chapter 2 information was presented as a portrait of a student body. The question raised at that point was how can a college or university with seemingly ever more restricted funding bases begin to contemplate how to act as a remedial or change agent for the large number of students who enter with considerable emotional "baggage." If the campus can address this tenth of Shneidman's characteristics, the consistency of life long coping patterns, by learning how students have managed their previous life crisis, it may be possible to change some of the many ineffective coping behaviors. This may seem a daunting task, but these efforts can and should be made. Whatever is done can produce some positive effect. As students are developing their perceptions of a campus, every positive effort can produce an effect upon the student body that may be immeasurable. We encounter that question we would all like answered. How many fewer suicidal actions have we had on the campus as a result of our efforts?

In all of this work, there is an essential, perhaps even the quintessential factor. That is the human being. Whether this person is a student, an electrical engineering professor, a graduate teaching assistant in history, a cook in the food service, a coach on a sports team, or the president of the institution, it is a real person who can act, interact, and react with another person. It is the person who can create a comfortable, trusting, and consistent relationship with the student. It is the person who respects the student and is genuine about his or her welfare. It is the person who will listen, and listen, and listen and then act to help the student through their crisis.

What is the student's perception of the campus response to suicide? Exactly what they see us do. How is the student's perception of this response formed? It is formed through what they see, what they hear and what they intuitively feel is happening on their campus. Does the campus response enable, deter or even prevent the student from seeking assistance when feeling depressed or suicidal? The student is enabled when he or she is empowered to talk about his or her depression and/or suicidal ideation and actions and to seek counseling. The student is enabled when the campus provides resources which act in the best interest of the student be that counseling in an out-patient setting or hospitalization and in-patient therapy including medications. The student is enabled when the actions taken are empowering and not punitive. The student is enabled when he or she is seen as an individual who has a significant problem in his or her life that needs resolution and not as someone who is "crazy." If these factors are not present, the student is deterred or prevented from seeking assistance.

We must empower every person on the campus to reach out to students who want to reach out their hands and have someone touch them and say, "I care." We must empower every person on the campus to be proactive and ready to ask, "Are you thinking about committing suicide?" We must empower every person on the campus to be proactive as well as reactive when they meet students who are contemplating or attempting suicide. And, we must empower every person on the campus to interact with students and listen to them as they tell of their grief following the suicide of a significant person in their life.

All of this means that our institutional programs, as excellent as they may be, must be backed up with human beings who genuinely care. Without this quality our institutions are like a Hollywood movie set. We look beautiful from the outside, our claims to fame are presented for everyone to admire. It all looks so wonderful and real until someone reaches for the doorknob and opens the door to what they believe is reality only to find it is a fiction, a mirage. It takes much work, many dedicated people and significant resources to create reality behind the door. If reality isn't there the student's perspective will be of the desert, not the promised land.

REFERENCES

1. M. L. Bernard and J. L. Bernard, Institutional Responses to the Suicidal Student: Ethical and Legal Considerations, *Journal of College Student Personnel, 21*:2, pp. 109-113, 1980.
2. I. Sivits-Luhring, *Institutional Policy Regarding Students with Mental and Life-threatening Physical Disorders,* UMR-ACUHO Research and Information Committee, Lincoln, Nebraska, 1988.
3. B. R. Hopkins and B. S. Anderson, *The Counselor and the Law,* AACD Press, Alexandria, Virginia, 1985.
4. R. B. Jr. Winston, S. Anchors, and Associates, *Student Housing and Residential Life: A Handbook for Professionals Committed to Student Development Goals,* Jossey-Bass, San Francisco, 1993.
5. R. H. Seiden, Suicide among Youth, Supplement to the *Bulletin of Suicidology,* December 1969.
6. J. L. Bernard and M. L. Bernard, Factors Related to Suicidal Behavior Among College Students and the Impact of Institutional Response, *Journal of College Student Personnel, 23*:5, pp. 409-413, 1982.
7. G. Pavela, Therapeutic Paternalism and the Misuse of Mandatory Psychiatric Withdrawals on Campus, *Journal of College and University Law, 9*:1, pp. 101-147, 1982-83.
8. G. Pavela, *The Dismissal of Students with Mental Disorders,* College Administration Publications, Asheville, North Carolina, 1985.
9. D. D. Gehring, The Counselor's "Duty to Warn," *The Personnel and Guidance Journal, 61*:4, pp. 208-210, 1982.
10. D. D. Gehring, The Dismissal of Students with Serious Emotional Problems: An Administrative Decision Model, *NASPA Journal, 20*:3, pp. 9-14, 1983.
11. R. H. Pate, Student Suicide: Are you Liable?, *American Counselor, 1*:3, pp. 14-19, 1992.

12. F. L. Hoffmann and X. Mastrianni, The Mentally Ill Student on Campus: Theory and Practice, *Journal of American College Health, 38*:1, pp. 15-20, 1989.
13. G. Amada, Coping with the Disruptive College Student: A Practical Model, *Journal of American College Health, 40*:3, pp. 203-215, 1992.
14. U. Delworth, *New Directions for Student Services: Dealing with the Behavioral and Psychological Problems of Students* (No. 45), Jossey-Bass, San Francisco, 1989.
15. V. L. Brown and D. A. DeCoster, The Disturbed and Disturbing Student, in *New Directions for Student Services: Dealing with the Behavioral and Psychological Problems of Students,* (No. 45), U. Delworth (ed.), Jossey-Bass, San Francisco, pp. 43-56, 1989.
16. H. L. Pruett and V. B. Brown (eds.), *New Directions for Student Services: Crisis Intervention and Prevention* (No. 49), Jossey-Bass, San Francisco, 1990.
17. M. Dannels and D. Stuber, Mandatory Psychiatric Withdrawal of Severely Disturbed Students: A Study and Policy Recommendations, *NASPA Journal, 29*:3, pp. 163-168, 1992.
18. H. J. Solky, J. E. McKeever, R. A. Perlmutter, and T. E. Gift, Involving Parents in the Management of Psychiatric Emergencies in College Students Far from Home, *Journal of American College Health, 36*:6, pp. 335-339, 1988.
19. P. W. Meilman, C. Manley, M. S. Gaylor, and J. H. Turco, Medical Withdrawals from College for Mental Health Reasons and their Relation to Performance, *Journal of American College Health, 40*:5, pp. 217-223, 1992.
20. E. S. Shneidman, *Definition of Suicide,* John Wiley & Sons, New York, 1985.
21. E. S. Shneidman, Commentary: Suicide as Psychache, *The Journal of Nervous and Mental Disease, 181*:3, pp. 145-147, 1993.
22. H. A. Murray, *Explorations in Personality,* Oxford University Press, New York, 1938.
23. A. H. Maslow, *Motivation and Personality,* Harper & Brothers, New York, 1954.

CHAPTER 10

Selected Resources

BOOKS

Alcohol, Drug Abuse and Mental Health Administration, *Report of the Secretary's Task Force on Youth Suicide,* 1989.
>   *Volume 1: Overview and Recommendations,* DHHS Pub. No. (ADM)89-1621.
>   *Volume 2: Risk Factors for Youth Suicide,* DHHS Pub. No. (ADM)89-1622.
>   *Volume 3: Prevention and Interventions in Youth Suicide,* DHHS Pub. No. (ADM)89-1623.
>   *Volume 4: Strategies for the Prevention of Youth Suicide,* DHHS Pub. No. (ADM)89-1624, Superintendent of Documents, U.S. Government Printing Office, Washington, D.C.

Alvarez, A., *The Savage God: A Study of Suicide,* Random House, New York, 1971.

Bolton, I., *My son . . . my son . . . A Guide to Healing After Death, Loss or Suicide,* Bolton Press, Atlanta, Georgia, 1983.

Bongar, B., *The Suicidal Patient: Clinical and Legal Standards of Care,* American Psychological Association, Hyattsville, Maryland, 1991.

Bongar, B., *Suicide: Guidelines for Assessment, Management and Treatment,* Oxford University Press, New York, 1992.

Centers for Disease Control, *CDC Recommendations for a Community Plan for the Prevention and Containment of Suicide Clusters,* MMWR, 37 (Supp. No. 5-6), Atlanta, Georgia, 1988.

Colt, G. H., *The Enigma of Suicide,* Summit Books, New York, 1991.

Curran, D. K., *Adolescent Suicidal Behavior,* Hemisphere, New York, 1987.

Delworth, U. (ed.), *New Directions for Student Services: Dealing with the Behavioral and Psychological Problems of Students* (No. 45), Jossey-Bass, San Francisco, 1989.

233

234 / PERSPECTIVES ON COLLEGE STUDENT SUICIDE

Dunne, E. J., McIntosh, J. L., and Dunne-Maxim, K., *Suicide and its Aftermath: Understanding and Counseling the Survivors,* W. W. Norton & Company, New York, 1987.

Evans, G. and Farberow, N. L., *The Encyclopedia of Suicide,* Facts on File, New York, 1988.

Farberow, N. L. (ed.), *Suicide in Different Cultures,* University Park Press, Baltimore, Maryland, 1975.

Farberow, N. L. (ed.), *The Many Faces of Suicide: Indirect Self-destructive Behavior,* McGraw-Hill, New York, 1980.

Hatton, C. L. and Valente, S. M., *Suicide Assessment and Intervention* (2nd Edition), Appleton-Century-Crofts, Norwalk, Connecticut, 1984.

Hopkins, B. R. and Anderson, B. S., *The Counselor and the Law,* American Association for Counseling and Development, Alexandria, Virginia, 1985.

Kushner, H. S., *When Bad Things Happen to Good People,* Schocken Books, New York, 1981.

Leenaars, A. A. (ed.), *Life Span Perspectives of Suicide: Time-lines in the Suicide Process,* Plenum Press, New York, 1991.

Lester, D., *Why People Kill Themselves: A 1990's Summary of Research Findings on Suicidal Behavior* (3rd Edition), Charles C. Thomas, Springfield, Illinois. (Note: This is an excellent annotated reference work.) 1992.

Lester, D., *The Cruelest Death: The Enigma of Adolescent Suicide,* The Charles Press, Philadelphia, Pennsylvania, 1992.

Maris, R. W., *Pathways to Suicide: A Survey of Self-destructive Behaviors,* The Johns Hopkins University Press, Baltimore, Maryland, 1981.

Mcintosh, John L., *Research on Suicide: A Bibliography,* Greenwood Press, Westport, Connecticut. (Note: This is an excellent reference work, 323 pages of listings on suicide.) 1985.

Oaks, J. and Ezell, G., *Dying and Death: Caring, Coping, Understanding* (2nd Edition), Gorsuch Scarisbrick, Scottsdale, Arizona, 1993.

Pavela, G., *The Dismissal of Students with Mental Disorders: Legal Issues, Policy Considerations and Alternative Responses,* College Administration Publications, Inc., Asheville, North Carolina, 1985.

Pruett, H. L. and Brown, V. B. (eds.), *New Directions for Student Services: Crisis Intervention and Prevention* (No. 49), Jossey-Bass, San Francisco, 1990.

Shneidman E. S. (ed.), *Essays in Self Destruction,* Science House, New York, 1967.

Shneidman, E. S., *Definition of Suicide,* John Wiley & Sons, New York, 1985.

Stillion, J. M., McDowell, E. E., and May, J. H., *Suicide Across the Life Span: Premature Exits,* Hemisphere, New York, 1989.

Sudak, H. S., Ford, A. B., and Rushforth, N. B. (eds.), *Suicide in the Young,* John Wright, Boston, 1984.

Wass, H., Corr, C. A., Pacholski, R. A., and Forfar, C., Death Education: An Annotated Resource Guide, Hemisphere, Washington, DC: 1985.

Whitaker, L. C. and Slimak, R. E. (eds.), *College Student Suicide,* Haworth Press, New York, 1990.

Worden, J. W., *Grief Counseling and Grief Therapy: A Handbook for the Mental Health Practitioner* (2nd Edition), Springer, New York, 1991.

Zinner, E. S. (ed.), *New Directions for Student Services: Coping with Death on Campus* (No. 31), Jossey-Bass, San Francisco, 1985.

JOURNALS

Crisis: International Journal of Suicide and Crisis Studies, Hogrefe and Huber, Toronto, Ontario, Canada.

Death Studies, Hemisphere, Washington, DC.

Illness, Crisis & Loss: Multidisciplinary Linkages, The Charles Press, Philadelphia, Pennsylvania.

Journal of Traumatic Stress, Plenum Press, New York.

Omega: The Journal of Death and Dying, Baywood, Amityville, New York.

Personnel and Guidance Journal, (Special issue on loss, *59*:6, 1981).

Suicide and Life Threatening Behaviors, Guilford Press, New York.

ORGANIZATIONS

American Association of Suicidology (AAS), 2459 South Ash, Denver, Colorado, 80222. (303) 692-0985.

Association for Death Education and Counseling (ADEC), 638 Prospect Avenue, Hartford, Connecticut 06105-4298. (203) 232-4825.

International Association for Suicide Prevention (IASP), Institut für Medizinische Psychologie, Severingasse 9, Vienna, Austria A-1090. (222) 483-568.

MEDIA GUIDELINES
(American Association of Suicidology)

News stories, articles, and dramatic presentations on the subject of suicide came under question in the last few years. The concern has been that such presentations may have stimulated some persons to attempt suicide. There is confusion about how the subject of suicide should be treated to minimize this danger.

As a service to the news media and to the people making public presentations on the subject of suicide, the Public Information Committee of the American Association of Suicidology offers the following guidelines. These are intended to be general statements to aid in a responsible presentation of information about suicide. It is hoped that they will serve to stimulate discussion between members of the American Association of Suicidology and people involved with informing the public.

1. To discourage imitative or copycat suicides, it is important to avoid or minimize:
   - reporting specific details of the method
   - descriptions of a suicide as unexplainable, e.g., "He had everything going for him."
   - reporting romanticized versions of the reasons for the suicide(s), e.g., "We want to be together for all eternity."
   - simplistic reasons for the suicide, e.g., "Boy commits suicide because he has to wear braces."

In addition, the print media can reduce the imitative effect by:

   - printing story on inside page
   - if story must appear on first page, print it below the fold
   - avoid the word "suicide" in the headline
   - avoid printing a photo of the person who committed suicide

It is important to report a suicide in a straightforward manner so that the suicide does not appear exciting. Reports should not make the suicidal person appear admirable, nor should they seem to approve of the suicide.

2. To encourage prevention of suicide, it is helpful to:
   - Present alternatives to suicide, e.g., calling a suicide prevention center, getting counseling, etc.
   - Whenever possible, present examples of positive outcomes of people in suicidal crises.

- Provide information on community resources for those who may be suicidal or who know people who are.
- Include a list of clues to suicidal behavior, e.g.:

Warning Signs of Suicide

Suicide threats
Statements revealing a desire to die
Previous suicide attempts
Sudden changes in behavior (withdrawal, apathy, moodiness)
Depression (crying, sleeplessness, loss of appetite, hopelessness)
Final arrangements (such as giving away personal possessions)

What To Do

Discuss it openly and frankly
Show interest and support
Get professional help

GUIDELINES FOR MEDIA INTERVIEWS
(American Association of Suicidology)

The following list of suggestions can help increase the educational aspect of the TV, newspaper, radio or magazine stories and minimize the potential dangers.

1. Set policies and make decisions regarding working with media before the occurrence of an emotional event such as a completed suicide.
2. Direct all media inquiries to one person who has been designated as spokesperson. This avoids confusion in times of crisis and ensures consistency in information given to the media.
3. Use clear, simple, layman terminology that the readers or viewers can understand.
4. Avoid being defensive. Do not treat the interviewer as an adversary. Acknowledge the difficulty of the media's role and take the position of helpfulness. If you do not know the answer to a question, find out and call back or put the interviewer in contact with another resource. Place media coverage high on your list of priorities and view it as an asset to your work.
5. Review statistics so you will not dispense erroneous information. Be sure you can back up facts and statistics with original resources.

6. Use caution if the interviewer requests to be put in contact with an attempter or survivor. Decide: 1) If it is in the best interest of the attempter or survivor and, 2) what would be the educational value of such an interview. Make contact yourself first and get permission to give the media person their name and telephone number or offer anonymity to protect them from future unwanted calls.

7. Make clear before being recorded or interviewed live that you do not think it will be appropriate to discuss details of the method or specific reasons of a particular suicide. Avoid sensationalizing or romanticizing. General information is more beneficial, e.g., guns are used in the majority of suicides, or most suicides follow a significant loss, etc.

8. Personal experiences and case studies can make a point more real and understandable, but be cautious not to reveal information that might break the confidentiality of a client.

9. Emphasize whenever possible the suicide warning signs, how to respond to someone who is threatening suicide, and where to go for help in your local community.

10. Do not insist on seeing questions ahead of the interview or to edit the final copy. Only what fits the purpose or theme and is of interest to readers or viewers will be used. Your willingness to be interviewed must show some trust. If you have too many doubts, refer the reporter to someone else.

11. Become pro-active with the media. Establish a relationship beforehand. Initiate a contact with a phone call or press release and establish yourself or your agency as a contact on the issue of suicide prevention.

About the Author

Ralph L. V. Rickgarn has an M.A. and an Ed.S. in counseling from the University of Minnesota, specializing in the area of suicidology. His interest in suicide developed during 20 years in student personnel work and with students in residence halls on both a small, private liberal arts campus and a major public university. He developed and was co-facilitator for a counseling group for students who had seriously considererd or attempted suicide. He is currently employed as Research & Staff Development Administrator for Housing Services at the University of Minnesota. He is a guest lecturer on the issues of suicide in the departments of sociology, educational psychology, mortuary science, general college, public health and the medical school at the University of Minnesota where he also teaches two classes for Resident Assistants in the Department of Psychoeducational Studies. He was awarded the J. C. Penny Golden Rule Award for outstanding volunteer work in the area of suicide education, prevention, intervention and postvention and the Gordon L. Starr Faculty/Staff Outstanding Contribution Award for contributions to the welfare of the student body at the University of Minnesota. He founded the Death Response Team at the University of Minnesota. He has been certified as a professional death educator and grief counselor by the Association for Death Education and Counseling (ADEC) and is co-chair of the Governmental Relations Committee of ADEC. He is a Board member of the Campus Violence Prevention Center and professionally affiliated with the American Association of Suicidology, American College Personnel Association and the Minnesota College Personnel Association. He has published a number of articles on suicide and violence on campus in various journals and books and serves as a consultant and trainer for programs related to the issues of suicide for elementary and secondary schools, religious organizations and colleges and universities.

Contributing Author

Dr. Barry Garfinkel is in the Division of Child and Adolescent Psychiatry. He has been with the University of Minnesota for ten years. Previously, he was with the Department of Psychiatry at Brown University where he was Director of Graduate and Undergraduate Medical Education in Child Psychiatry. Dr. Garfinkel was born and grew up in Winnipeg and is a Canadian Citizen. He received his medical degree at the University of Manitoba and training in adult and child and adolescent psychiatry in 1974 at the University of Toronto. Dr. Garfinkel's clinical and research interests are in the areas of depression and suicide in children and adolescents, and pharmacological research in children and adolescents with Attention-Deficit Hyperactivity Disorder. He is currently studying suicide risk factors in youth, the prevalence of suicide attempts, suicidal communication and school-based suicide prevention programs. He has published articles in the areas of depression, suicide, Attention Deficit Disorder, and the pharmacological treatment of emotional disorders in children and adolescents.

Index